Masculine/ Feminine or Human?

An Overview of the Sociology of Sex Roles

Janet Saltzman Chafetz

UNIVERSITY OF HOUSTON

F. E. PEACOCK PUBLISHERS, INC.
ITASCA, ILLINOIS

Masculine/Feminine or Human?
An Overview of the Sociology of Sex Roles

Table of Contents

Preface

Since I am not a "value-free scientist," this book is not a "value-free" endeavor. I am deeply committed to the basic goal of maximizing the opportunities for all human beings to develop to the fullest extent possible their own unique talents, interests, and predilections. My particular interest is in bringing about changes that will encourage males and females to explore and develop their human potentials more fully, as opposed to maintaining the stereotyped masculine and feminine roles foisted upon them by virtually every aspect of this society— as well as most others. In short, I am concerned not merely with "women's liberation," but with "human liberation," although I profess to be a "member" of the former social movement.

This book comprises an effort to delineate the parameters of the newly emerging field of the sociology of sex roles. I am attempting to describe the present and recent past state of affairs in this connection, and at the same time to prescribe much needed changes in that state of affairs, some of which have already been begun. A virtual mountain of recent publications exists pertaining to the problems of females in contemporary American society, and the genesis and possible solutions of these problems. Parallel literature about the male role comprises little more than an ant hill. Moreover, literature examining the two sex roles in their complementary aspects is practically nonexistent. Yet it would appear that when two role complexes are as tightly interwoven and interdependent as the sex roles, it makes no sense to explore one in isolation from the other.

In my view, both roles are constrictive and costly for many, if not most, human beings, although for very different kinds of reasons. To the extent that there are social problems relating to one sex, it is inconceivable that they would not involve counterparts in the other, and to begin to understand and cope with the problematic aspects of either sex role necessitates a broad view of the entire area. It is crucial first to understand the nature of these stereotyped roles, how they are sustained and transmitted, what their implications or human "costs" are for all of us, and who profits (and in what ways) by their continued existence. Such issues of "social statics" comprise a large segment of this book. It is also important to examine emerging trends that may (hopefully) undermine traditional sex roles and allow for the emergence of a society of *humans* whose lives are based on achieved rather than ascribed characteristics. In this I am exploring phenomena of social change.

This book is designed primarily for undergraduates, to be used as a brief overview and starting point in newly developing courses throughout the nation in the sociology of sex roles. It arises chiefly out of my own experiences in trying to teach such a course; I have found it difficult to locate reading that is other than polemical and/or centered almost exclusively on the feminine sex role. I am also of the opinion that this topic should not be tucked away in courses of its own, into which people already committed to the values implicit in the subject matter recruit themselves. Rather, it must find its way into the broader curriculum. Thus this text should be useful supplementary reading in education, counseling and social work curricula, and other sociology courses such as Introductory, Social Problems, Minorities, Stratification, Social Movements, Social Psychology, and Marriage and Family. In light of this, I have attempted to integrate as many relevant broadly sociological theories and concepts as possible.

Sociology has long been primarily a male field. Courses in it are usually taught by males, utilizing texts written by males. If we take our own discipline seriously, we should understand that all human knowledge (including our own) is partial in that it represents perceptions from some particular vantage point. Given contemporary social definitions, males and females tend to learn to perceive reality in somewhat different ways. Therefore, a masculine point of view will logically be partial, as will a feminine one; both are ultimately needed. Materials in virtually all courses must be expanded to comprise an understanding of reality as it appears from a wide variety of perspectives. It is my hope that by integrating material from the sociology of sex roles into the broader curriculum the discipline may begin to overcome its myopia. To the extent that this endeavor is a success, those of us who specialize in sex roles and women's studies should find ourselves superfluous. The true measure of this subfield is how long it takes for the "normal" curriculum to expand to take account of sex role phenomena, thus making our courses unnecessary.

Intellectual debts for a work such as this cannot be counted. How can I thank the scores of women whose frank discussions during various feminist meetings have inspired many of my ideas? Or the 75 students who put up with my first fumbling efforts at teaching the sociology of sex roles at Trinity University, and whose papers, as well as class participation and out-of-class discussions, contributed so much to my thinking and to the material presented herein? There are countless other students as well who, knowing of my interests, have contributed ideas and references. I specifically thank the secretarial staff of the Graduate School of Social Work, University of Houston for their help; Patricia Sampson for her work as research assistant; Barbara Brown, Henry Chafetz, Richard Vogel, and Kathleen Kemp for their careful reading and comments on early drafts of this book; and Kathleen Kemp for devoting hours to discussing many of the issues raised in the text and, most of all, for calling my attention to yet more material I should read and consider. I am particularly indebted to my friend and colleague Barbara Polk for the challenging and stimulating ideas she expressed during many delightful hours of discussion running the course of four years. Finally, my deepest appreciation goes to the University of Houston, whose Faculty Research Initiation Grant and Publications Committee Grant provided me the leisure and resources with which to write this book.

JANET SALTZMAN CHAFETZ

Houston, Texas
May, 1973

Chapter 1

Gender or Sex Role?

If you tried to predict the lives 25 years hence of newborn babies in a hospital nursery, half snuggled under blue blankets and half under pink, a variety of images might come to mind. Those wrinkled little creatures under the pink nylon might become young wives in their computerized kitchens fixing a high protein soybean gruel for their toddlers or teachers facing 20 youngsters at their desk-console computers. They might be scurrying around some hospital in white pantsuits administering the doctor's orders, or sitting at a typewriter transcribing a boss's letters. That's about it. The babies under the blue blankets, however, would be engaged in so many different pursuits it would be difficult to describe them all. There they are, building, reading, lecturing, writing, barking orders, peering down microscopes, fixing machines, fighting fires, standing in a courtroom, a shop, a hospital, an office, a factory, a field.

It can be imagined that a doctor or physical scientist would comment on such images as follows:

> I never cease to marvel that nature has provided so marvelously for the different kinds of needs humans have by allowing for two sexes of such radically different physical and mental structures. The natural compassion, passivity, and nurturing instincts of women, arising

1

from their childbearing and childrearing functions and sustained by a delicate hormonal system, harmonize so beautifully with the innately greater aggressiveness, strength, and energy of the male of the species. *Vive la difference!*

A social scientist, on the other hand, might be more likely to observe:

What a crime that our culture dictates so strongly the possibilities of individuals on their birth day! For no inherent reason these infants have already been started on a long and complex path of learning designed to ensure that each gender will be restricted in a variety of ways from fulfilling the potentialities of its individual members. But times are changing. . . .

The images and reactions just described point up two issues. First there is the obvious fact of the importance of the ascribed characteristic of sex in determining many, if not most, aspects of the future life of every individual. Our society pays constant lip service to an equal-opportunity ethic by which achieved statuses are supposed to be all important. From the very start of life, however, we in fact run two separate but not equal competitions, one for males and one for females (as we do with other groups with immutable characteristics, such as race). This phenomenon, indeed, comprises the substance of most of the rest of this book. The second issue is whether or not such ascribed differences are in any way necessary, given some innate nature for the two sexes. This chapter seeks some answers to this question.

Differentiating Gender and Sex Role

To begin such a discussion, it is necessary to make the crucial distinction, often obliterated in everyday thinking, between *gender* and *sex role*. Almost all human beings (and, for that matter, all animals above a very low order on the evolutionary scale) are born with a more or less clearly identifiable gender as male or female. For most people, the minute they are born the fact of their maleness or femaleness is obvious, as indicated by physical attributes including distinctions in gonadal, chromosomal, and hormonal characteristics. When, occasionally, these various indicators of gender do not agree, it is an indication that such individuals are not totally of one or the other gender. In some cases, infants with consistent gender characteristics can be misidentified at birth due to distortions of the genitals. Raised as members of the opposite gender, they find it difficult if not impossible to function like other members of their own sex when the mistake is later discovered. This problem attests to the strength of sex role identification in determining human behavior.

Sex role is a different order of phenomenon than gender. The relevant terms are not "male" and "female," which are gender terms, but "masculine" and "feminine." It does not require a very astute social observer to notice that from very early childhood to death, people act differently according to sex. Most females display, to a greater or lesser extent, a set of behavioral, temperamental, emotional, intellectual, and attitudinal characteristics identified, in a given culture at a given time, as feminine. Similarly, most males display, to a greater or lesser extent, a set of different characteristics defined as masculine. These learned characteristics can be conceptualized together under the rubric "sex roles."

Sociologists attach a specific meaning to the term "role." Most introductory texts define it in terms of a cluster of socially or culturally defined expectations that individuals in a given situation are expected to fulfill. At any given time for any given individual born into a culture, the roles are a given in the sense that they exist outside of that individual. Confronted by a set of socially and culturally prescribed roles, the individual is pressured, rewarded, and punished to accept and internalize certain roles and not others during the process of socialization. This process will be discussed at length in Chapter 3. Here, it is sufficient to understand that the concept "role" centers on two fundamental phenomena: (1) roles are defined more or less precisely by society and presumed to apply to all individuals in a given category (e.g., all people who sign up to take a course are expected to accept the prescribed role of student), and (2) roles are more or less well learned responses by individuals. The main implication of these two aspects of the definition of "role" is that given role definitions are subject to change over time and space. The expectations centered around the role of student in our society today differ in significant ways from those associated with that role 100 years ago, or in China or, probably, at some future date in America. Also, it should be noted that roles are *more or less* well defined. They vary on at least two continua: they may be more or less precise in the expectations they prescribe, and the number of such expectations may be many or few. Moreover, individuals vary according to the extent to which they learn or internalize their roles. The more completely they do so, the more conformist they are.

It should be clear that when the terms "masculine" and "feminine" are used, it is assumed that the characteristics in question are socially prescribed and individually learned, and hence changeable, phenomena; they are not innate to the organism. Since they are not innate, they cannot be directly related to gender in any necessary fashion. Thus, if passivity is considered part of femininity, as opposed to femaleness, it is conceived as learned and, therefore, potentially unlearnable.

The points of view expressed at the beginning of the chapter by the physician and the social scientist might be reconceptualized to a question: Where does gender leave off and sex role begin? Are some behavioral and temperamental differences innate to the two genders, or are they all aspects of sex role? The argument in the pages to follow will be this: Given present evidence, no precise line between organism and environment, gender and role, can be drawn. However, the burden of proof rests with those who would argue for the innate quality of virtually any behavioral, attitudinal, emotional, or intellectual trait.

The term "instinct," when used in reference to humans, has long been in disrepute among students of human behavior. Indeed, many are reluctant to apply the term to any of the higher primates. Instead, terms such as "need disposition," "behavior tendencies," and so on are currently employed. This is not merely a matter of semantics. According to a dictionary's primary definition, an instinct is "an inborn tendency to behave in a way characteristic of a species; natural, unacquired mode of response to stimuli. . . ." Conceptually, an instinct can be viewed as a behavioral pattern programmed into the genetic structure of a species, much as a computer is programmed to respond in given ways to particular stimuli. There is virtually no important *adult* human behavior that is so programmed. Sucking, on the part of an infant, probably is; the mode of acquisition, preparation, and consumption of food by human adults certainly is not. Sexual behavior patterns among monkeys, apes, and humans are learned, not innate, behaviors. Where in human behavior do we find a counterpart of the elaborate and, within species, identical, mating rituals of many birds? Or the work patterns innate to the ant or bee?

Humans can survive so well in a wide variety of environments and under conditions of drastic change precisely because they lack such rigidly patterned responses; they are a highly adaptable species. It is imperative that humans eat, drink, reproduce, and so forth, but the ways in which they go about doing these things are culturally developed and transmitted, and they vary tremendously from one culture to another. Humans are provided with a diffuse sexuality, but there is no innate mechanism that specifies the appropriate sexual partner, not to mention the form of sexual behavior. The history of the ways in which human mothers have treated their children seems to present ample evidence that there is no such thing as a "maternal instinct." Moreover, "needs," unlike "instincts," can with a very few exceptions (e.g., nutritive and eliminative needs) be ignored, unfulfilled, or sublimated by individuals, and, although there will always be some sort of psychic and/or physical "cost" involved in ignoring them, it won't normally destroy the organism.

The question, then, isn't whether males and females are innately different at the instinctual level—whether males are instinctively "aggressive" and females innately "passive" or "maternal." A more sophisticated approach considers whether the two genders are equipped with divergent need dispositions which could be ignored or culturally mitigated. Not only is the evidence on this issue obscure, but it is virtually impossible to devise methods of study that would yield the kind of data necessary to answer such questions with any degree of surety. Humans are brought up by other humans, and after a very short period of time it is virtually impossible to separate the learned from any unlearned components of the behavior of an individual. However, on the basis of cross-cultural and even cross-species studies, some individuals have tried to distinguish gender and sex role components. A few of these formulations will be considered in the following section.

Speculations on Need Dispositions

Social theorists have often grounded their work in certain assumed innate tendencies common to humans. In Marx's assumption of a "species being" by which humans must be creative in their labor to be fully human, W. I. Thomas's "four wishes" of new experience, security, recognition and response, or even Pareto's "residues," to mention but a few, there is a common theme: humans do not come to the world with a complete *tabula rasa*.

Although the majority of social scientists in the past half century or so have tended to deny in practice virtually any influence other than "environment" on the development of the individual, only a second of thought would show such an approach to be preposterous. The human species represents no radical break in the evolutionary chain; it is not a species apart. Humans have some attributes that are more highly developed than other species (e.g., brains), and others that are less so (e.g., sense of smell). But all aspects of the human body are distinctly related to other species, particularly, of course, other primates. It is also clear that many animals, including most primates, have some sort of rudimentary "culture" in the sense that they learn certain behavior patterns from other members of their communities. Moreover, it is obvious that most, if not all, species do in fact possess certain innate behavioral tendencies, whether instinctual or less rigidly patterned. To assume that there are no remnants of such tendencies in *Homo sapiens* is simply anthropocentric. But even if we are more humble in our approach, the virtually unanswerable questions remain: What is the nature of these behavioral tendencies in humans? How strong are they? And, for the present text, the crucial question: Do they vary within the species by gender?

Margaret Mead: Tweedle Dee and Tweedle Dum

Margaret Mead has been directly and indirectly concerned with such questions for over 35 years. Indeed, the vacillations of her ideas have been a pretty accurate gauge of public opinion on the "woman question" during this period. For this reason, she is amply discussed and lampooned by many of the recent "feminist" authors (Bird, 1968,

p. 176; Friedan, 1963, chap. 6). But she is also one of the few
scholars to devote much attention to trying to cope with these issues.
Her two most important works for the present purposes are *Sex and
Temperament in Three Primitive Societies,* published originally in
1935, and *Male and Female,* which appeared nearly 15 years later.
Her more recent views have been presented in a variety of speeches,
interviews, and articles in popular magazines.

The overriding impression gained from her study of three "primitive
societies" in New Guinea (Mead, 1969) is one of virtually total cultural conditioning of human "temperament." In two of three cultures
males and females do not seem to differ in temperament, while strong
sex-linked behavior patterns are evident in the third. Division of labor
along gender lines is evident in all three. Mead argues that individuals
differ innately in temperament along a continuum. A given culture
takes only one or two parts of that continuum and makes it the norm
for one or both sexes, condemning those who fall elsewhere on it to
life as a deviant. However, gender is not relevant to one's place on
the continuum and, thus, members of both sexes may find themselves
deviant in any given society. The same individuals, of course, would
not necessarily be deviant in another culture.

The general nature of the similarities and differences between the
sexes in these three cultures comes as a shock to those who assume
the Western pattern to be "natural" and somehow inviolate. At the
risk of distortion, the simplest way of characterizing the sexes in these
cultures is as follows: among the Arapesh, both sexes resemble our
stereotypical contemporary femininity; among the Mundugamor, they
both appear to approximate our norm of masculinity; and finally,
among the Tchambuli, the females are "masculine," the males
"feminine."

The Arapesh of both sexes are peaceful, cooperative, and passive,
overwhelmingly concerned with "growing" things and people. Males
as well as females are said to "bear children." Long before the actual
birth of a child, the fetus is believed to grow and develop during the
first several weeks only by the continual participation of the father in
adding his sperm to mix with the mother's blood, thus producing the
individual in the womb. Postnatal rituals pertaining to the growth and

development of the infant also involve the father as intimately as the mother.

The Arapesh male's "maternal" behavior doesn't begin with the fathering of a child. While still little more than a boy, after his initiation, he receives a young girl as a bride. His task is then to "grow" her—namely, feed her, protect her, and train her. Eventually they engage in sexual intercourse when both are ready, and they thus are married. His authority over her then is no more or less than that of a parent over the child it has nurtured. Where this arrangement breaks down due to premature death of one of the partners or for some other reason, a later marriage is never really successful, because the husband has not "grown" his wife and, therefore, has no truly legitimate claim to her.

Mead makes it clear that barring a few exceptions who find themselves truly outcast, both male and female Arapesh "are neither strongly nor aggressively sexed . . ." (p. 157). Even the role of authority figure is so repugnant to the Arapesh that they have institutionalized ways of selecting an individual male and, from childhood, training him to be more aggressive. He is more pitied than envied by those whom he will eventually lead.

The formerly cannibalistic Mundugamor present a picture that is almost diametrically opposed to the Arapesh. Mead summarizes the Mundugamor ideal of character as "identical for the two sexes; . . . both men and women are expected to be violent, competitive, aggressively sexed, jealous, and ready to see and avenge insult, delighting in display, in action, in fighting" (1969, p. 213).

The family structure of the Mundugamor is such that intense animosity between husband and wife, father and son, mother and daughter, same-sexed siblings, and co-wives is institutionalized. Moreover, the hostility, distrust, and aggressiveness formalized in the family structure extend outward and pervade the entire community, giving it a highly competitive and even violent atmosphere. The Mundugamor are well prepared for this by their early childhood. Pregnancy is viewed by both the future parents as a disaster, and the future mother is ignored by her husband, who often uses this opportunity to find a new wife. When the infant arrives, the father is prepared to virtually hate a male; similarly, the mother will despise a female. Moreover, the mother is less than attached to the idea of being a mother at all. She rarely comforts the child or has warm bodily contact with it (unlike the Arapesh); she suckles it as little as possible and then weans it early and abruptly.

Very little attention is given to the third tribe of this study, the Tchambuli. The image of the two genders that emerges, however, is one of differentiation along lines essentially opposite to our own. Artistic ability, petty jealousy, sensitivity, nervousness, and emotional dependence are words descriptive of the males. The females are casual but efficient and competent, virtually running all necessary domestic and economic functions. They have *de facto* control of the important real property, in spite of the existence of formally patrilineal institutions. Moreover, it is the female who plays the role of sexual aggressor; the male "holds his breath and hopes . . ."; he is "not so urgently sexed" as the female (pp. 241–42).

From these findings Mead concludes that

> . . . many, if not all, of the personality traits which we have called masculine or feminine are as lightly linked to sex as are the clothing, the manners, and the form of head-dress that a society at a given period assigns to either sex . . . the evidence is overwhelmingly in favor of the strength of social conditioning (1969, p. 260).

About fifteen years later, in 1949, Mead came to somewhat different conclusions. In *Male and Female* (1970), she reviews her work on four tribes in addition to the three discussed above, paying particular attention to comparisons and contrasts to sex roles in then-contemporary America. In this long, rambling, and often contradictory work, psychoanalytic thought (which will be discussed later) is influential. Mead is now concerned to show how basically different bodies and reproductive functions *must* affect other aspects of the personalities (temperaments) of the two genders. Here she talks about "the different gifts of each sex" and the "special superiorities" of each. She is not convincing. Nowhere does she present serious cross-cultural evidence that any *particular* personality trait is necessarily gender linked.

Mead's arguments pertaining to females seem to rest on the invalid assumption that mothers must do the mothering (i.e., bearing and raising children are both necessarily female functions). Given the present state of science, all children must be borne by females, but raising children is certainly not a sex-linked function by biological necessity. Other than breast feeding, females are no better equipped to raise children than males. Mead argues from the basis of this fallacious assumption that women have a "special superiority in those human sciences which involve that type of understanding which until it is analyzed is called intuition." (We all "know" from folk culture that women are "naturally intuitive"!) The point is, whoever actually raises a child probably becomes more "intuitive," "sensitive," "humane" and so forth in the process. But anatomy does not dictate that it be the female who does the child raising, society does, and especially today when so few women nurse their young for very long, if at all.

Mead's discussion of males gives further evidence of her essentially nonbiological assumptions. She assumes that because men are not tied to the act of reproduction in anything but a very passing manner, they must "compensate" by being creative in everything else. Doubtless there is an element of veracity to this reasoning; "womb envy" will be a topic of further comment. It is a desire to be *creative* that is here basic to the organism, however, and presumably this is a *human* characteristic, not a male one. Many, but by no means all, females are able to fulfill this need via motherhood, especially in cultures that define motherhood as creative. Presumably, however, those females who, for whatever reason, do not procreate are as competent and creative as males in everything else but reproduction.

Mead is also concerned with ensuring male sexual desire. Her argument is that sexual intercourse and hence reproduction of the species does not require sexual desire on the part of the female, while, for obvious anatomical reasons, it does for the male. Therefore, anything that systematically reduces male sexuality is to be avoided, more or less like the plague. The question to be asked of Mead is: What kinds of things destroy male sexual desire in otherwise "normal" heterosexuals? The answer is that essentially anything that males perceive as threatening to their *masculinity* tends to have that effect. As discussed earlier, masculinity, as a sex role term, is defined by a given culture and thus is subject to change. In short, I suggest that concern for male sexual desire indicates support for the sex role status quo. Since any systematic deviation from sex role definitions, particularly by females, will often be perceived by males as a "threat" to masculinity and may result in impotency, Mead's orientation necessarily sees such deviations as "bad." This is a crucial point and one worth exploring a little further.

Assume for now that we really are concerned with ensuring human reproductivity (which might seem questionable at this point in history), or at least with heterosexual sexuality. Obviously, males must achieve and sustain erections to accomplish sexual intercourse; no such limitation is placed on the ability of the female to function as a sexual partner—at least minimally. The literature on male impotence is vast, but most of it is medical or psychological. The problem here is sociological. We are not concerned with why one man may be impotent, but with cases where impotence may be widespread in a society. In an era of changing sex roles, especially for females, is it not conceivable that widespread male impotence will result? Certainly it is, in the short run. If, for instance, millions of females become the primary source of income, when masculinity has heretofore been defined as provider and femininity as homebody, then their male mates and co-workers may find themselves similarly threatened and similarly impaired sexually. Whether or not this has in fact occurred recently in our society is a moot question, but the issue involved is important.

The problem is the confusion of gender and sex role by society. The only 100 percent sure component of maleness in all societies is male sexuality, that is, sexual satisfaction via erection of the penis and subsequent ejaculation. When other components are added to the definition of masculinity, the potential for trouble begins. (This same logic also applies to the feminine role.) Thus, for instance, in our society the artistic or sensitive male, the male who adores children and would like to teach kindergarten or stay home and raise his own, the male who has a mate in a higher status and better paid job than his (to mention but a few) begins to wonder about his essential maleness. He doesn't ask whether he deviates from "society's arbitrary norms," but rather whether he deviates from "nature's rules." He has confused society's (temporary) definition of masculinity with the essentially unchangeable reality of his maleness. His ability to function as a male thus suffers—unnecessarily. It is only when we sort things out and separate gender from sex role that the latter can change without affecting the functioning of the former.

Judging by the evidence presented by Mead in the two works considered here, the conclusions of the second can be all but ignored. The impression remains that although "temperaments" vary between individuals and different cultures institutionalize vastly different "ideal temperaments" for each or both sexes, there is no innate core temperament that can be attributed to one sex as against the other. Mead, the *cultural* anthropologist, remains just that.

Sigmund Freud: Biology Is Destiny—Almost*

No chapter concerning gender identity and sex roles could ignore Freud's theories of psychosexual development. His contributions to the study and understanding of human sexuality have had a profound impact on 20th-century Western thought. Many of Freud's concepts and principles are currently accepted as generalized knowledge, and his theories and vocabulary have found their way into the popular idiom. Unfortunately, such popularization can reduce theory to slogans, and the initial concepts become subject to severe distortions. Partly because of such distortions and partly on the basis of their own merits, Freud's ideas have recently been subject to angry rejection by feminists, as will be reviewed more fully in Chapter 3. Here the discussion will be confined to trying to understand Freud's own notions of the relationship of biology to culture in psychosexual development.

Freud was a Victorian living in a Victorian age, and he displayed the paternalistic and authoritarian qualities characteristic of the role of the physician. That these personal qualities should be reflected in his writings is to be expected. However, his writings covered a period of over four decades during which he wrote prolifically, frequently reconceptualizing, reordering, and discarding earlier concepts which he felt did not hold up under scrutiny. In that vast corpus of writing, statements may be found to support virtually any point of view on

---

* This section was written with the late Dr. Allyn Zanger.

the subject at hand. It is impossible to follow here the development of Freudian thinking in any detail, but an effort will be made to highlight basic concepts as they relate to an understanding of gender and sex role. Brenner (1957), Jones (1961), Lidz (1968), and Waeldner (1964) give greater detail. Freud's own article "Three Contributions to the Theory of Sex" (1938) is the basis for part of the following discussion.

Freud postulated the existence of drives or "libido" which, when operative, produce a state of tension which impels the individual to activity. The activity itself is mediated by experience, learned behavior, and reflection. It is not predetermined. He conceived of drives as possessing three major components: a source, an aim, and an object. The source was conceived of as biological in nature; the aim as tension reduction; the object as the product of learned or environmentally determined experiences. Thus sex as a drive impels an individual to seek gratification through some sort of sexual activity. The plasticity of the object of the drives is important in understanding the readiness with which objects can be substituted for one another in the event that the original object becomes associated with anxiety. The object of the sexual drive may be a heterosexual object, a homosexual object, an inanimate object (as in fetishism), or any other kind of object which the individual has learned through his or her unique life experiences to regard as nonthreatening and gratifying. It is clear from Freud's writings, however, that all these responses are not equally "normal" and "healthy," thus implying more emphasis on biological than cultural components. At any rate, Freud tried to maintain the position that *both* constitutional or biological factors and experiential or cultural factors interact dynamically to produce behavior, "normal" as well as "neurotic."

Biological maturation unfolds from conception in a largely predetermined manner that is species specific. The sequence of maturation is a given, but it is somewhat variable in terms of individual differences and the impact of the family as representative of the cultural environment. Paralleling physiological maturation is psychosexual development, which is the emotional and mental aspect of personality as it is shaped by the interaction of biology and culture. The cultural element is conceived by Freud in narrow terms—namely, the family.

In the course of development from infancy to adulthood the sexual activities motivated by drives change according to an inborn biological schedule, culminating in "mature" sexual needs that are normally characterized by heterosexuality. However, the evolution of sexuality is heavily influenced by parental inputs at every stage of development.

Freud conceived of sexual development as following approximately this scheme: (1) the three stages in early childhood, oral, anal, and genital, culminating in the Oedipus (including Electra) complex; (2) a latency period, namely a brief prepubertal stage evidencing a revival of oral and anal strivings; (3) puberty, and (4) a genital stage characteristic of adult sexuality. It is the prelatency stages that, in Freudian thinking, are crucial for determining adult behaviors.

In the first two stages of early childhood psychosexual development (oral and anal) there is no differentiation of the genders, although genetic and hormonal influences may predispose the child at birth to basic patterns of passivity or activity which enter into the subsequent development of male or female sex role characteristics. At approximately three years of age the child begins the third and most important stage, the genital, having reached a stage of physiological development where erogenous gratification is clearly focused in the genital area. With the biological sensitization of the genitals, children develop a keen interest in their anatomy and begin to substitute genital masturbation for thumb sucking and to manifest curiosity around differences in sexual anatomy. These stages comprise the biological component in Freud's thinking.

Within the family parents find that the child is no longer asexual but a relatively uninhibited creature with clear sexual qualities. They generally can no longer relate to the child as a neuter but begin thinking of it as either a boy or a girl, and the "cultural" element enters the picture. Until this point, Freud thinks the psychosexual development of boys and girls is identical. Recent research indicates he was incorrect in this, a matter to be discussed more fully in Chapter 3.

According to Freud, the "Oedipus complex" arises out of the wish or expectation of the child that the mother, who has always gratified needs in the past, will also gratify these new drives in some fashion. The crucial variable is how both parents respond to this new development. Generally, the child soon becomes aware that parents do not respond with delighted enthusiasm to sexual overtures. Depending upon the quality of the parental responses on the one hand and the primitive state of the child's cognitive development on the other, a boy will generally develop a fear that the parents will deprive him of the sexual organ which he now so highly prizes. This is "castration anxiety," according to Freudian theory, which helps to inhibit conscious expression of incestuous fantasies. At the same time, the boy begins to identify with the sex role of his father in an effort to emulate this person who possesses both the "bigger and better" penis and the object of the child's fantasies, namely, the mother. Such sex role identification elicits approval and thus reinforces the learning.

The girl (like the boy) receives gratification through mastabatory activities, becomes sexually curious, and so forth. Physiologically, it is the clitoris that is the area of greatest excitability. There is a tendency to compare herself unfavorably with the more obvious appendage of the boy. Children, at least in Western culture, have already assimilated a "bigger means better" mentality at that age—the essence of the Freudian concept of "penis envy." It is also quite likely that little girls associate the greater power and privilege of males with this obvious characteristic of maleness and thus envy the possessor of a penis and wish for one of their own. Freudian theory presents a tortuous scheme in an effort to describe the girl's shift of love object from mother to father, while yet retaining an identification with the mother. In essence, Freud said the girl renounces the mother for having deprived her of a penis and turns her interest to the father in a fantasy of possessing the father's penis. This is the "Electra complex." It is only when she later substitutes a desire for a (male) baby for the desire for a penis that she will have reached true "maturity" and, of course, mental "normalcy."

Freud repeatedly referred to the rather defective development of the superego (conscience) in females and its lack of stability, apparently convinced that women lacked the most important incentive for superego formation, namely, the castration fear. This was based on his observations that the girl does not usually repress her desire for the father as completely as the boy represses his erotic feelings for his mother. This deficit in superego development is supposedly reflected in the female's lack of a sense of social justice and in her narcissism. A feminine identity, Freud claimed, is established only when the wish for a penis is replaced by the wish for a child, which is directly related to female masochism, and when clitoral orgasm is renounced for vaginal orgasm (a nonsensical dichotomy, according to modern medical science). In many of Freud's writings activity is associated with masculinity and passivity with femininity, with frequent blurring of the distinction between gender and sex role. As a consequence of his biological orientation, it was never clarified whether these "feminine" qualities are biologically or culturally determined.

Freud did not consistently postulate radically different innate biological qualities for males and females, although many of his concepts were sufficiently ambiguous to leave that possibility open, and many of his followers have so interpreted them. Rather, he concentrated on the dynamic interplay between biological development and the reactions of those closest to the growing child, its parents. A critical analysis of his approach and those of the army of his followers will be left for a later section of this book.

Lionel Tiger: Vive la Difference!

One of the newer targets for the wrath of feminists is Lionel Tiger's recent *Men in Groups* (1970). In an impressive *tour de force* Tiger, another anthropologist, cites evidence from a large variety of social scientific and biological sources to support his basic contention that there is an innate, biological propensity for human males to "bond." Moreover, he argues that this bonding, resulting as it does in cohesive, all-male groups, is vitally linked to male dominance and political power.

Ethologists (students of nonhuman animal behavior) have produced a veritable outpouring of research reports in recent years. Much of their discussion has centered around two related phenomena, territoriality and status hierarchies within nonhuman communities. Beginning with Robert Ardrey's *The Territorial Imperative* (1966), some efforts have been made to generalize the findings of ethology to the human species. In Ardrey's book this was done primarily by analogy, and the resulting argument was weak and unconvincing. Tiger has presented a more cogent argument based on studies of various human groups and communities, as well as ethological evidence. Tiger begins his analysis with the now generally accepted argument that *Homo sapiens* evolved as a basically hunting species which, given limited biological equipment, pursued game in groups. Given the rigors of childbirth and rearing that preoccupied the female, these hunting groups were all male. The female who did pursue the hunt was less likely to pass on her genes since there was greater risk to her life, as well as to the lives of her young, than there was to her sisters who remained behind. Over time, Tiger argues, a nonerotic, male-male link parallel to and equally important for the survival of the species as the male-female link developed and became biologically "programmed" into the genetic structure. Bonding became a general male genetic characteristic, he continues, because it would have resulted in a breeding advantage to individuals who had it. To the extent that bonded males were more efficient hunters and better able to protect their communities, they would be more successful in leaving offspring (Tiger, 1970, chap. 3). Given the lack of evidence substantiating the existence of an innate male-female "bond," I find it difficult to understand precisely what kind of mechanism Tiger might be referring to when he talks of male bonding. The concept appears quasi mystical.

Tiger has noted many ramifications of such male bonding. He claims that aggression "is directly a function and/or outgrowth of corporate male interaction" (p. 247). Aggression by a group of bonded males serves to strengthen ingroup cohesion and cooperation, a general phenomenon long recognized by sociologists (Coser, 1964; Sumner, 1959). There is also obvious stratification in male groups. Such groups, to be efficient for hunt, war or, in complex contemporary societies, economic, political, and religious enterprises, must be both cooperative and hierarchical; somebody needs to be more or less in charge, and others must be prepared to follow. According to Tiger, females are not found in positions of leadership because, given male bonding, they simply do not provide the "releasers" for followship behavior (pp. 96–97 and 258). In fact, he does not find women to be politically active in any context to any great extent, and he suggests that this may be because political activity rests on the basis of male groups and an innate, presumably male, territoriality.

Territoriality, a characteristic found in a number of animal species, consists of either individual (male) or community (both sexes, usually male dominated) possession of a piece of real estate which is protected from invasion by other members of the same species. In the case of individual territoriality, a male, by virtue of the territory he holds, attracts one or more mates; he permits no other males access to his "turf." In communal territoriality, a group holds a territory and defends it against invasion by other groups of the same species. In these species there is often a relatively elaborate status hierarchy, especially among mature males, with the breeding advantage going to the highest status males. Although most extant higher primate species do not seem to be territorial at all, Ardrey (1966) argues that *Homo sapiens* is. Moreover, although other species are either individually or communally territorial, Ardrey seems to suggest that humans may be both, with the home and the nation alike constituting territory to be defended. Tiger appears to tentatively accept Ardrey's unsubstantiated argument that *Homo sapiens* is territorial and links this to male bonding and male dominance of political activity.

The burden of Tiger's argument does not concern territoriality, however. It is best summarized in his own words:

> The hypothesis here is that in the most general political case, defense needs and for social order are satisfied most effectively by soliciting subordinate or cooperative relationships with adult males. Thus, females of all ages and pre-adult males will seek subordinate relationships with adult males who will protect them when the group is attacked and who will enforce social order when internal disturbance occurs. . . . The hypothesis contains the proposition that the defenders and policemen must be males (1970, pp. 109–10).

From this it would seem that Golda Meir and Indira Gandhi must be mistaken about their gender! Female subordination is nothing more or less than a fact of genetics, in this view. Of course, as an anthropologist Tiger cannot really accept such extreme conclusions. He pays due lip service to the strength of sociocultural phenomena and suggests that females may in fact function in ways perhaps more "natural" to males, given "explicit selfconscious provision of special facilities by a concerned, sensitive, and willing community" (p. 112).

The same logic applies to the occupational sphere, according to

Tiger, in which there is virtually everywhere "an inverse relationship between the status of occupations and the participation of females" (p. 142). Moreover, " 'Female' implies tasks involving specific inter-actions of a personal or quasi-personal kind [e.g., taking care of the family] while 'male' implies activities on a larger scale . . . with greater direct and active relevance for communal integrity and social dominance" (pp. 146–47). In arguing this Tiger ignores the fact that the greater physical strength of males could allow them to appropriate power and privilege, regardless of any quasi-mystical force such as bonding.

Most of the rest of *Men in Groups* is devoted to extensive docu-mentation of the male bonding phenomenon as revealed in sports, secret societies, initiation rites, war and so on. Tiger shows how males "court" other males and "validate" their maleness through interaction, often of an aggressive, even violent nature. Forms of communal female interaction and ceremony are virtually ignored. Tiger presents the reader with a large array of exemplary material, but nowhere does he make any pretense of really "testing" his hypothesis, let alone "proving" it. Moreover, recent research comparing male and female patterns of social participation fails to support Tiger's thesis (Booth, 1972).

Alternative Ideas on the Origin of Patriarchy

Tiger's basically biological explanation for male political and eco-nomic dominance constitutes the gender approach to an analysis of sex-differentiated behavior. There is little question as to the existence of certain extraordinarily widespread regularities in the area of male dominance. Virtually everywhere there is division of labor by sex. The tasks assigned to the female or male sex vary tremendously, so that what is masculine in one place and time is feminine in another, and vice versa (with a few possible exceptions). The division of labor is practically universal, however, and it seems to be related in almost all societies to the institution of patriarchy. The overwhelming major-ity of human societies about which we have any information have been patriarchal, at least to some extent. Even where cultures have been found to be matrilocal and/or matrilineal, in the definitions of male versus female tasks, the former are more prestigeful. Moreover, *final* authority for decision making seems virtually everywhere to be a male prerogative. There are some exceptions to this pattern, but they appear to be extremely limited in number. The question is, why are prestige and authority nearly universally male prerogatives? Tiger offers one possible explanation. An alternative explanation, while also based on gender considerations, concentrates more explicitly on sociocultural factors; this is the sex role approach. Any answer to this question must go back to the dawn of human development and, therefore, must be speculative. With this in mind, I offer the following conceptualization of the development of male dominance. It appears to make at least as much sense as Tiger's.

As humans evolved from their primate ancestors they lost many physical advantages. The prehensile tail that enables the monkey to scramble from tree to tree, safe from ground predators, disappeared; eyesight and hearing became markedly inferior to those of many mammals; protective fur coats and strong jaws and teeth were lost; and the size and strength characteristics of some higher primates were diminished. In short, humankind became the physically vulnerable creature called by Desmond Morris (1967) "the naked ape." All this was traded in for the apposite thumb and, most crucially, a markedly increased brain capacity.

Over the millenia, this vulnerable naked ape could only survive (not to mention thrive) by substantially increasing its brain capacity. The enlarged size of the skull necessary to contain the bigger brain presented a practical problem: How was such a skull to pass through the birth canal? One possible solution was for the pelvic region of the female to so broaden that she would be rendered virtually immobile throughout her life. But evolution followed another path: human infants were born in a relatively underdeveloped state. Thus, at birth the human brain is only 23 percent of its final adult size (Morris, 1967, p. 29). The extremely long dependence period of the human child is the result.

The consequence of this long-term dependency, however, was a different kind of immobility for the female. One need not postulate any maternal instinct to understand that the helpless child was primarily dependent on the mother, and only indirectly so on the father.

As in all mammal species the infant lived on its mother's milk, and in humans this was true for a considerable period. Given almost constant pregnancies and biologically dependent children, females were often incapable of readily supplying themselves with the requisite food, shelter, and protection. In this connection, it is important to realize that *Homo sapiens* was evolving not in the lush jungles of its primitive herbivorous ancestors, but in the desolate savannas that were replacing them.

During the evolutionary process, another important biological change was occurring. In nonhuman species that reproduce sexually the female of the species is sexually receptive only at certain periodic intervals, namely, during "heat." Perhaps because of the dependence of the human infant and thus of its mother, or perhaps for some other reasons, the human female evolved the capacity to receive sexually and enjoy a male at any time. The estrus cycle disappeared. Undoubtedly, this ability of humans of both sexes to enjoy sex at any time played an important role in the creation of relatively permanent mating bonds, a very rare phenomenon among other species and absent in other primates. Essentially, then, the human family probably grew out of an exchange of sexual accessibility by females in return for provision of food, shelter, and protection by males (Morris, p. 54 ff.). This, in turn, helped to ensure the survival of the young during their long dependency. So far this approach offers little that Tiger would dispute. However, in her intriguing book *The Descent of Woman,* Elaine Morgan (1972) recently questioned this entire interpretation of human prehistory. She claims that neither sexuality nor economic dependence of females encouraged the creation of the mated pair in humans. In fact, females supplied the vast bulk of the total food supply by gathering fruits, nuts, roots, and so forth. Moreover, in losing the estrus cycle, Morgan argues, human females lost much of their sexuality.

Assuming the more orthodox interpretation, the question arises how male dominance or patriarchy arose from the exchange of sexual accessibility for creature needs. By its very nature the exchange is somewhat unequal. Individual males (as well as females) could survive quite well without sex. Females with young, however, could not readily survive, nor could their offspring, without males. Thus, as

Shulamith Firestone (1970, pp. 8–9) argues, a power differential is built into the human "biological family," whether that family is monogamous or structured in some other manner. Without the reinforcing mechanisms of most cultures, this power differential might have remained negligible. Indeed, there seems to be good reason to believe that in the earliest societies females had a substantial amount of prestige and, perhaps, power (Gough, 1971, pp. 768–69). Many if not most major early deities were probably fertility goddesses. It is even likely that knowledge of the male's function in reproduction was altogether lacking. After all, it is no mean intellectual feat to logically connect an act of sexual intercourse with some symptoms that appear a number of weeks later and a delivery occurring nine months after the fact!

It seems likely that to primitive humans the act of giving birth must have appeared to be a spectacularly mystical and creative phenomenon, although also quite frightening, as various taboos pertaining to postpartum and menstruating women in preliterate tribes attest. It is not at all farfetched to suggest that early males suffered acute "womb envy" (Stannard, 1970). It should be no cause to wonder that males, simultaneously frightened and strongly attracted by the birth process, attempted to appropriate virtually all other mystical, status-conferring, and culturally defined creative activity for themselves. They usually succeeded by default. It is from this "mass sublimation" that patriarchy, which was mildly inherent in the biological facts of life for the species, gained a powerful grip. Cultural patterns were then established granting males, by virtue of their inability to bear children, all manner of rights and privileges, eventuating in the replacement of the fertility goddess by the male god of war and the hunt.

By the time males discovered that they played a role in reproduction, patriarchy was already entrenched and self-reinforcing. In fact, for a long time, even into the 19th century, Western patriarchal culture had produced a medical "science" convinced that the male carries a miniature but complete baby in his sperm, the female merely supplying an appropriate environment for its early development (Stannard, 1970, p. 28). The creativity of the reproductive act, having first been viewed (erroneously) as female, was made into an exclusively male function, with the resulting offspring being defined by law and custom as the father's possession. Thus to this day a legitimate child is an infant who bears its father's name. All infants have an identifiable mother; we only grant full status, however, to those whose paternity is well assured. As a friend recently quipped, "maternity is a fact, paternity only a rumor." It was, indeed, a short step then to institutionalize a wide range of restrictions on females by which "proper" paternity of offspring was ensured. Patriarchy was in full swing, with virtually every social and cultural institution helping to support it.

The interesting possibility exists that even the size and strength differential between the sexes was, in origin, a culturally induced phenomenon. In many animal species the sexes are not differentiated by size or physical strength. Moreover, there are some human cultures where males and females are built about the same, such as the Balinese studied by Mead (1970, p. 106). It is conceivable that once patriarchy was instituted, culturally defined notions of beauty came to favor strength and large size in males, and weakness and petite structure in females. Such definitions of beauty, marvelously supportive of patriarchal social institutions, would lead to selective reproduction favoring small, weak females and big, strong males. This difference, then, would feed back and support male power and prestige.

If the above thesis is correct, an innate leadership-followership component of male bonding by which some males provide the proper "releasers" to attract followers, while no females are inherently capable of doing so, is needless. The core of my argument hinges on an essentially psychosocial phenomenon: males envied females their supposed "creative" function and were able to appropriate power and, ultimately, status because females could find sufficient psychic fulfillment in this particular function to care little about the others. I am merely assuming that there is some sort of innate *human* tendency to want to be creative, in whatever terms this is defined by the group. This approach is similar to one implied by Mead's discussion reviewed earlier.

Hormones, Chromosomes, and Behavior

No chapter considering the question of the extent to which male-female behavioral and psychological differences are innate or learned would be complete without a word about the possible effects of hormones. Three facts are clear in this respect: (1) males and females have different amounts of the various sex-related hormones in their systems, (2) sex hormones do enter the brain and affect its activity, and (3) research is scanty and inconclusive as to what the specific behavioral ramifications of nos. 1 and 2 might be. Judith Bardwick's *Psychology of Women* (1971, chap. 2) is a good source of information on this topic.

Hormones are chemical substances secreted into the bloodstream by the endocrine glands. The primary male sex hormone is testosterone, one of a group of hormones known as androgens. Females secrete this hormone also, but in small amounts. In the female there are a number of important sex hormones, the release of each of which is related to the menstrual cycle. Two of the most important are estrogen and progesterone (which are also present in small amounts in males). The former is chiefly responsible for the development of female secondary sex characteristics and for preparing the uterus for ovulation and possible conception. The latter is important in maintaining a state of pregnancy and for signaling the end of the menstrual cycle if impregnation does not occur.

Right before menstruation the levels of both estrogen and progesterone are low. Given the repeated finding that most women experience premenstrual depression, irritability, fatigue, crying spells, hostility, anxiety, and so forth, regardless of their "normal" psychological state, it would appear that hormonal levels probably do influence the psyche. Specific reactions to the cycle vary according to the mental health of the individuals, but nearly all women seem to undergo substantial cyclical patterns of emotional variation. Moreover, the same psychological symptoms appear in most women at two other times when the estrogen and progesterone levels are low: during menopause and immediately after childbirth. Other findings cited by Bardwick reported "passive-receptive tendencies and a feeling of well-being correlated with progesterone production, and active heterosexual striving correlated with estrogen production" (1971, pp. 28–29). She also suggests that feelings of maternal nurturance toward infants are biologically grounded in the high levels of estrogen and progesterone present during pregnancy (pp. 33–35). It is, however, quite possible (especially in Western cultures) that females have been told since childhood that they can *expect* to experience these different mood swings during their cycle, during menopause and after childbirth, and such information itself serves to create a self-fulfilling prophecy. If this is the case, cultures, not hormones, create the emotional variation. The male is generally not thought to undergo cyclic hormonal and related psychic changes, although recent research casts doubt on even this assumption. Estelle Ramey (1972) has recently presented evidence from a number of studies which suggest that males are also influenced by a hormone cycle of approximately 30 days which affects mood. At any rate, levels of testosterone definitely do vary between men, and it appears that there may possibly exist an important behavioral correlate of this variation. A recent study (Kreuz & Rose, 1971) of a sample of prisoners led to the following tentative conclusion: "The findings suggest that testosterone may be related to a history of assault, and to the occurrence of more violent or aggressive criminal behavior during childhood through adolescence" (p. 16). However, testosterone level did not appear to be related to adult behavior in this study. Bardwick offers some supporting evidence concerning the behavioral effects of male hormones on the behavior of rhesus monkeys. Baby female monkeys whose mothers had been injected with male hormones before giving birth "displayed much more 'rough and tumble' play than normal females and exhibited as much chasing behavior as males" (1971, p. 85). They also showed more aggressive behavior. Even more convincing is some research she cites with reference to humans: "If testosterone is administered to normal adult females we find that their . . . levels of physical activity and their general level of aggressiveness may increase to levels normally found in males" (p. 89).

Finally, a word should be added concerning sex chromosomes and behavior. The female of the species has her sex determined by the XX chromosome, the male by the XY. It has become common knowledge since Ashley Montagu wrote *The Natural Superiority of Women* in 1952 that because of the generally more important role of the larger X chromosome, of which females have two compared to only one for males, the latter are much more vulnerable to a wide variety of genetically transmitted disorders, such as hemophilia and color blindness (1968, chap. 5). Montagu lists about 60 such disorders, 30 of which are "serious" (pp. 76–78). Males also die more frequently pre- and postnatally. But more important for our purposes are the recently emerging findings concerning those few males whose sex chromosomes are XXY. Preliminary studies seem to indicate that such men may be particularly prone to violence and aggressive behavior. Prison inmates seem to manifest this characteristic more frequently than a "normal" sample; one of the more notorious XXY's was mass murderer Richard Speck. These traits may, however, result from the psychological ramifications of the fact that such males are sterile and frequently somewhat abnormal in external sex-related characteristics.

The conclusions to be drawn from findings concerning hormones and chromosomes point once again to the need for keeping the biological component in mind when assessing human behavior—sex role or otherwise. On the basis of the research cited, there may be reason to say males, or at least those with extra X chromosomes or testosterone, have a greater inherent bent for aggressive, even violent behavior than females (which is not to deny the existence of these traits in the latter). Similarly, some aspects of maternal behavior, especially shortly after childbirth, may be innate to the female endocrine system.

One set of additional facts is relevant to this discussion. It seems evident that babies are born with somewhat differing "temperaments"—some are cranky, some pacific, and so forth. Most differences noted do not appear to be related to gender, but a few do. At birth it seems that, generally, females show greater motor passivity than males (i.e., they are less physically active), and they are more sensitive to a greater number of physical stimuli (Bardwick, 1971, p. 93; Lynn, 1972, p. 243). Whether such differences are directly related to hormones, chromosomes, or something else has not been established, but surely they would tend to elicit different responses from parents and others in contact with the infant which might be expected to feed back, strengthening and reinforcing sex differences. Bardwick concludes:

> It is not, then, that children are born with a built-in set of responses that will determine their behaviors irrespective of environmental reactions. Nor is it true that children are 'tabula rasa,' or blank clay, destined to be molded solely by the imprint of a parental . . . hand. Predispositions to respond and to perceive similar stimuli may be

significantly different between the sexes because of genetically determined differences that have their roots in physiology. The endocrine data and the infant animal and human studies lead to the assumption of general behavioral tendencies that are sex linked. . . . The behaviors of the organism, whether animal or human, will be responded to, rewarded, punished, or ignored in the process of socialization. I suggest that most cultures may be reinforcing behavior tendencies or predispositions *characteristic* of the sexes (1971, p. 95).

Heredity or Environment: Some Conclusions

During the course of this chapter a number of studies and hypotheses have been reviewed pertaining to the basic questions: What if anything inherently differentiates males and females? Are the only too obvious differences frequently noted no more than sociocultural whims? The answers to these questions are very little clearer now than they were at the outset; relevant research is scanty and highly inconclusive, while speculation abounds. In very general terms, however, it is possible to draw a few conclusions.

First, it is clear that the vast majority of the behavioral and psychological characteristics designated as masculine or feminine in any given culture are not innate to the genders. If they were, the amount of cross-cultural variation noted by Mead, among others, would be virtually impossible to explain.

Second, the data pertaining to hormones, and chromosomes in particular, lead to the conclusion that some few innate tendencies probably do differ by gender. However, I think it is also safe to conclude, with Tiger, that sociocultural factors can be institutionalized that virtually obliterate the effects of any such innately different tendencies between the genders. This is because such traits are not "instinctual" but, at most, predispositions to behave in certain ways, and are therefore modifiable.

One other conclusion can be drawn. Whatever innate behavioral and psychological differences may exist between the genders, they are a matter of degree, not kind. Males are not aggressive and females passive; if anything, males may be somewhat more *inclined* to aggressiveness than females. Similarly, females may be at times more inclined to nurturing behavior toward infants than males would be, although the latter presumably have some inclination in this direction as well. The issue of the nature and types of intergroup differences will be considered further in the next chapter.

These conclusions are best summarized in Bardwick's argument that most cultures reinforce those differences that may be inherent in the genders. In effect, Freud's theories allow for much the same conclusion. It is my contention that such "reinforcement" is far and away the most important element in determining gender-linked behavior and psychology. Put simply, sex role is a much more crucial factor than gender.

References

Ardrey, Robert. *The Territorial Imperative.* New York: Delta Books, Dell Publishing Co., 1966.

Bardwick, Judith. *Psychology of Women: A Study of Bio-cultural Conflicts.* New York: Harper and Row, 1971.

Bird, Caroline. *Born Female: The High Cost of Keeping Women Down.* New York: David McKay Co., 1968.

Booth, Alan. "Sex and Social Participation." *American Sociological Review* 37 (April 1972): 183–93.

Brenner, Charles. *An Elementary Textbook on Psychoanalysis.* Garden City, N.Y.: Doubleday & Co., 1957.

Coser, Lewis. *The Functions of Social Conflict.* Toronto, Canada: Free Press Paperback, 1964.

Firestone, Shulamith. *The Dialectic of Sex.* New York: Bantam Books, 1970.

Freud, Sigmund. "Three Contributions to the Theory of Sex." In A. A. Brill (ed.), *The Basic Writings of Sigmund Freud,* pp. 553–632. New York: Random House, 1938.

Friedan, Betty. *The Feminine Mystique.* New York: Dell Publishing Co., 1963.

Gough, Kathleen. "The Origin of the Family." *Journal of Marriage and the Family* 33 (November 1971): 760–70.

Jones, Ernest. *The Life and Work of Sigmund Freud.* Abridged and edited by Lionel Trilling and Steven Marcus. New York: Basic Books, 1961.

Kreuz, Leo, and Rose, Robert. "Assessment of Aggressive Behavior in a Young Animal Population." *Psychiatric Spectator* 7 (August 1971): 15–16.

Lidz, Theodore. *The Person.* New York: Basic Books, 1968.

Lynn, David B. "Determinants of Intellectual Growth in Women." *School Review* 80 (February 1972): 241–60.

Mead, Margaret. *Sex and Temperament in Three Primitive Societies.* New York: Dell Publishing Co., 1969; first published 1935.

Mead, Margaret. *Male and Female: A Study of the Sexes in a Changing World.* New York: Dell Publishing Co., 1970; first published 1949.

Montagu, Ashley. *The Natural Superiority of Women.* New York: P. F. Collier, 1968; first published 1952.

Morgan, Elaine. *The Descent of Woman.* New York: Stein and Day, 1972.

Morris, Desmond. *The Naked Ape.* New York: Dell Publishing Co., 1967.

Ramey, Estelle. "Men's Cycles." *Ms.* (Spring 1972): 8–14.

Stannard, Una. "Adam's Rib, or the Woman Within." *Trans-Action* 8 (November–December 1970): 24–35.

Sumner, William G. *Folkways.* New York: Dover Publications, 1959, first published 1906.

Tiger, Lionel. *Men in Groups.* New York: Vintage Books, Random House, 1970.

Waeldner, Robert. *Basic Theories of Psychoanalysis.* New York: Schocken Books, 1964.

Chapter 2

Stereotypes and Stigmas

Human beings try to make sense out of their world by lumping together a variety of individual cases, labeling them, and then reacting to categories of phenomena. If they didn't do this, they might quite literally "blow their minds." It is certainly impossible for people to react to the myriad stimuli around them on an individual basis; their brains would overload and the circuits would burn out. Therefore they categorize phenomena on the basis of an outstanding attribute or a few salient features that a number of individual cases seem to have in common. Often they then proceed to react to the category rather than the individual phenomenon.

This process of prejudging or stereotyping is as true of reactions to other humans as it is to any other phenomenon. Particularly when we don't know people well, we tend to react to them on the basis of a small number of relatively obvious characteristics. Chief among these are probably gender, race (or ethnicity), dress (or life style in general), occupation (or social class), and age. Up to a point, there is nothing the matter with this; indeed, we could hardly function socially without making some assumptions about people. Moreover, up to a point, stereotyping is "true." For whatever reasons, people who are similar on any one or more of those key characteristics *tend* to be similar in other ways as well. The problem arises when we take our categories too seriously; when we say that since females (blacks, old people, poor people, and so forth) tend to do so and so, a *particular* individual can be expected to do the same. It is worse yet when the characteristic is judged negatively by those doing the categorization. At this point, prejudgment becomes prejudice. When we behave toward an individual on the basis of that prejudice, we are guilty of discrimination.

In concrete terms, it is one thing to make the more or less factually accurate observation that most females in contemporary America are not ambitious for promotions entailing great amounts of authority and responsibility. It is quite another thing to say, on that basis alone, that Jane Doe doesn't want a promotion in her job. And it is inexcusable, in a society dedicated to equal opportunity for all, to then fail to promote Ms. Doe on that basis alone. An excellent detailed discussion of these distinctions is provided in Gordon Allport's classical work, *The Nature of Prejudice* (1958).

Categorical Differences

Allport (p. 94 ff.) presents a useful fourfold distinction of types of categorical or intergroup differences. Two (or more) categories of people can differ in a given characteristic in these ways: (1) a J-curve of conformity behavior, (2) a rare-zero differential, (3) overlapping normal curves of distribution, and (4) a categorical differential. Most male-female differences are probably of the third type. The four categories are hypothetically illustrated in Figure 2.1.

The J-curve of conformity behavior occurs when practically all members of a group have a characteristic in common while a few do not. Thus, for instance, if most (say, 80 percent) young American males play football fairly regularly, 15 percent play only occasionally, and 5 percent never, a graph (frequency polygon) of this would resemble a J (Figure 2. 1A). A J-curve shows that a particular attribute is highly characteristic of a specific population. It distinguishes one group from another when both do not behave in a like manner. Thus American females, few of whom ever play football and almost none of whom play regularly, would not fit this curve.

FIGURE 2.1

FOUR TYPES OF CATEGORICAL DIFFERENCES*

A. J-curve depicting frequency of football playing among American males.

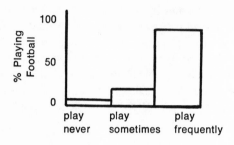

B. Rare-zero differential of hemophilia.

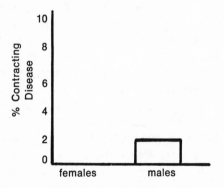

C. Overlapping normal curves of height distribution.

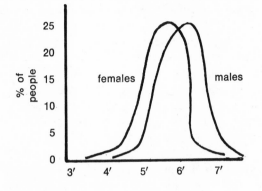

D. Categorical differential of suicide rates.

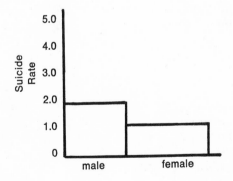

*All numbers are hypothetical.

The second type of difference of the rare-zero differential (Figure 2.1B). This occurs when a very small number in one group possesses a given trait, but no one in the other group does. An example of this is the relatively rare disease hemophilia, which strikes only males (although females are carriers).

Probably the most common kind of difference between groups is that represented by overlapping normal curves (Figure 2.1C). The trait in question is distributed normally within each of two or more groups, but the arithmetic means of the various groups differ, as do the modes and medians. Examples of this are legion. Comparisons of height and weight between the genders have this characteristic. "Passivity" and "aggressiveness" (whatever these may mean) are also probably distributed in this way, with the mean for males being somewhat lower on the former and higher on the latter than for females. Concretely, this means, in terms of aggressiveness, that both males and females vary between being highly aggressive and very unaggressive. However, the *group* average for males is somewhat higher, signifying that a greater number of males is found in the higher ranges of aggressiveness than females and, conversely, a smaller number is found in the lower ranges. Nonetheless, a substantial number of females will be equally or more aggressive than a substantial number of males. How substantial this overlap is will depend on how far apart those group means fall and what the standard deviations are. Generally speaking, however, differences within one group (in this case a gender) will be greater than differences between groups; there is more difference between the most aggressive and least aggressive males than between most males and most females (see Brenton, 1966, pp. 48–50).

Allport's fourth type is the categorical differential (Figure 2.1D). In this case, the various groups compared all have some of the given characteristics (unlike the rare-zero type), but genuine differences exist in the extent of the trait. It differs from overlapping normal curves by being a discontinuous variable; that is, it does not fit a normal curve. An example of such a phenomenon would be the suicide rates of males compared to that of females. Members of both groups kill themselves, but the rates differ.

Pinpointing and describing group differences and beliefs about them is a crucial first step in understanding how they arise, what they mean to members of the different categories, and how they are sustained. This chapter and the next will attempt to develop these understandings with reference to contemporary American sex roles.

Prejudgments of Contemporary American Sex Roles

The number of traits males and females are said to differ on are legion. Most such differences are considered to be so obvious, in fact, that little or no actual research exists to document the degree of difference that exists.

Table 2.1 lists a large number of such traits subdivided into six general types, plus a residual "other personal characteristics" category. This list grew out of the work done by 13 small groups (five to six people per group) of students of both sexes who discussed the question: "What kinds of words and phrases do you think *most Americans* use to characterize males compared to females, or "masculinity' versus 'femininity' ? "

TABLE 2.1

SEX ROLE STEREOTYPE TRAITS

Characteristics	Masculine Traits	Feminine Traits

I. Physical	Virile, athletic, strong*
	 Sloppy, worry less about
	   appearance and aging
	 Brave
		Weak, helpless, dainty,
		   nonathletic*
		 Worry about appearance
		   and aging*
		 Sensual
		 Graceful

II. Functional	Breadwinner, provider*	Domestic* Maternal, involved with children* Church-going

*Attribute listed by five or more of the groups.

SEX ROLE STEREOTYPE TRAITS—continued

Characteristics	Masculine Traits	Feminine Traits
III. Sexual	Sexually aggressive, experienced* Single status acceptable; male "caught" by spouse	Virginal, inexperienced; double standard* Must be married, female "catches" spouse Sexually passive, uninterested Responsible for birth control Seductive, flirtatious
IV. Emotional	Unemotional, stoic, don't cry*	Emotional, sentimental, romantic* Can cry Expressive Compassionate Nervous, insecure, fearful
V. Intellectual	Logical, intellectual, rational, objective, scientific* Practical Mechanical Public awareness, activity, contributor to society Dogmatic	Scatterbrained, frivolous, shallow, inconsistent, intuitive* Impractical Perceptive, sensitive "Arty" Idealistic, humanistic*
VI. Interpersonal	Leader, dominating* Disciplinarian* Independent, free, individualistic* Demanding	Petty, flirty, coy, gossipy, catty, sneaky, fickle* Dependent, overprotected, responsive* Status conscious and competitive, refined, adept in social graces* Follower, subservient, submissive
VII. Other Personal	Aggressive* Success oriented, ambitious* Proud, egotistical, confident Moral, trustworthy Decisive Competitive Uninhibited, adventurous	Self-conscious, easily intimidated, modest, shy, sweet* Patient* Vain* Affectionate, gentle, tender, soft Not aggressive, quiet, passive Tardy Innocent Noncompetitive

*Attribute listed by five or more of the groups.

All attributes listed were mentioned by at least 2 of the 13 groups. Group members were specifically instructed to ignore their own particular impressions, if possible, since they were assumed to be somewhat more sophisticated on the subject than "most Americans." The sample taking part was anything but random. First, the students had recruited themselves into a course entitled "Sociology of Sex Roles," given at a small, private university. They were overwhelmingly white, although there were a few blacks and Mexican-Americans. They were mostly middle to upper-middle class in family background, and about two thirds to three quarters were female. Finally, since the school is located in Texas, some regional biases were probably present. A somewhat less biased sample of graduate social work students at another Texas university arrived at almost the same stereotypes of masculinity and femininity when asked the same question, however.

Given the biases of the sample, a number of interesting observations can still be made on the basis of this relatively comprehensive list of traits stereotypically assigned to the sexes. The first of these is the manner in which some of these traits can be related to Allport's typology of categorical differences. Those words and phrases that were mentioned by at least five of the groups and had counterparts for both sexes are largely of the overlapping normal curves (ONC) variety, as shown in Table 2.2. This means that many, if not most, members of one gender will have at least some traits assigned stereotypically to the other. More precisely, a large proportion of each gender will have high levels or "scores" on variables assigned categorically (primarily as J-curves) in the popular imagination to the opposite gender. The potential confusion that this can cause is obvious, as members of both sexes can be led to wonder "What's the matter with me? Why am I a 'masculine' female (or a 'feminine' male)?"

Making prejudgmental or stereotypical assertions about groups does not necessarily entail negative connotations. In the case of the sex role traits cited, however, a curious difference between the masculine and feminine lists is evident in this respect. In any language, words take on an emotional content over and above their definitions per se. This affective dimension is a function of prevailing cultural values. There are many more blatantly negative connotative words used to describe femininity than masculinity, and somewhat fewer positive terms. It must be recalled that one of the biases of the sample was overrepre-

TABLE 2.2

TYPES OF CATEGORICAL DIFFERENCES BETWEEN SOME SEX ROLE TRAITS

Masculine Traits	Feminine Traits	Categorical Difference Type
Athletic, strong	Weak, nonathletic	Overlapping normal curve ONC
Worry less about appearance and aging	Worry about appearance and aging	ONC
Breadwinner	Domestic	Categorical difference
Sexually experienced	Virginal	Categorical difference
Unemotional, stoic	Emotional, sentimental	ONC
Logical, rational, objective, intellectual	Scatterbrained, inconsistent, intuitive	ONC
Leader, dominating	Follower, subservient	ONC
Independent, free	Dependent, overprotected	ONC
Aggressive	Passive	ONC
Success oriented, ambitious	Easily intimidated, shy	ONC

sentation of females. Among the words listed with reference to masculinity, only "sloppy" and "egotistical" are clearly negative in connotation in this society, and the former is trivial. "Proud," "ambitious," "aggressive," "dogmatic," and a few others are somewhat negative, depending on the context in which they are used and the values of the individuals using them. Consensus on the values represented by these terms is lacking. Large segments of our society would find these traits very agreeable, but substantial numbers would define them as disagreeable. Generally speaking, however, the words used to describe the masculine role are quite positive: "practical," "logical," "experienced," "brave," "adventuresome," "confident," "trustworthy," and so on.

The tone of the words used to describe femininity is considerably different. Such terms as "petty," "fickle," "coy," "sneaky," "status conscious," "frivolous," "shallow," and "vain" are very negatively charged in this society. The positively charged words are innocuous compared to their masculine counterparts. Females are said to be "idealistic, humanistic" rather than a "contributor to society"; "innocent" rather than "adventurous"; "patient" rather than "ambitious"; and "gentle, tender, soft" rather than "moral, trustworthy." Thus a general, if not too precise, impression emerges that the masculine sex role stereotype is a positive thing, and the feminine one either negative or passive. A basic dualism is, in fact, displayed toward the female, who is simultaneously held to be "sexually passive, uninterested" (the Virgin Mary image) and "seductive, flirtatious" (the wicked Eve tempting poor innocent Adam). This theme runs throughout the history of Western civilization, and our mores concerning "good" and "bad" females have no parallels for males.

The question arises at this point whether any other evidence exists that the sex role stereotypes depicted above are indeed held by Americans. The answer is yes. Phyllis Chesler (1971a, p. 97) reports that a study of 79 psychotherapists, 46 male and 33 female, revealed the following description of the "mentally healthy adult female": "submissive, emotional, easily influenced, sensitive to being hurt, excitable, conceited about appearance, dependent, not very adventurous, less competitive, unaggressive, and unobjective." Moreover, she "dislikes math and science." This description was generally agreed upon by both the male and female therapists. Although the masculine traits were not listed, Chesler notes that "clinicians have different standards of mental health for men and women. Their standards for a 'healthy adult man' looked like those for a 'healthy adult'; but healthy women differed from both. . . ." (p. 97).

Myron Brenton reviews common masculine stereotypes in an excellent chapter in *The American Male* entitled "The Masculinity Trap" (1966, chap. 2). Some of the supposed masculine characteristics he discusses include "aggressive-sadism"; "violence"; a tendency to "stifle . . . intuition, tenderness, and sensitivity"; "stoicism"; "protectiveness" concerning females; a feeling that the financial burden is the male's alone; "mechanical ability"; "athletic prowess"; "courage" and "bravery." Similarly, Jerome Kagan and Howard Moss (1962) define the masculine role model in such terms as "sexually active," "athletic," "independent," "dominant," "courageous," and "competitive." Their feminine model includes the traits of "sexual timidity," "social anxiety," "fearing and avoiding problem situations," and "pursuing homemaking activities rather than career ones." Thus, although some of the individual words differ, the general images of the two roles are quite consistent with each other and those of the students cited above.

An exercise to show just how stereotyped our notions of the two genders are involves taking some descriptive material pertaining to a member of one sex and systematically substituting the other sex in all references. Jennifer Macleod (1971) did this in an article "advising" new bridgrooms:

> Oh, lucky you! You are finally bridegroom to the woman of your dreams.
> But don't think for a minute that you can now relax and be assured automatically of marital happiness forever. You will have to *work at it*. While she may have eyes only for you *now*, remember that she is surrounded every day by attractive young men who are all too willing to tempt her away from you. And as the years go by, you will lose some of the handsome masculinity of youth. . . .

Macleod proceeds to state a number of specific recommendations to prevent the wife from being "tempted to stray," such as:

> . . . You should always be available to your wife whenever she wants you. It is of course your husbandly prerogative to say no, but you will be wise never to do so unless you are really ill, for that may tempt her to turn to other men. . . . She cannot do without sex. . . .
> . . . Now for a subject that may seem trivial: your appearance and dress. Don't overlook it. . . .
> Every woman likes to be proud of how attractive her husband is, so dress to please her. . . .

To reinforce the point (and also because these quotes are fun!), consider the following from a local newsletter for a women's liberation group in Albuquerque, New Mexico:

Mr. Herb Dennish, an attractive young man of 27, spoke to the June meeting. . . . Mr. Dennish was informally attired in tan slacks and a navy blazer, with a lemon-yellow shirt. He wore a fashionably wide navy tie with yellow stripes centered by red pinstripes. His jewelry was all gold: watch, two sleeve buttons, a wide wedding band, and a class ring.
   Mr. Dennish spoke on the Model Cities program and the new Youth Opportunity program. He is the Assistant Model Cities Director. . . .
   Mr. Dennish is the husband of Janie Dennish, who has a doctorate fellowship. . . .

The Media and Sex Role Stereotypes

Perhaps the most generalized reflection of extant sex role stereotypes can be found in the mass communications media, which both reflect and reinforce various contemporary realities, including sex role definitions. These media include television, newspapers, magazines, movies, and popular music, among others.

In Chapter 2 of her classic *The Feminine Mystique,* Betty Friedan (1963) discussed findings from an analysis of women's magazines from the late thirties to 1960, especially *Redbook, McCalls,* and *Ladies Home Journal.* She documents the rapid demise of "happily, proudly, adventurously, attractively career women" as heroines after World War II and their replacement by heroines "Occupation: housewife." (The historical phenomenon involved here will be discussed in Chapter 6.) During the fifties virtually all of the stories and articles centered around the housewife, who is told that in her role she is "expert in a dozen careers simultaneously," such as "business manager, cook, nurse, chauffeur, dressmaker, interior decorator, accountant, caterer, teacher, private secretary . . . [and] philanthropist" (p. 36). She is informed that "great men have great mothers," and warned that careers and higher education lead to "masculinization" and concomitant danger "to the home, the children dependent on it and to the ability of the woman as well as her husband to obtain sexual gratification" (p. 37). Typical titles of articles from this era were: "Femininity Begins at Home," "Have Babies While You're Young,"

"How to Snare a Male," "Are You Training Your Daughter to Be a Wife?" "Why G.I.'s Prefer Those German Girls," "Really a Man's World, Politics," "How to Hold On to a Happy Marriage," "Don't Be Afraid to Marry Young," "Cooking to Me Is Poetry," and so on. Friedan notes that "by the end of 1949, only one out of three heroines in the women's magazines was a career woman—and she was shown in the act of renouncing her career and discovering that what she really wanted to be was a housewife." By 1958, Friedan could find no heroines "who had a career, a commitment to any work, art, profession, or mission in the world, other than 'Occupation: housewife.' " Moreover, "even the young unmarried heroines no longer worked except at snaring a husband" (p. 38).

Friedan goes on to state that the heroines get constantly younger "in looks, and a childlike kind of dependence." Their only vision of the future is to have more babies; the only "active growing figure in their world is the child" (p. 38). Their problems consist of how to get their allowances increased, how to fight those "devil" career women who threaten to steal their husbands, and, occasionally, how to squash their own dreams of independence and a life of their own (p. 40). "The end of the road," writes Friedan, "is the disappearance of the heroine altogether, as a separate self and the subject of her own story. The end of the road is togetherness, where the woman has no independent self . . . ; she exists only for and through her husband and children" (p. 41).

Politics, national issues, science, and virtually every idea concerning the world beyond the family were absent from the only material that most females read, according to studies. Not surprisingly, where the magazine writers and editors of the preceding era were female, in the era of the "feminine mystique," as Friedan calls it, they were replaced by males (p. 47). As a final, if subtle, insult, "the very size of their print is raised until it looks like a first-grade primer" (p. 58).

Two recent studies of magazines tend to support Friedan's findings. In a brief study of fictional heroines in three women's magazines in 1957 and 1967, Margaret Lefkowitz (1972) found strong support of the "happy housewife" syndrome. She concluded that "changes in real-life American women" are not yet reflected in short-story heroines in women's magazines (p. 40). Lovelle Ray (1972) intensively studied four women's magazines and the men's magazine *Playboy* throughout the late sixties for their image of females and found considerably more diversity of role models than Friedan had earlier. These were mostly reflected in the nonfiction articles, in which females were portrayed in a variety of occupational fields. However, strong support for the traditional feminine stereotype was still obvious in all five magazines. Ironically, the supposed career-girls magazine *Cosmopolitan* was as guilty as the others or more so in its total emphasis on "catching a man" (pp. 47–53).

In one of the very few books to concern itself seriously with the masculine sex role, Brenton (1966, pp. 126–28) briefly discusses media stereotypes of the father in terms of "The Dagwood Bumstead Syndrome." Cartoons, magazine articles, and especially TV commercials and situation comedies portray the father as "a well-meaning idiot who is constantly outwitted by his children, his wife, and even his dog"; he is "the village imbecile." This degrading stereotype differs drastically from the masculine stereotype discussed earlier, but that may well be because what is being discussed here is the male as *father*. The father role (unlike the mother role) is not considered central to the masculine sex role definition, which is rather grounded in the male as breadwinner or worker. It is on the job or during his leisure activities "with the guys" that the contemporary male has dignity, importance, and a host of positive stereotypes associated with him, not in the home. This topic will be explored further in Chapter 5.

An examination of a variety of media in 1971 demonstrated that, impressions of recent changes in sex role definitions notwithstanding, the masculine and feminine stereotypes noted above continue to be consistently presented. Working mostly in teams of two, nearly 80 students examined sex role portrayals in movies, popular music, magazines, TV shows and commercials, and newspapers. In addition, some studied children's books, TV shows and toy catalogs. Their findings pertaining to adult audiences are discussed in this section.

Popular Songs

Today's young adults are considered by many to be more willing to experiment with new ideas, roles, structures, and so on than their

TABLE 2.3

CHARACTERISTICS RELATED TO SEX ROLE STEREOTYPING IN
CONTEMPORARY ROCK LYRICS

Characteristic	Male (percent)*	Female (percent)*	Total N**
Sexually aggressive	41	5	
Sexually passive	0	9	219
Politically involved	14	3	201
Conformist	6	6	
Nonconformist	23	9	215
Intellectual	15	3	
Nonintellectual	2	2	204
Unmalleable, rigid	28	3	
Malleable, adaptable	6	3	202
Egotistical	24	3	
Nonegotistical	7	1	202
Sensitive	15	20	
Insensitive	5	1	203
Does domestic work	3	7	
Does not do domestic work	23	3	205
Adventuresome	33	5	
Not adventuresome	1	2	201
Uses drugs	19	2	
Does not use drugs	1	0	199

*Percentages represent the proportion of the total number of references in which the characteristic is present; e.g., 41% of 219 total showed males being sexually aggressive. Omitted from the table in each case is the large percentage of songs in which the variable in question is not mentioned.

**Total N is greater than the 197 songs sampled due to multiple counts for some songs (e.g., a song with both a sexually aggressive male and a sexually passive female).

parents and grandparents. Surely, if any medium could be expected not to reflect traditional sex role definitions, it would be the one that is most specifically and explicitly created and consumed by youth: popular songs. However, the same medium that protested war, pollution, racism, and middle-class materialism, and extolled peace, love, drugs, and a generally more free and humane life style, continued to reflect very traditional sex role stereotypes.

Two students, Steve Hudson and Wes Hoover, sampled 19 albums for a total of 197 different songs from the field of contemporary rock. They excluded instrumentals and concentrated on the lyrics. Some of the most popular groups of the era were included: The Rolling Stones; Jefferson Airplane; Crosby, Nash and Stills; the Beatles; Santana; Grand Funk Railroad; Cream, to mention but a few. Their analysis of the content of the songs concentrated on ten dimensions, as reported in Table 2.3.

The most striking finding in this table is manifested by the uniformly small percentage of females in any category; the majority of songs dealt only with males, and females were simply of little or no concern. Indeed, the only category with a substantial percentage of females is the stereotyped trait of "sensitivity." The more explicitly defined masculine role is characterized as sexually aggressive, nonconforming, somewhat more intellectual, rigid or unmalleable, and egotistical. Males' activities consist of anything other than domestic work; they are frequently adventurous and considerably more likely than females to use drugs and be politically active (probably components of adventuresomeness and nonconformity). A glance back at Table 2.1 will show a strong similarity between this characterization and stereotypical masculinity.

TABLE 2.4

CONFORMITY TO THE FEMININE STEREOTYPE IN 33 POPULAR SONGS

Stereotypical Traits	Percent Conforming to Stereotype	Percent Not Conforming	Percent Not Mentioned in Song
Domestic	33	0	66
Passive	66	9	24
Flirtatious	45	3	51
Insecure	36	27	36
Inconsistent	18	0	81
Idealistic	30	0	69
Dependent	54	27	18

In another study of 33 songs popular during the three years preceding the study, students Christine Hauser and Becky Hanson found widespread support of both masculine and feminine stereotypes. Table 2.4 shows the relevant data concerning the feminine stereotype. Except for "insecure" and "dependent," females are rarely portrayed as not conforming to a stereotyped trait, while in five out of the seven traits at least one third of the songs manifested definite conformity. Especially noteworthy is the fact that in two thirds of the songs females are pictured as "passive."

TABLE 2.5

CONFORMITY TO THE MASCULINE STEREOTYPE IN 33 POPULAR SONGS

Stereotypical Traits	Percent Conforming to Stereotype	Percent Not Conforming	Percent Not Mentioned in Song
Breadwinner	57	3	39
Aggressive	66	0	33
Unemotional	39	33	27
Rational	66	6	27
Demanding	69	6	24

Similarly, Table 2.5 shows data concerning five supposed masculine traits. Here, as with Hudson and Hoover's findings, the masculine role is more sharply defined than the feminine. Of five stereotyped traits, four were sustained in well over 50 percent of the cases. For only one characteristic, "unemotional," did a substantial proportion break the stereotype. Males emerge as aggressive, rational, demanding creatures who "earn the bread."

Published Media

The youth culture is also reflected in "underground" newspapers. Students Nancy Spencer and Sara McMillan studied six of these papers, beginning with staff makeup. They found that the proportion of males ranged from 50 to 85 percent, with most papers staffed by well over two thirds males. More importantly, "in none of these newspapers was a female an editor or in any apparently top administrative position. . . ." They then concentrated on the personal ads, most of which were "seeking some kind of personal relationship," and found that there were many more males seeking females than vice versa— not unusual in a culture where mating is generally accomplished through male initiative. Their general findings further support stereotypical notions of both sexes:

> Since sex is the overriding interest of males for females, there is also concern that the girl be attractive physically. . . . The desire for intellectual qualities was secondary if mentioned in addition to sex, and the exception when mentioned alone. Several advertisers . . . were looking for females who would boost their egos . . . so they advertised for submissive or passive females. The female advertisers also often sought sex in males, but in addition mentioned the financial security that would ensue from a lasting relationship.

In short, the male is seeking an attractive, ego-boosting "playmate," the female a solid "meal ticket."

In written media oriented toward older, middle-class Americans, it is not surprising that blatant sex role stereotyping is the rule. In their analysis of three news magazines, *Time, Newsweek* and *U.S. News and World Report,* students Melanie Hardy and Ricky Meador found that females were seldom mentioned. When present they were portrayed as "sex objects." More striking was their observation that even great females were discussed in the context of a related male. Thus, the leader of India was patronizingly referred to as "Nehru's strong-willed daughter Indira." Equally striking was the treatment of the Berrigan plot, in which the brothers were described as "masterminding" the plot and the equally involved Sister Elizabeth MacAllister was termed a "gentle idealist."

Lack of objectivity, a complaint often leveled against the news media, is borne out by a finding reported by Ronald Morales, a student who analyzed the sports pages of a San Antonio newspaper. He found the following adjectives used to describe male athletes: "huge," "tremendous," "great," "bruiser," "tough," "brilliant," "courageous," "cool." Compare these to their counterparts for female athletes: "pretty," "slim," "attractive," "gracious," "lanky brunette," and "lovely."

Indeed, whenever athletes are the subject in the various news media, females are routinely referred to as "girls" or "ladies," and males as "men." We hear about "men's" and "ladies'" golf and tennis and "men's" and "girls'" Olympic teams, never about "boy's" professional football or "gentlemen's" hockey teams. It is also relevant to consider the content of that part of the newspaper known as the "women's pages." Society news, wedding and engagement announcements, recipes, exercises, beauty hints, health, and child-care columns abound, but a single word concerning legal, political, intellectual, or economic matters is seldom to be found. In fact, it is curious indeed that newspapers have "women's pages" but not "men's."

One final study pertaining to sex roles as reflected in newspapers is worthy of note. Student John Nairn analyzed 11 comic strips according to the frequency with which selected stereotypical traits were assigned to male and female characters. Again, male characters emerge as aggressive, completely nondomestic, mechanical, independent, and athletic. They are considerably less frequently emotional, gossipy, and well-groomed than female characters, but more frequently intellectual and responsible. Female comic strip characters, by contrast, are passive, domestic, emotional, dependent, nonathletic creatures, given to gossip and an inability to do mechanical things. Nairn concludes that "at their best they [comic strips] mirror the sexual stereotypes of our society. At their worst they blow them completely out of proportion."

A number of students attempted to replicate the research on magazines reported by Friedan that was discussed above. The easiest way to summarize the rather substantial student findings pertaining to magazines oriented to a feminine readership is that they are supposedly *for* females but *about* males. Article titles in 1971 seemed almost identical to those listed by Friedan; the sole function and purpose of females was still viewed as finding a husband and becoming a housewife and mother. By way of helping to achieve this, women's magazines abound in beauty hints. Thus, in ads cited by Donyn Bird and Nancie Wakefield, women are asked, "Are you a disappointed brunette?" They are informed, "He'll love you for introducing him to the House of Pancakes," and told that some product "makes your eyes just one thing, sexy, very, very, sexy."

Magazines such as *Mademoiselle, Cosmopolitan, Glamour, Mc-Call's, Vogue,* and *Ladies Home Journal* offered little by way of intellectual stimulation. Bird and Wakefield did come up with one article about "politics." It dealt with Judy Agnew, who was quoted as saying "I don't get involved in politics and issues, but I enjoy my role!" With reference to careers for females, Bird and Wakefield found the following:

> The magazines attempt to appear objective in dealing with the female role by publishing advertisements of possible college and career choices. Yet their subjectivity becomes apparent when it is realized that the careers suggested are those of airline stewardess, nurse, fashion designer, and interior decorator; the colleges proposed to train women for these occupations only. It is interesting to note that these advertisements are discreetly "hidden" in the back of the magazines, possibly to avoid offending or leading astray those women who [are or] hope to be housewives.

How is masculinity pictured in women's magazines? In sharp contrast to femininity. Students Kathy Brown and Janie Johnston summarized this image in terms of males being "well-rounded, active, aware individuals who represent something almost god-like around which a woman may center her life." The male is, first and foremost, a provider. "He conceives of his roles and his wife's roles as being clear-cut and well-defined; his place is in the business world and hers is at home. . . . He is a leader, is independent . . . is generally success-oriented and ambitious, as well as egotistical and proud." Even in an article about two-career marriages, the male of the couple is always presented as better educated than his well-educated wife, and older— "a type of superiority." Bird and Wakefield also point out that the various "serious" articles on health, psychology, and so forth are inevitably written by male authorities.

If magazines oriented to feminine audiences define femininity in terms of homemaking and motherhood, and masculinity in terms of husband-provider, what then is the image presented by magazines aimed at masculine audiences? Quite a different one. Indications of this come from a study by Jean Franklin and Wayne Ramsey of both a men's magazine (*Playboy*) and a women's magazine (*Good Housekeeping*). They found that where 60 percent of the males in *Good*

Housekeeping cartoons were portrayed in provider-husband roles, only 15 percent were so portrayed in *Playboy*. *Playboy* males were most frequently (53 percent) "fornicators" and "adulterers." Conversely, 100 percent of the cartoons in *Good Housekeeping* portrayed females as wives and/or mothers, compared to a mere 7 percent in *Playboy*. *Playboy* was more apt to perceive females, like males, as adulterers and fornicators (two thirds).

Ironically, it seems that criticism by feminists notwithstanding, *Playboy* engages in somewhat less sex role stereotyping than women's magazines do. This conclusion was also implied by Ray in her study of four women's magazines and *Playboy* (pp. 48–57). While one may seriously question the desirability of treating anyone primarily in terms of a sex object, at least *Playboy* distributes this somewhat between both genders, although undoubtedly emphasizing the female in this capacity. Indeed, the female in men's magazines is relatively rarely depicted as homemaker; she is often employed, albeit as secretary or in some other stereotypical feminine job.

Nonetheless, all student papers dealing with men's magazines emphasized that in all contexts males were viewed stereotypically as dominant, sexually aggressive, even exploitative, independent souls, and females often as passive and subservient, and always as beautiful adornments. Females are routinely utilized, often in various states of undress, to sell products to males. In fact, a student, Bennie Oglesby, concluded from his study "that women are being correlated with the ownership of the products in the ads: if you get the car or shoes, the girl is yours too."

Unlike women's magazines, men's are *for* and *about* their own gender. The females presented are perhaps fantasy escapes from the homemaker-wife-mother, and, of course, its corollary, the husband-provider-father. The fantasy is also a stereotype: she is the "temptress Eve" of that radical dichotomy assigned the feminine stereotype. This stereotype is, in some very crucial ways, similar to the other, more traditional one. Females are subservient to males in both and orient themselves primarily to males for their identity. But they are also different. The fantasy stereotype emphasizes a somewhat broader variety of roles for females and allows for freer and even more aggressive behavior, at least in the sexual realm.

Movies and Television

Student studies of motion pictures revealed the sole exception to the strong emphasis on sex role stereotyping by the media. While manifesting stereotypical traits to some extent, pictures making the rounds of theaters in the spring of 1971 were at least moving away from such stereotypes. The data presented in Table 2.6 were developed from a study of 20 scenes in each of five films by students Denise Perez and Harry Edwards. As in the other cases, male characters were more frequently dominant, strong, and active and less frequently emotional than female characters. However, two other phenomena are noteworthy. First, substantial proportions of male characters clearly did not conform to the relevant stereotypical traits. Thus, 41 percent were submissive, 35 percent emotionally free, 35 percent helpless, and a third were even passive. Conversely, almost a third of the females were found in three of the four categories representing nonconformity with the feminine stereotype.

Television, the most influential communications medium, does not

TABLE 2.6

CHARACTERISTICS RELATED TO SEX ROLE STEREOTYPING IN FIVE MOTION PICTURES (total 100 scenes)

Characteristics	Male Characters (percent)	Female Characters (percent)
Dominance	45	29
Submission	41	36
Not applicable	14	35
Emotional freedom	35	54
Emotional restraint	51	14
Not applicable	14	32
Strength	49	32
Helplessness	35	28
Not applicable	16	40
Active	55	32
Passive	32	23
Not applicable	13	45

manifest the trends evident in motion pictures. Blatant sex role stereotyping in both programming and commercials is overwhelmingly the case.

Two student studies concerning commercials unearthed consistent findings. In general, males do the actual selling, but primarily to customers presumed to be female. In a study of 50 prime-time commercials, Lark Lands and Jerry Brennan found that while 26 were aimed solely at a feminine audience and only 12 at a masculine one (the other 12 being oriented to a general population), 62 per cent of the narrators were male. Moreover, even in commercials selling products to females, almost two in three narrators were male. Similarly, Michele Parker and Debby Lemm's study of household-product and car commercials found that the central figure in the commercial was male twice as often as female. Lands and Brennan's study also showed that among those commercials oriented to masculine consumers, 76 percent had only males in the commercials. The analogous figure for female-oriented commercials is 46 percent; most, in other words, had at least one male character.

The behavior of the characters also supports sex role stereotyping. Lands and Brennan analyzed the "type of voice" used by the narrator and found that virtually all of the males were either "factual" or "aggressive-sales pitchy." Only one female fell into these categories; they were overwhelmingly characterized as either "seductive" or "soft-spoken." Relatedly, Parker and Lemm found that 24 percent of the female characters were "silent," a category that held no males. They also examined the physical movement of the characters and found that over half the males, but only 6 percent of the females, moved "constantly," while 47 percent of the females and only 14 percent of the males moved "little."

There are also a number of other ways in which stereotypes pertaining to sex roles are expressed in television commercials. For instance, where 41 percent of the "sales pitches" delivered by females in the Parker-Lemm study emphasized the ease, comfort, and luxury of the item, none of those delivered by males did. Conversely, 86 percent of the male-delivered commercials emphasized performance of the product, compared to only 29 percent for the females. Lands and Brennan reported that two thirds of the commercials aimed at females had a domestic setting compared to only one case for males. They also found that the containers of the various products reflected sex role stereotyping: "Women receive their products in containers which are delicate, artistically shaped, softly colored, and often fragile. The corresponding adjectives used to describe women are obvious. Men's containers are sturdy, square, bold-colored, and generally non-breakable. Again, the correspondence is obvious."

What can we conclude from all this? Males, as portrayed in TV commercials, are considered practical in their consideration of consumer products, active, knowledgeable, and presumably more convincing as salespeople. As Lands and Brennan state, advertisers obviously believe that men are "trusted and believed much more often than women." Females emerge as more concerned with personal appearance and sex appeal. By now, these traits should be sounding somewhat familiar.

A brief look at two other student studies of TV programs is in order. James Frost and David Terway studied the characters in five urban, prime-time TV series: "Mission Impossible," "Mannix," "The Interns," "The Young Lawyers," and "The Smith Family." They viewed each one twice, noting that in most of the ten shows "token" female professionals were present, but males "totally dominated every program." Indeed, "the male did not so much dominate the female, but rather there simply were no females to speak of. . . . Almost all important roles, both good and bad, were male roles." Males emerged from this study as intellectually and financially independent, leaders, and professionals; females as nonprofessionals, followers, and, frequently, dependent.

George Gallegos studied only the feminine role as it appeared in a half dozen daytime soap operas. He found that 66 percent of the female characters were "passive," 53 percent "dependent," 80 percent "emotional," 80 percent "expressive," and 66 percent "practical" and concluded that only in the final case was the feminine stereotype not upheld. Soap operas probably reflect the fantasy existence of substantial numbers of avid female viewers (as *Playboy* does for many males). In light of this, the seemingly strong adherence to traditional stereotypes is interesting. The question that remains to be studied concerns the corresponding female fantasy of the masculine sex role.

The stereotypes that are reflected so clearly in the media are reinforced and legitimized in a number of ways in our society, including the legal, religious, academic, scientific, linguistic, and even medical realms. More detailed discussion of how sex role stereotypes are reinforced will be undertaken in Chapters 3 and 4. Some of the implications of sex role stereotypes for people pressured to conform to them are considered in the next section.

Some Individual Costs of Sex Role Conformity

It is probably true that very few individuals conform totally to their gender-relevant stereotypes. Roles of all kinds, as explained in Chapter 1, are sociocultural givens, but this is not to say that people play them in the same way. Indeed, individuals, like stage actors and actresses, interpret their roles and create innovations for their "parts." The fact remains that there is a "part" to be played, and it does strongly influence the actual "performance."

It is also important to note that the precise definitions of sex role stereotypes vary within the broader culture by social class, region, ethnicity, and other subcultural categories. Thus, for instance, more than most other Americans the various Spanish-speaking groups in this country (Mexican-American, Puerto Rican, Cuban) stress domesticity, passivity, and other stereotypical feminine traits, and dominance, aggressiveness, physical prowess, and other stereotypical masculine traits. Indeed, the masculine sex role for this group is generally described by reference to the highly stereotyped notion of *machismo*. In fact, a strong emphasis on masculine aggressiveness and dominance may be characteristic of most groups in the lower ranges of the socioeconomic ladder (McKinley, 1964, pp. 89, 93, 112). Conversely, due to historical conditions beyond their control, black America has had to rely heavily on the female as provider and, more often than the rest of society, as head of the household. Thus, the feminine stereotype discussed above has been, until the recent advent of Black Muslimism and other radical Black Power ideologies, less a part of the cultural heritage of blacks than whites (Staples, 1970). It is also clear that, at least at the verbal level, both sex role stereotypes have historically been taken more seriously in Dixie than elsewhere (see Scott, 1970, especially chapter 1). Although today this difference is probably declining, along with most other regional differences, personal experience leads me to conclude that it nonetheless remains. The pioneer past of the Far West, where survival relied upon strong, productive, independent females as well as males, may have dampened the emphasis on some aspects of the traditional feminine stereotype in that area of the country. Another subculture, that of the "hippies," has radically redefined the meaning of masculinity, although leaving the feminine stereotype virtually unchanged.

Much research remains to be done by way of documenting differences in sex role stereotypes between various groups, but there is little doubt that such differences exist. It is important to note, however, that, with the exception of explicitly countercultural groups such as the "hippies," even among subcultures with relatively strong traditions of their own the cultural definitions of the dominant society exert substantial pressure toward conformity. Minorities—namely all those who are not part of the socioculturally dominant white, northern European, Protestant, middle and upper classes—exist within a society that defines them to a greater or lesser extent as inferior. To some degree such definitions are internalized by many members of the various minority groups and accepted as valid, a phenomenon known in the literature on minority groups as racial or ethnic "self-hatred" (Adelson, 1958, pp. 486, 489; Allport, 1958, pp. 147–48; Frazier, 1957, pp. 217, 226; Simpson & Yinger, 1965, pp. 227–29).

To the extent that individual minority members engage in such group self-hatred they are led to attempt, within the limits of opportunity and the resources allowed by the dominant group, to "live up to" the norms and roles of the dominant society. Given limited economic opportunities, the result is often a parody of the values and behaviors of the dominant society, as exemplified by the strong emphasis on aggression, sexual exploitation, and physical prowess by lower class males of most ethnic groups and by the generally larger number of children born to lower class females than to those in the middle class. Similarly, large numbers of blacks, many highly educated and involved in radical politics, have accepted the negative (and false) description of their family structure as "matriarchal" propounded by

Daniel Moynihan (1965) and other whites. Moreover, many black males and females are now engaged in efforts to change this structure to conform to the major cultural pattern of male as dominant partner and breadwinner, and female as subservient homemaker. However, less biased research (Hill, 1971; Rhodes, 1971) suggests that the traditional black family structure is and has been very functional in enabling the black to survive in this society. This structure is not the pathological, weak, disorganized entity usually conveyed by the term "matriarchy."

Individuals of all levels of society who reject traditional sex role stereotypes are labeled "nonconformist" and subjected to the wrath of most members of the society. The treatment of longhaired males a few years ago by police, possible employers, and ordinary citizens speaks eloquently of the "cost" of nonconformity, as does the "wall-flower" status of competitive, intellectually or career-oriented females. But costs are also paid by those who generally conform to sex role stereotypes (or any other kind, for that matter), and these are usually more "hidden."

Perceived Costs and Benefits

Students in a sex role class were asked to form single-gender groups to discuss the advantages of the opposite sex role and the disadvantages of their own. This exercise was a replication of the study done by Barbara Polk and Robert Stein (1972) at a northern university, using 250 students of highly diverse backgrounds, and the results parallel theirs almost exactly. Results of the class study are reported in Tables 2.7 and 2.8.

When the advantages and disadvantages of the sex roles are compared the most striking finding relates to the relative length of the various lists. There seem to be many more disadvantages adhering to the feminine role as perceived by females than to the masculine role as perceived by males (or else the females were simply and stereotypically more loquacious!). Conversely, more advantages are seen as accruing to the masculine role by females than to the feminine role by males. More relevant to the question of costs, however, is the finding that the perceived advantages of one sex are the disadvantages of

TABLE 2.7

DISADVANTAGES OF SAME SEX ROLE AND ADVANTAGES OF OPPOSITE
ONE AS PERCEIVED BY MALES*

Male Disadvantages	Female Advantages
Can't show emotions (P)	Freedom to express emotions (R)
Must be provider (O)	Fewer financial obligations; parents support longer (S)
Pressure to succeed, be competitive (O)	Less pressure to succeed (P)
Alimony and child support (O)	Alimony and insurance benefits (S)
Liable to draft (O)	Free from draft (S)
Must take initiative, make decisions (O)	Protected (S)
Limit on acceptable careers (P)	
Expected to be mechanical, fix things (O)	
	More leisure (S)
	Placed on pedestal; object of courtesy (S)

*Letters enclosed in parentheses refer to a fourfold categorization of roles:
   P = Proscription
   O = Obligation
   R = Right
   S = Structural benefit

the other. If it is a masculine disadvantage not to be able to show emotions, it is a feminine advantage to be able to do so. Likewise, if it is a feminine disadvantage to face limited job opportunities, the converse is a masculine advantage. Summarizing similar findings, Polk and Stein conclude: "The extent to which this relationship exists strongly suggests that there is general agreement on the desirable characteristics for any individual, regardless of sex" (p. 16).

Polk and Stein's fourfold categorization of role components as rights, obligations, proscriptions, and structural benefits is useful in examining the nature of specific perceived costs and benefits of the two roles. According to Polk and Stein, "Rights allow the individual the freedom to commit an act or refrain from an act without receiving sanctions for either choice" (p. 19). Obligations and proscriptions are different in that individuals are negatively sanctioned, in the first case for not doing something, in the second for doing it. Structural

TABLE 2.8

DISADVANTAGES OF SAME SEX ROLE AND ADVANTAGES OF OPPOSITE ONE AS PERCEIVED BY FEMALES*

Female Disadvantages	Male Advantages
Job opportunities limited; discrimination; poor pay (P)	Job opportunities greater (S)
Legal and financial discrimination (P)	Financial and legal opportunity (S)
Educational opportunities limited; judged mentally inferior; opinion devalued; intellectual life stifled (P)	Better educational and training opportunities; opinions valued (S)
Single status stigmatized; stigma for divorce and unwed pregnancy (P)	Bachelorhood glamorized (R)
Socially and sexually restricted; double standard (P)	More freedom sexually and socially (R)
Must bear and rear children; no abortions (in many places); responsible for birth control (O)	No babies (S)
Must maintain good outward appearance; dress, make-up (O)	Less fashion demand and emphasis on appearance (R)
Domestic work (O)	No domestic work (R)
Must be patient; give in; subordinate self; be unaggressive; wait to be asked out on dates (P)	Can be aggressive, dating and otherwise (O)
Inhibited motor control; not allowed to be athletic (P)	More escapism allowed (R)

*Letters enclosed in parentheses refer to a fourfold categorization of roles:

   P = Proscription
   O = Obligation
   R = Right
   S = Structural benefit

benefits refer to "advantages derived from the social structure or from actions of others" on the basis of gender alone (p. 21). Each advantage and disadvantage listed in Tables 2.7 and 2.8 is followed by a letter in parentheses which represents my judgment as to whether that characteristic is a right (R), a proscription (P), an obligation (O), or a structural benefit (S). Masculine disadvantages consist overwhelmingly of obligations with a few proscriptions, while the disadvantages of the feminine role arise primarily from proscriptions, with a few obligations. Thus females complain about what they can't do, males about what they must do. Females complain that they cannot be athletic, aggressive, sexually free, or successful in the worlds of work and education; in short, they complain of their passivity. Males complain that they must be aggressive and must succeed; in short, of their activity. The (sanctioned) requirement that males be active and females passive in a variety of ways is clearly unpleasant to both.

The nature of the types of advantages seen as accruing to the two roles by the opposite sex supports the stereotyped dichotomy between activity and passivity still further. Females are seen as overwhelmingly enjoying structural benefits, namely, advantages that accrue to them without reference to what they do. Males believe females have only one right. Females believe males also enjoy structural benefits but have considerably more rights, namely, choices of action or inaction. These findings generally agree with Polk and Stein's, who found that altogether the masculine role had 14 obligations compared to 8 for the feminine; 6 rights compared to 0; 4 proscriptions compared to 15; and 6 structural benefits compared to 4 (pp. 20–21, Table 2).

The many costs of being female and feminine are increasingly being aired publicly. The often less obvious costs of being male and masculine can be summarized in a student's own somewhat melodramatic and confused but deeply felt words:

> I, a 20th-century American male, feel trapped, suppressed, suffocated by an uncaring, stereotyping . . . society. My individuality is labeled queer and my interests unnatural because the idea of seeing a baseball game . . . does not send me into euphoric ecstasy. I feel bitterness for the conforming role nature has forced me to bear. Then again, nature is not to blame, it is our . . . society. . . . My problem [is that I am] . . . myself with a veneer of overt masculine, . . . emotionless behavior, all aimed toward the affirmation of my masculinity. By far the most tragic fact of this role playing which most American men portray is the fact that we lose sight of our true beings. If we concentrate on appearing as a brute masculine, bicep-

oriented expanse of wall-to-wall ego, then we cease to be caring, compassionate human beings. . . . I feel compelled to display or affirm my masculinity. This in itself implies insecurity; but I am not insecure. . . . I do not need a football game, a wild boar hunt, or rippling biceps and triceps to prove my masculinity. I feel the societal pressure, however, and this embitters me.

I am a male. I am not uncaring. . . . I am not devoid of emotion. I can cry; I can laugh; I can feel. I cannot suppress these facts of my being and don the stereotyped male sex role.

Why is it that
We cannot know
Ourselves?
We block out facets
Of personal experience
That could make
Life worth living.
What is going to be the
Destruction of man?
His war or his psyche?

Economic Costs and Benefits

Another interesting and relevant exercise can be done with the material on stereotypes generated by the students. Referring to the list of stereotypical traits presented in Table 2.1, one could ask how helpful or costly such traits would be for one who would compete successfully in the highest echelons of our economy and society.

Robert Hodge, Paul Siegel, and Peter Rossi (1966) studied the relative prestige of a large number of occupations in the United States and found that the four most prestigious were: U.S. Supreme Court Justice, physician, scientist, and state governor. Table 2.9 summarizes the data on which stereotypical traits are clearly helpful in attaining and performing well in these occupational roles and which are harmful. While the designation as "helpful" or "harmful" for some few traits is debatable, the overall picture probably is not. Stereotypical feminine traits patently do not equip those who might try to live up to them to compete in the world of social and economic privilege, power, and prestige; the exact opposite is the case for masculine char-

TABLE 2.9

SEX ROLE TRAITS HELPFUL AND HARMFUL IN ACQUIRING AND PERFORMING
WELL IN PRESTIGIOUS OCCUPATIONAL ROLES*

Stereotyped Traits	Harmful	Helpful

Masculine	Sloppy
	Dogmatic
		Breadwinner, provider
		Stoic, unemotional
		Logical, rational, objective,
		   scientific
		Practical
		Mechanical (for scientist and
		   physician)
		Public awareness
		Leader
		Disciplinarian
		Independent
		Demanding
		Aggressive
		Ambitious
		Proud, confident
		Moral, trustworthy
		Decisive
		Competitive
		Adventurous

Feminine	Worry about appearance and age Sensual Domestic Seductive, flirtatious Emotional, sentimental Nervous, insecure, fearful Scatterbrained, frivolous Impractical Petty, coy, gossipy Dependent, overprotected Follower, submissive Self-conscious; easily intimidated Not aggressive, passive Tardy Noncompetitive	Compassionate Intuitive Humanistic Perceptive Idealistic Patient Gentle

*Traits not classifiable as either "helpful" or "harmful" are omitted.

acteristics. Where 15 feminine traits are classified as "harmful," only 2 masculine ones are so designated. Conversely, where 17 masculine traits are classified as "helpful," the analogous figure for feminine traits is 5. The cost of femininity for those who would enter the world outside the home could scarcely be more clear: The more a female conforms, the less is she capable of functioning in roles that are other than domestic.

Some Other Costs

A number of other problems—medical, psychiatric, educational and legal—differ by gender and undoubtedly reflect the pressures of sex role stereotyping. Chapter 4 will give a more thorough discussion of the direct costs of discrimination against females in the realms of economics, politics, and other institutional areas. Here the costs that males and females pay for conformity will be briefly discussed.

Basically, sex role stereotyping affects people's "heads." That is to say, a good many of the costs are mental, and other problems, medical and behavioral, result from the psychological effects.

Betty Friedan, speaking of white, mostly middle-class, middle-aged, married females, called it "the problem that has no name" (1963, chap. 1). She describes the female's psychological malaise:

> It was strange stirring, a sense of dissatisfaction, a yearning that women suffered. . . . Each suburban wife struggled with it alone. As she made beds, shopped for groceries, matched slipcover material, ate peanut butter sandwiches with her children, chauffeured Cub Scouts and Brownies, lay beside her husband at night—she was afraid to ask even of herself the silent question—"Is this all?" (1963, p. 11).

Basically, Friedan's argument is that conformity to stereotyped domesticity (the "feminine mystique") has dearly cost large numbers of intelligent, educated, once active and dynamic females. They fled to psychiatrists asking why, with all they have (lovely house, children, loving husband), they are dissatisfied with life, empty, bored, looking forward to nothing, and complained to their doctors of being tired all the time, a symptom usually regarded as psychosomatic. They turned in large numbers to tranquilizers, barbituates, and alcohol (although the vast majority of drug addicts and alcoholics remain male). And, most tragically, their frustration may have resulted in a generation of children who were unable "to endure pain or discipline or pursue any self-sustained goal of any sort," children with "a devastating boredom with life" (pp. 24–25). Alcoholics Anonymous estimates that there are one million female alcoholics—largely housewives. Their children have a much higher probability of being in trouble with the police by age 16 than the offspring of working mothers (Tiffany, Cowan, & Tiffany, 1970, p. 49).

According to the stereotype, females are trained to conceive of themselves as feminine only to the extent that they are loved by males and devote their lives to mates and children. Friedan indicates that even with "storybook" marriages, women are often frustrated. There are other ramifications of this phenomenon. Although males commit suicide more often than females, females unsuccessfully attempt suicide far more often than males (Sexton, 1969, p. 6), a trend which seems recently to be changing (*Time,* March 20, 1972, p. 47). Is this mere "feminine ineptitude?" I think not. The pressures of the masculine role may be harsh enough to lead many men to forsake life, as witnessed also by the fact that suicide rates, along with impotence and mental illness rates, are very high among unemployed males, namely those not fulfilling the primary masculine role of provider (Sexton, 1969, p. 6). Among women, however, a suicide attempt is conveying less a desire to end life than a plea for love and attention from significant (male) others. Serious suicides usually "succeed." That females succeed less often implies that self-destruction is not the goal at all.

Most teen-age delinquency and even adult crime is committed by males (Sexton, 1969, p. 7), probably in the process of establishing their "masculine" prowess and independence (Brenton, 1966, pp. 64–66). Increasingly, male crime is associated with a drug habit, a problem somewhat less prevalent among females. The few delinquent adolescent females are nearly all in fact, if not as of legal record, "guilty" of breaking sexual mores; they are "unmanageable," meaning they are guilty of promiscuity, prostitution (a means of supporting a drug habit for many), or unmarried pregnancy. Adolescent boys are virtually never institutionalized on such grounds. Especially among adolescent girls attempting to work through problems of identity, promiscuity and premarital pregnancy probably represent attempts to gain male attention and affection, so crucial to their self-definition as "feminine." By way of an interesting footnote to this discussion, changing definitions of the feminine role may be affecting crime and delinquency rates of adolescent girls and women. Recently more females are being adjudged delinquent, and for a wider variety of reasons (Brenton, 1966, p. 201). It seems that behaviors that had heretofore been defined as "sick" when engaged in by females are being redefined as grounds for arrest, as they long have been for males.

One final cost some females pay for conformity should be mentioned. As we have seen, the feminine role is clearly linked to domesticity, meaning, probably more than anything else, child bearing and rearing. It is little wonder, then, that females suffer relatively high rates of mental breakdown at about the time their last child leaves the "nest." Since this usually coincides with menopause, many have viewed the biological changes as directly or indirectly "causing" the breakdown. I think it is rather the fact that women lose their primary, indeed, almost sole functional role at this time of their life and see very little in their future. Pauline Bart's (1970) study of middle-aged women in mental hospitals showed that prior intense involvement with the mother role was closely related to serious depression. It is interesting to note that in highly traditional societies where the role of grandmother is revered and respected, females do not seem to suffer psychological problems at menopause (Dowty, 1972). Further supporting this interpretation is the fact that males undergo severe mental problems at about 65 or during prolonged periods of unemployment, namely when stripped of their only important functional role, that of worker and provider. There is no relatively abrupt biological change that can serve as an explanation for this phenomenon among males.

There are some further costs of the masculine role. It is well known that males have a life expectancy that is shorter by several years than that of females, and there is a much higher mortality rate for males between the specific ages of 18 and 65 than for females. Some of the reasons for this are probably closely related to sex role phenomena. First, males suffer many more accidental deaths (Sexton,

1969, p. 9): in sports, on dangerous vehicles like motorcycles, and through violence. Part of the definition of masculinity is personal bravery and adventuresomeness. Such traits are, if anything, actively discouraged among females. Under the circumstances, it is little wonder that males die more frequently for the kinds of reasons enumerated.

Over and above accidental deaths are deaths from diseases that probably reflect, in part, the masculine emphasis on competition, success, and productivity. The pressures on males to "succeed" in a highly competitive world of work create tremendous stress; in the final analysis, few males can ever sit back and say "I've arrived; I am a success; now I can relax." So strong is the work and success ethic for males in our society that even millionaires feel compelled to "produce," in the sense of active participation in the economy. Among the large numbers of males doing less competitive but more repetitious labor, the pressure to persist day in, day out, year after year, in highly alienating work results from the sex role requirement that they provide for their families the best they possibly can in material terms. Heart attacks, strokes, high blood pressure, and other circulatory illnesses probably result in part from such pressures. They undoubtedly also contribute to the much higher rates of alcohol and drug abuse among males, which in turn hasten death, and they are reflected in the higher male suicide rate. The proscription on expressing emotions entailed in the masculine role definition probably exacerbates the stresses inherent in the obligation to support a family—financially and emotionally—and to succeed in an often highly competitive "rat race."

Young males, perhaps even more than their elders, suffer a number of costs in the process of trying to establish their masculine identity. According to Sexton (1969, p. 6), as children males outnumber females in mental institutions at a rate of 2 to 1. This ratio is reversed in adulthood, according to Chesler (1971 b, p. 747). Male youth are far more frequently adjudged delinquent; they comprise the vast majority of school discipline "problems"; they have reading and general learning problems about twice as frequently as girls (Sexton, 1969, p. 10). Sexton argues that the major cause of all these problems is to be found in the vast discrepancy between what boys are encouraged to be as masculine creatures and what they are required to do as students. School requires sitting still, rather passively, and carrying out the orders of an authority figure who is generally female. Meanwhile, male children are being urged to accept "values such as courage, inner direction, certain forms of aggression, autonomy. . . . adventure, and a considerable amount of toughness . . ." (p. 15). Moreover, they are learning that they are "better than girls," whom they must protect and help, while subjected to the direct authority of female teachers. They either conform to their sex role stereotype and become learning and school "problems" or conform to school requirements and are considered by their peers as "sissy," or they buckle under the pressure of conflicting expectations. Such pressures clearly do not exist for most girls, whose sex role stereotype dovetails nicely with the behavior required by schools.

It is clear that our society does in fact define stereotypically a host of traits as belonging almost exclusively to one or the other sex roles. In short, it creates a radical dichotomy of human types, despite both the many differences between individuals of the same gender and the many similarities between people of opposite genders. From birth on we are all encouraged to assume a self-definition and certain behaviors that may or may not be congruent with our natural proclivities, and which, at any rate, express only half, if that, of our human potential. It is abundantly clear that this is a costly procedure for everyone involved, in a myriad of ways.

References

Adelson, Joseph. "A Study of Minority Group Authoritarianism." In Marshall Sklare (ed.), *The Jews: Social Patterns of an American Group*, pp. 475–92. Glencoe, Ill.: Free Press, 1958.

Allport, Gordon. *The Nature of Prejudice*. Garden City, N.Y.: Doubleday Anchor Books, 1958; first published 1954.

Bart, Pauline. "Mother Portnoy's Complaints." *Trans-Action* 8 (November–December 1970): 69–74.

Brenton, Myron. *The American Male*. Greenwich, Conn.: Fawcett Publications, Inc., 1966.

Chesler, Phyllis. "Stimulus/Response: Men Drive Women Crazy." *Psychology Today* 5 (July 1971) (a), pp. 18 ff.

Chesler, Phyllis. "Women as Psychiatric and Psychotherapeutic Patients." *Journal of Marriage and the Family* 33 (November 1971): 746–59 (b).

Dowty, Nancy. "To Be a Woman in Israel." *School Review* 80 (February 1972): 319–32.

Frazier, E. Franklin. *Black Bourgeoisie*. Glencoe, Ill.: Free Press, 1957.

Friedan, Betty. *The Feminine Mystique*. New York: Dell Publishing Co., 1963.

Hill, Robert B. "The Strengths of Black Families." Unpublished manuscript, July 1971.

Hodge, Robert; Siegel, Paul; and Rossi, Peter. "Occupational Prestige in the United States: 1925–1963." In Reinhard Bendix and S. M. Lipset (eds.), *Class, Status and Power*, pp. 322–34. 2nd ed. Glencoe, Ill.: Free Press, 1966.

Kagan, Jerome, and Moss, Howard. *Birth to Maturity: A Study in Psychological Development*. New York: John Wiley & Sons, 1962.

Lefkowitz, Margaret. "The Women's Magazine Short-Story Heroine in 1957 and 1967." In Constantina Safilios-Rothschild (ed.), *Toward a Sociology of Women,* pp. 37–40. Lexington, Mass.: Xerox College Publishing, 1972.

Macleod, Jennifer. "How to Hold a Wife: A Bridegroom's Guide." *Village Voice*, February 11, 1971, p. 5.

McKinley, Donald G. *Social Class and Family Life*. Glencoe, Ill.: Free Press, 1964.

Moynihan, Daniel P. *The Negro Family: The Case for National Action*. Washington, D.C.: U.S. Department of Labor, 1965.

Polk, Barbara Bovee, and Stein, Robert B. "Is the Grass Greener on the Other Side?" In Constantina Safilios-Rothschild (ed.), *Toward a Sociology of Women*, pp. 14–23. Lexington, Mass.: Xerox College Publishing, 1972.

Ray, Lovelle. "The American Women in Mass Media: How Much Emancipation and What Does it Mean?" In Constantina Safilios-

Rothschild (ed.), *Toward a Sociology of Women*, pp. 41–62. Lexington, Mass.: Xerox College Publishing, 1972.

Rhodes, Barbara. "The Changing Role of the Black Woman." In Robert Staples (ed.), *The Black Family*, pp. 145–49. Belmont, Calif.: Wadsworth Publishing Co., 1971.

Scott, Anne Firor. *The Southern Lady*. Chicago: University of Chicago Press, 1970.

Sexton, Patricia Cayo. *The Feminized Male*. New York: Vintage Books, 1969.

Simpson, George E., and Yinger, J. Milton. *Racial and Cultural Minorities*. 3rd ed. New York: Harper and Row, 1965.

Staples, Robert. "The Myth of the Black Matriarchy." *Black Scholar* 1 (January–February, 1970): 8–16.

Tiffany, Donald; Cowan, James; and Tiffany, Phyllis. *The Unemployed*. Englewood Cliffs, N.J.: Prentice-Hall, 1970.

Time magazine staff, "Situation Report," March 20, 1972.

Chapter 3

The Bringing Up of Dick and Jane

A baby is born knowing nothing, but full of potential. The process by which an individual becomes a creature of society, a socialized human being reflecting culturally defined roles and norms, is complex and as yet imperfectly understood. It is evident, however, that most individuals eventually reflect societal definitions more or less well; most males born and raised in America will someday think and behave like other American males in many important ways and not, for instance, like their Japanese counterparts. Through the socialization process humans come to more or less completely internalize the roles, norms, and values appropriate to the culture and subculture within which they function. Cultural definitions become personal definitions of propriety, normality, and worthiness. Because internalization of cultural definitions is less than total for most people, social control mechanisms are brought to bear by some individuals and social groups to encourage others to conform to expectations. Control mechanisms range from such severe forms as physical punishment inflicted by the state (imprisonment and even execution), to social ostracism or unwillingness to hire job applicants, to such mild forms as ridicule.

Underlying both the socialization process and the concomitant use of social controls is the assumption that people learn to conform by the application of sanctions. Sanctions may be positive, in which case they are known as "rewards," or negative, when they are known as "punishments." Generally, people learn more completely and retain things longer when rewards rather than punishments are employed. By their nature, however, social control mechanisms utilize largely negative sanctions, and therefore they function as relatively ineffective teaching techniques. The socialization process itself is typically comprised of a mixture of both types of sanctions. The proportion of rewards to punishments during this process varies according to such factors as ethnic subculture and social class, as well as the personalities of the individuals involved. Thus the extent to which individuals will internalize social norms and roles varies, although the fact that rewards are normally utilized to some extent helps to ensure substantial success for the process.

Human interaction is crucial to the process of personality development. A newborn infant has no concept of self. By the time a child enters school, it has begun to develop a fairly coherent picture of who it is and what the appropriate behaviors are for that identity. The process of developing this picture is probably never-ending, but by adulthood it is usually subject to relatively less change than it was earlier.

The classical explanation for how an individual's identity emerges is that offered by the symbolic interactionists, dating back a half century or more to George Herbert Mead (1934) and Charles H. Cooley (1909), among others. Through interaction with "significant others," primarily parents and, later, peer groups, children come to form an idea of self consisting of "three principal elements: the imagination of our appearance to the other person; the imagination of his judgment of that appearance, and some sort of self-feeling such as pride or mortification" (Cooley, 1909, p. 152). Cooley called this the "looking glass self." In developing this approach further, Mead emphasized the key role of language in the interaction process. He believes children first develop a sense of "I," namely, a basic awareness of self as actor and organism. Later the "Me" develops, which consists of an understanding and internalization of how others perceive the child. The "me" is the social component of the personality; it entails the internalization of roles, norms, and values presented by society and is in many ways similar to Freud's superego. It is learned by the child through role-playing—taking the role of the other in negotiating human interactions. This is only possible through the manipulation of symbols, that is, language. In this way the child eventually learns the organized attitudes and expectations of larger social groupings, called by Mead "the generalized other." Stated in its simplest form, children learn who they are and internalize what they are expected to be by trying to put themselves in the place of others and experience themselves as others perceive them. This is possible only through the use of symbolic communication.

Two other related concepts are relevant to a discussion of the socialization process. W. I. Thomas's (1923) renowned concept of the "definition of the situation" entails recognition of the fact that if human beings define a situation as real, then, regardless of objective reality, the fact of defining it in that way has real social consequences. If, for instance, a boy is told that "boys are athletic," regardless of the truth of this assertion it will have a real impact on that child's behavior and expectations of himself. Robert K. Merton (1957) was essentially noting the same phenomenon when he developed the notion of the "self-fulfilling (or defeating) prophecy." Merton's concept applies to those cases where the act of predicting something helps to ensure that the phenomenon in question will (or will not) occur. Thus, for instance, the girl who is told she will never be strong (because girls aren't) will probably take no steps by which she could become strong. When later she lacks strength, a self-fulfilling prophecy will have been realized.

This chapter will primarily be concerned with the ways in which children and adolescents learn to internalize the sex role stereotypes discussed in Chapter 2 and the control mechanisms employed to reinforce these stereotypes.

The Captive Audience: Childhood

The first crucial question of the parents of a newborn baby is "What is it? a boy or a girl?" Only later will they be concerned with any other attribute of the infant, even its physical condition; the first priority is to establish its gender. Indeed, almost immediately, gender identity is permanently stamped on the child by the name it is given.

When the proud new father lifts his infant he might jostle it just a little if it's a boy; he will pet and cuddle it if it is a girl. In the months that follow mother will speak to the infant more if it happens to be female—and later everyone will wonder why it is that young girls show greater linguistic skills than boys (Lewis, 1972, p. 54). Father will continue to play a bit rough with the infant if the child is male. Both parents will discourage a male toddler from "clinging"—but not his sister. Indeed, recent research shows that up to six months of age male infants receive more physical contact from their mothers than do female babies (probably because they value a male child more), while after that males are more quickly and totally discouraged from such contact than females (Lewis, 1972, p. 56). The parents will tell little Dick, but not little Jane, that "big boys don't cry." They will devote hours to combing *her* hair and putting decorations in it and will bedeck *her* with jewelry, but they will look with horror on *his* games with mother's lipstick or clothes. Jane will soon be attired in dresses and told not to get dirty and not to do anything that will let her "underpants show"; Dick will be in trousers with no such restrictions—and later everyone will say that girls are innately less physically coordinated and strong than boys. And so begins the life and training of these new human beings.

The description of the early treatment of infants can provide useful insights in terms of the concepts developed above. First, from birth the nature of the interaction between parents and children differs markedly according to the gender of the child. If, indeed, the interaction process is crucial to the development of a self-image, it is clear that those of males and females will eventually be quite different. The parents of the little girl relate to her as a breakable object to be carefully tended, protected, and beautified; the little boy's parents treat him as self-reliant, physically active, even "tough," and not very emotionally expressive. These images are undoubtedly learned by the children. In addition, they are verbally instructed and sanctioned for doing or refraining from certain things according to gender. Finally, these restrictions and encouragements serve to "define reality" for the children in self-fulfilling ways. If little Jane is assumed to be weak, in need of protection, and an ornamental thing, she will be clothed in apparel reflecting these attributes and informed not to do anything out of keeping with her attire. Unable to swing on the jungle gym and still live up to her parents' image of her and the strictures they impose, she will most certainly fail to develop her muscles; ultimately, she will indeed be weak, in need of protection, and engrossed in her own appearance.

In taking a closer look at the process by which young children are thought to internalize their gender-relevant sex roles, David Lynn's excellent short text *Parental and Sex Role Identification* (1969) is useful. A vast quantity of child development literature is reviewed, and 38 propositions are developed to summarize the relevant theory and research. Lynn's approach to the subject is only one of many, but it is more sociologically relevant than most. For a somewhat more technical and detailed discussion, see Eleanor Maccoby's fine collection of articles entitled *The Development of Sex Differences* (1966).

Lynn begins by asserting that both male and female infants usually establish their initial and principal identification with the mother, an identification that neither gender ever loses entirely (pp. 21–23). This is predicated on the assumption, true in the majority of cases in this society, that the mother functions as the infant's chief caretaker. It is important to note that any change of that norm would invalidate this proposition. At any rate, having established this identity, the female child can continue it and, in so doing, learn the "appropriate" sex role behavior. To the extent that "identification" strongly entails imitation, young Jane need only copy her mother to be rewarded. In this way she quickly begins to internalize the feminine role behavior expected of her.

Little Dick, however, faces a serious problem. Given the relative absence of male figures during his waking hours, the male toddler is hard pressed to find out what he is supposed to do. Early in life his mother begins to sanction him negatively for imitating many of her ways. In this society the father is absent so often the child cannot imitate him, and when he is present, he joins the mother in punishing the boy for being "too feminine." Indeed, he usually surpasses the mother in this, perhaps because of his own sex role insecurities and a resulting fear of homosexuality. The result is that where Jane identifies easily with her mother, Dick must identify with a cultural definition of masculinity that he pieces together from peers, media, a series of don'ts from his parents, and so on (Lynn, 1969, pp. 23–26). In fact, according to Lynn, peers are more important in shaping the identity of males than females (p. 92). The boy finds out that "boys don't cry," "boys don't cling," and so on, but often on the basis of negative sanctions from parents and peers. Given the lesser efficacy of punishments compared to rewards in the socialization process, it is not surprising that males have greater difficulty establishing their sex role identities than females. They also fail in this endeavor more frequently, are more anxious about it throughout their lives, and are more hostile toward the opposite sex (Lynn, 1969, pp. 57–64).

The ramifications of this duality are everywhere. Male fear of and hostility toward homosexuality finds little parallel among females, nor does the hang-up of "proving one's masculinity." Girls are far less concerned about the label "tomboy" (and, in fact, often wear it with pride) than boys are about "sissy." Undoubtedly, too, there is a relationship between this phenomenon and the kinds of problems presented by school-aged boys.

There are other implications of the two rather radically different methods of early sex role learning. Jane, it will be recalled, learns by imitation and positive reinforcement. Dick, on the other hand, has to make a mental effort to comprehend what he is supposed to be, and he more frequently receives negative sanctions. One result, according to Lynn, is that throughout their lives females rely more on affection, or demonstrate a "greater need for affiliation," than males. Males develop greater problem-solving abilities because of this early mental exercise. Moreover, they become more concerned with internalized moral standards than females, who in turn rely more on the opinions of others (Lynn, 1969, chap. 4).

It is important to bear in mind that this duality is predicated on the relatively constant presence of the mother and, conversely, the relative absence of the father. This is certainly the typical (although hardly necessary) American pattern. If this pattern were reversed, all of the traits discussed as common to one or the other gender would need to be reversed as well. In examining the relationship of family structure to sex role learning, Lynn offers a series of other arguments (Lynn, 1969, chap. 5). The "normal" family is assumed to consist of a close mother and *moderately* distant father. A moderately distant father is close enough to provide some model for the young boy, as well as the motivation to use that model, but sufficiently remote to require the mental effort on the part of the boy that was discussed above. Boys with either very close or very distant fathers will not develop analytical skills superior to those of the average girl. In the first case, the boy will directly imitate the father, much as the girl does the mother. In the second, the intellectual effort (and lack of motivation) may be just too great to cope with. Conversely, girls with more distant mothers and/or fathers as caretakers will develop analytical skills commensurate with those of the average male. Certainly, the assumption made by many that the best way to bring up any child, regardless of gender, is with a constantly present mother must be open to serious question.

In our society males have considerably more prestige, power, and freedom than females. Little children are not oblivious to this fact. Thus, again according to Lynn (1969, pp. 65–78), although boys experience initially much greater sex role identity problems than girls, as time goes on they become more firmly identified with the masculine role. Females, however, do not do so with reference to the feminine role. Indeed, a larger number of girls show preference for the high prestige and powerful masculine role than boys do for the feminine role, as witnessed by the relative numbers of "tomboys" and "sissies." Pushing this logic a step further, it is likely that given the higher prestige of the masculine role, homosexuality and sissyishness may appear as a kind of betrayal, while lesbianism and tomboyishness may appear as more or less understandable imitations of a superior status role. This would help to explain the far greater social antipathy to the former than the latter (see Progrebin, 1972). Similarly, feminine fashions often "ape" masculine ones, but the opposite rarely occurs. The whole notion of transvestism basically applies to males only; no one blinks an eye at a female in jeans, a shirt, and boots or sneakers, much less suggests that she is a transvestite, but a male in a skirt (unless he is Scotch or an ancient Roman) is a different matter.

It is clear that parents play a major role in the process of socialization in general and the communication of sex role identity and behavior in particular. Moreover, it is clear that children have established a firm notion of their sex role by about age 3, if not earlier. By this age, little Dick is already objecting to certain things because they are for girls, and Jane is happily imitating mother with her dolls and tea parties. However, a view of human development that claims that any identities or behavior patterns are irrevocably set for life by that age seems to me to be myopic. Life for most humans *is* change, to a greater or lesser degree. If such changes are slow relative to those occurring in the first years of life, they nonetheless exist and, cumulatively, may sometimes acquire substantial dimensions. Any such changes away from patterns established by parents must logically be initiated from some source outside the home environment. If society at large provides strong, even coercive supports for identities and behaviors learned early in life from parents, they will be further reinforced rather than changed. This seems, by and large, to be the case with reference to sex roles, inasmuch as most parents reflect stereotypical sex role definitions. The following sections will consider some of these reinforcing and control mechanisms as they act on the child.

Language

George Mead's (1934) ideas pertaining to childhood socialization, in which he stresses the important role of symbolic communication or language, were discussed briefly at the beginning of this chapter. The words and grammatical constructions available to any people are shaped by, and in turn strongly influence, their perceptions of the world and therefore themselves. It is difficult to conceptualize phenomena for which we have no words. Likewise, we are apt to pay more careful attention to phenomena for which we have adequate linguistic expression.

For the English-speaking population as well as for many others, gender is an overwhelmingly important fact of language (and therefore of life). While most if not all languages probably have words to distinguish the genders, English makes it almost impossible *not to* so distinguish in discussing humans. This is true even if the gender involved is not known or is irrelevant to the topic. We do not have a gender-free singular pronoun to refer to a human; "it" is not generally used for this purpose. Thus, when speaking of another person, at least in the singular, we either use the name (which is gender-linked) or "he" or "she." I have conspicuously tried to avoid assigning gender when it is not called for in this book and have found it a difficult task requiring constant attention (and rewriting). Moreover, it could involve incorrect grammar, because the only non-gender-linked pronoun is plural ("they"). If I begin a sentence with reference to "a child" and then need to refer back to it with a pronoun, I should use the singular "he" or "she," but I am tempted to use "they." One means of avoiding irrelevant uses of a gender-specific pronoun is to avoid using the singular altogether. Kate Millett and Casey Swift (1972) have suggested the institution of a new singular "common gender" to overcome this problem. It would consist of "tey" (he or she), "ter" (his or her), and "tem" (him or her).

The procedure of linguistically categorizing by gender seems so "natural" that we rarely question it. In discussing this issue in a manuscript in progress, Barbara Polk and Robert Stein raise the question of structuring pronouns on, for instance, the basis of age. We would then talk about "over" and "under" a certain age rather than "he" and "she"!

Many other words, particularly adjectives, are gender-linked. We rarely speak of "beautiful" males and "handsome" females, and when we do, the male is very young and the female somewhat old; in short, both are desexed. To call a woman "ambitious" or "aggressive" is an insult, but to say either of a man is a compliment. The opposite is the case with such words as "sensitive" and "intuitive." Even many objects and animals are generally associated with one of the genders, as Polk and Stein point out. Ships are feminine, as are hurricanes; cats are feminine, rats and dogs masculine (except if we insult a female by calling her a "bitch"). Indeed, everyone who sees our fluffy white male cat insists on calling him "her," while in the next breath the same people refer to our female dog as "him." Gender is everywhere evident in occupational names: salesman/sales-woman, waiter/waitress, poet/poetess, not to mention titles such as king/queen, duke/duchess, Mr./Mrs., Miss, Ms. A visitor from another planet noting this would find us quite obsessed with iden-tifying people first and foremost by gender, and this would be true not merely of the English-speaking but of most language groups.

Such identification, however, does not merely separate the gen-ders; our language makes the male the basic reality and, in Simone de Beauvoir's (1953) words, the female the "other." Where I have talked about "humans," "people," and *"Homo sapiens,"* most people in our culture would use the equally correct term "men." Indeed, *homo* means precisely that; the root of "human" is "man." Even the root of "female" is found in "male," and of "woman" in "man." The problem discussed above with reference to the singular pronoun is not solved by approximately equal reference to "him" and "her" when gender is unknown or irrelevant; the masculine form is uni-formly used. We have *his*tory to learn; in anthropology classes we study Peking *man* and Neanderthal *man;* in other social science courses, economic *man* and political *man.* Economists speak of *man*-power; organizations have chair*men*; police go on *man*hunts; and utilities are found in *man*holes. We even pronounce couples man (not husband) and wife (not woman)!

In her marvelous chapter in *Adam's Rib* entitled "Society Writes Biology," Ruth Herschberger (1954; also see Stannard, 1970) dem-onstrates how the language used by medical science "under the guise of objective fact" consistently "animates" the male part in the repro-ductive cycle and "deanimates" the female. Thus, for instance, the identical process is called an "erection" for males and "congestion" for females. Similarly, the terms "impotence" and "frigidity," both of which represent the same basic physiological phenomenon, convey very different images. In the first case there is a lack of power or activity; in the second, merely an unpleasant environmental factor.

In summary, our language does two things in relation to sex role learning. First, it constantly focuses attention on gender. Second, it does so in such a way as to imply that females are less than fully human, or at least that males are the model of humanity. Surely, this must have an impact, if subtle, on little Jane and Dick as they learn the language while they are learning their appropriate sex role identities and behaviors.

Play

The importance of play in teaching children the roles and values of society has been stressed by George Mead (1934), as well as by the famous Swiss child psychologist Jean Piaget (1932). As children move from solitary play, which usually consists of imitative role-playing (mother, fireman, truck driver), to organized games with other children, they gradually come to understand that society is based on a system of rules and interlocking roles; in Mead's terminology, they learn about "the generalized other." The play and games characteristic of a society contribute rather substantially to socializing children into their particular sociocultural milieu.

Past a relatively early age, children are usually segregated by gender in their play groups, which function almost as little "subcultures" with their own norms and roles. Nonetheless, these groups strongly reflect the broader culture and serve, by and large, to reinforce sex role stereotyping. From an early age boys' groups engage in more competitive team games with more elaborate rules than girls' groups do.

Young girls alone play "house"; this is probably also one of their most frequent activities together. They also play games that are relatively uncomplex and have few rules, like jump rope and hopscotch. Neither of these consists of any team effort, and both are only minimally competitive. Girls frequently "practice" twirling and cheerleading as they get a bit older, or they might engage in arts and crafts or dancing, activities which are not competitive and do not have elaborate rules. Sports considered appropriate for females include swimming, skating, and horseback riding, all of which have few rules and often no competition. Also considered appropriate are golf and tennis, both of which have less elaborate rules than popular male sports and usually do not entail team effort.

Meanwhile, their brothers have organized or been organized to play baseball, football, and basketball, all quite elaborate games emphasizing the strong need for intrateam cooperation, strategy development, and interteam competition. Popular also is some form of "guns" (cowboys and Indians, cops 'n robbers), again usually a competitive team effort.

Girls are systematically barred from most team sports, which are increasingly organized by adults through schools and Little Leagues. According to Booth (1972, p. 184), laws in some states forbid inter-school athletic competition to female teams. As Booth explains the effects of male participation in team sports: "Team competition fosters and provides social conditions favorable to friendship formation. . . . Furthermore, in team activities a boy learns group procedures and practices which he can later apply to role performance. . . . Thus, . . . team activities develop social initiative in males" (p. 184). One would also have to conclude from this that females generally fail to learn these same traits, which undoubtedly hinders them in any attempt to compete with males later in the broader society.

The division of play by gender is strongly supported by toy and game manufacturers, who undoubtedly sell more if sister Jane needs an entirely different set of toys from brother Dick's. How else can one explain the existence of "boy's" and "girl's" bikes? The bar on a boy's bicycle is dangerous for both boys and girls, but the average boy would sooner walk than risk being seen on a girl's bike and labeled "sissy"! To say the least, this constitutes a very profitable situation for bicycle manufacturers and retail stores.

When students in a sex roles class did content analyses on toy catalogs from Sears, Montgomery Wards, Creative Playthings, and a few local department stores, they found an emphasis on sex role stereotyping. Another perusal of a Creative Playthings catalog found that while this company conspicuously avoided sex-typing the toys in the written descriptions, the pictures were another matter altogether. In the bulk of cases the boys pictured were quite actively playing with the toy in question; girls pictured were usually watching a boy play or, at best, were seated at a table using only their hands. These impressions are only somewhat borne out by the findings reported in Table 3.1 from a study by students Diana Black and Betsy Mellus of three catalogs, including Creative Playthings. Boys are indeed pictured more frequently as physically active and mechanical, and girls as more physically passive, but the differences are quite small. The

TABLE 3.1

SEX ROLE CHARACTERISTICS AS PICTURED IN THREE TOY CATALOGS

Characteristic	Percent of Male Children Pictured	Percent of Female Children Pictured
Physically active	18	14
Physically passive	17	23
Mechanical or manipulative	23	17
Competitive	6	5
Vocational	8	6
Emotionally expressive	27	34
Number of children pictured	132	64

outstanding fact to be noted in this table is that altogether boys are pictured more than twice as frequently as girls.

A study of Christmas toy catalogs from Sears and Wards by students Janna Wilder and Deborah Scott found marked gender-related differences, beginning with the division into "boys' " and "girls' " sections. The girls' sections are full of dolls of every description, particularly baby dolls. Full sets of household goods, from dishes to toy vacuum cleaners and ovens, are also displayed. In the costume section little Jane finds she can be a nurse, a bride, a fairy princess, a ballerina, a majorette, or a cowgirl in a skirt. There are pages showing makeup kits, manicure sets, and other "beauty aids." The boys' sections are full of athletic gear, technological toys (tractors, building materials, etc.), toy soldiers, guns, and cars. Boys' dolls are Joe Namath, G. I. Joe, and an astronaut. A boy doctor is pictured with a girl nurse; boys are pictured being served "tea" by girls. Boys' costumes include a marine, superman, an astronaut, a race car driver, a policeman, and a football player.

Altogether, there were 356 female dolls and only 68 male; 4 girls playing the organ or piano compared to no boys; 6 boys playing guitars or drums and no girls; 13 boys but only 1 girl riding a toy; 29 boys but no girls operating a model vehicle (train, car, tractor, etc.); 29 boys and only 2 girls operating construction toys; and so on. To the extent that these toys are preparing their users for adult roles, it is clear that they are doing so in a most stereotypical fashion. Girls are being trained to be mothers, helpmates, and homemakers, or for one of a very limited number of "feminine" occupations. They are also encouraged to care for their appearance, although not particularly for the development of their muscles. Boys are patently not being trained for a major role most will eventually play: fatherhood. They are encouraged to consider a myriad of occupational possibilities and to develop their bodily strength and coordination, but not particularly to care for their appearance.

In another analysis of toy catalogs, students George Bronson and Ben Herring studied the types of toys and games advertised for the two genders according to age. They found that those designed for toddlers (under 3) were not particularly differentiated for boys and girls. Beginning in the preschool category (ages 3–6) and reaching virtually 100 percent by elementary school age, toys and games were found to be stereotypically gender linked. Finally, games oriented to adults (over 20) again showed relatively very little gender differentiation. In short, during the age when sex role learning is most salient, toys and games are oriented toward reinforcing stereotypical notions of masculinity and femininity, but not before or after that period.

Media

In the preceding chapter several studies of communications media oriented toward adults were examined to see whether or not they *reflected* stereotypical notions of sex roles. TV and books oriented to children can also serve to *teach* or reinforce learned sex roles of a possibly stereotypical nature. Children have a less well-developed capacity than adults to judge what they see and hear and to reject some or all of it. What is presented to them by various media will tend to be taken seriously as "truth." Thus, whatever influence such stereotypes in adult media might exert on the behaviors and self-images of parents, similar material oriented to children will undoubtedly have a vastly greater impact on young Jane and Dick.

When two students, Judy Moore and Eric Charlton, studied 100 TV commercials aired during children's shows in February 1971, their findings duplicated those concerning commercials for adults. For instance, 79 of 83 narrators were male; 17 females were depicted engaged in domestic activities compared to only 5 males; 8 males and no females were doing something mechanical; and 40 males but only 4 females were physically active. Males were dressed casually more than two thirds of the time, whereas females were overwhelmingly dressed more formally. Twenty-two males and only 2 females were portrayed in provider roles and, conversely, 16 females but no males were shown as economically dependent. Finally, 15 females were shown responding to social pressure, compared to only 3 males.

In analyzing the husband-wife relationships portrayed, Moore and Charlton found that "The male was invariably pictured as being independent and intelligent. He almost always had the competitive drive, the self-confidence, and the judgment necessary to control the life of his mate. The female, however, submits to the male authority and assumes a dependent posture." In terms of the mother-father role complex, "The roles . . . were dichotomized and distinct. The father was usually shown taking the children out to play while the mother stayed at home to watch over the babies."

Concern with sex role stereotyping in children's media has been evidenced by women's liberation groups. Complaints by various groups regarding the TV program "Sesame Street," which has succeeded so well in avoiding racial stereotypes, have been voiced against its blatant sex role stereotypes. The following was discovered in a survey of elementary school readers by a group affiliated with the National Organization for Women (NOW) called Women on Words and Images (1972): a heavy preponderance (5:2 ratio) of boys' stories; younger sister–girl "ninny" syndrome; older and taller boys outnumbering girls in most illustrations; smarter boys with greater initiative and achievement; fathers who work and play creatively with children; aproned mothers in supportive and passive roles; men depicted in a wide variety of roles and activities; women almost exclusively depicted as mothers and teachers. These same types of stereotypes were discovered in an intensive examination of award-winning picture books for preschoolers (Weitzman, Eifles, Hokada, and Ross, 1972).

Several students examined books designed for preschool and grammar school children. The findings of these studies repeat those already discussed and, therefore, will be reviewed only briefly. The findings of a study of 27 preschool books by students Johnnie Stark and Cathy Carter are shown in Table 3.2; they speak for themselves. Similar findings were reported by students Betsy Taylor and Nancy Weaver in their study of 15 picture books for preschoolers: 80 percent of the main characters were male; there were three times as many books oriented to male readers as female; only 1 nondomestic role was portrayed for female characters, namely, teaching, compared to 15 separate occupations represented for males; and male characters were depicted as active 100 percent of the time, females only 53 percent.

An analysis of grammar school texts by students Donna Harris and Ivett Quattlebaum drew similar conclusions. Males were far more frequently pictured and discussed in the text as physically active.

TABLE 3.2

SEX ROLE STEREOTYPES AS REFLECTED IN 27 PRESCHOOL CHILDREN'S BOOKS

Characteristic	No. of Books in Which Female Characters Exhibit Characteristics	No. of Books in Which Male Characters Exhibit Characteristics
Functional role		
Provider	1*	17
Domestic	18	3
Unclassifiable	8	7
Play activity		
Physically active	3	14
Physically passive	10	3
Unclassifiable	14	10
Personality		
Dominant	3	11
Passive	13	3
Unclassifiable	11	13
Intellectual		
Realistic, logical, objective	2	10
Idealistic, illogical, subjective	15	8
Unclassifiable	10	9

*Schoolteacher

Moreover, they had a wider variety of functional roles to fulfill than females. Comments and examples in school texts can also be very revealing of sex role stereotypes. One book urged: "You should mend your papa's handkerchief," and a girl is pictured doing it. We can all remember the arithmetic examples that read something like: "Jane is making cookies. She had two cups of sugar and her mother gave her two more. How many cups of sugar does Jane now have?" But "Dick was playing with his 28 model cars and gave four to his younger brother. How many model cars does Dick have now?"

One recurring finding in these studies of children's media is that many more males were portrayed than females. This could be a reflection of the fact that both males and females in our society find males much more interesting characters, capable of doing a wider variety of things and doing them well. An alternative explanation relating to the sex role learning process discussed by Lynn and reviewed above is also possible. Recall that little boys need to piece together their concept of masculinity from a variety of sources, where young girls need only imitate a model readily available to achieve femininity. Books, toy catalogs, and TV can all be viewed as instruments representing a model of masculinity to the growing boy for his emulation. It is patently clear that such a model is highly stereotyped.

Stereotyping also persists in texts used during the later years of education. In a study of high school history books and a second-year Spanish text, students Diana Phillips and Pat Steed found clear evidence that females were portrayed as domestics and caretakers of children, males as workers of all types; females were pictured as frequently passive, males as generally active. Most striking, 98 percent of the people discussed in one history book were male; such an illustrious woman as Madame Curie was found only in the context of a sentence in which Monsieur Curie was said to have been "assisted by his wife." In another history book, in which females comprised only 3 percent of the entries, famous females like Amelia Earhart, Catherine the Great, and Queen Victoria were absent. Where Boy Scouts and the YMCA were discussed, their female counterparts were not mentioned. The author of *Frankenstein,* Mary Wollstonecraft Shelley, was introduced as the poet Shelley's wife, and, again, Madame Curie was presented as her husband's helpmate.

School

If Dick and Jane have had "normal" parents, that is, parents functioning more or less within their stereotyped sex roles, and if they
play with peers, look at TV, and are read the typical preschool
books, they will arrive at school pretty firmly entrenched in their
respective stereotyped sex roles. When they get there, as we have
seen, their books will reinforce this further; so, generally, will their
teachers, counselors, and administrators (Andreas, 1971, chap. 2).

In many schools today girls still are not permitted by school administrators to wear slacks or pants of any variety. Attired in dresses,
little girls will obviously be less willing to engage in a variety of play
activities designed to develop strength, stamina, and coordination.
On many a school playground they may be observed using the jump-
ropes provided by their teachers or the swings, while the little boys
are climbing the jungle gym or already beginning to play baseball
and football. Even where girls are engaged in some sort of ball game
(usually segregated from the boys), they find it hard to devote themselves to it wholeheartedly. Picture Jane sliding into second base on
her bare legs, skirt flying! While Jane is finding it difficult to play such
games, Dick is discovering that if he can't play them well, his friends
and even teachers will make life rough for him. All this is exacerbated by the fact that having matured earlier, the little Janes are likely
to be stronger, taller, and better coordinated than the little Dicks, who
nevertheless have already learned to consider themselves physically
superior to girls.

Boys and girls are separated and treated somewhat differently in
a variety of other ways during grammar school. They are often lined
up separately for assemblies and such, separated in seating arrangements, and placed on opposing teams for spelling bees and other
competitions. Such separation supports the desires for exclusiveness
of little boys, who generally already understand their superior social
status. Girls serve the cookies and punch during school parties, while
boys move the furniture and carry the books (Progrebin, 1972, p.
27). Boys are permitted to engage in considerably more physical
activity and make more noise in the classroom (Howe, 1971, p. 81).
The sexes are probably most frequently separated throughout the

school years for discussions of hygiene and sex education, a procedure designed to ensure poor communication between the genders later on the subject of sex. When boys "put girls down," as they often do at that age, teachers (female usually) frequently say and do nothing to correct them (Baumrind, 1972, p. 166), thus tacitly encouraging their notion of superiority. According to studies cited by Florence Howe (1971, p. 81), teachers assume that girls "are likely to 'love' reading and to 'hate' mathematics and sciences," and the opposite is expected of boys. Here are some self-fulfilling prophecies on the way to becoming realities.

As Dick and Jane progress through school, she will learn figure-watching exercises in gym while he is climbing the ropes; she will play a variety of basketball requiring little movement or contact while he risks a broken nose to prove how good and brave an athlete he is in contact sports; she will giggle when she strikes out at softball and her pals will hardly care (nor will her teacher), while he will be ostracized if his coordination is lacking. After school, while Dick is trying out for school teams in football, baseball, track, or basketball, Jane is learning such ancillary activities as cheerleading, twirling, and "dancing" with a large group of her friends.

Past grammar school the curriculum itself becomes somewhat "sexregated." At many schools girls are required to take cooking and sewing and occasionally typing; woodworking and machine shop are required of boys. Frequently school administrators do not permit students to take the course designed for the opposite sex, and certainly they are not encouraged to do so by peers or teachers. A number of legal battles are currently being fought over such practices as people have become increasingly aware that males need to know how to cook and sew, and females should be able to fix basic machinery and make simple things—and some boys and girls even *like* such "inappropriate" activities!

By junior high, too, school counselors are strongly encouraging males and females in different career directions. It was not too many years ago that black and brown youngsters were systematically discouraged by their "counselors" from seeking a college education or setting their sights on white-collar jobs. By and large such racist practices have ceased in very recent years. Their sexist counterparts have not. College-bound girls are still frequently counseled into considering "typically feminine" curricula such as nursing, teaching, and home economics, and avoiding "masculine" fields like engineering, law, or business. Conversely, boys are urged to consider engineering, business, medicine, and so forth, and to eschew the fine arts, grammar school teaching, and other "feminine" fields. A good science student will be urged into high school science teaching if female; if male, into engineering, "pure" science, or medicine. Non-college-bound girls are pushed into typing courses to prepare them for secretarial futures, while their brothers are encouraged to become such things as mechanics. The possibility of a male secretary or a female mechanic never seems to occur to counselors. Indeed, when there is doubt as to whether or not the youngster should pursue a college education, counselors frequently encourage males and discourage females.

Counselors defend such practices on the basis of what youngsters may "realistically" expect to face in the future: marriage, child care, and a lack of opportunity in a number of career fields for females, and the need to support a family at the highest income and status levels possible for males. "Realism," however, has always been an excuse for maintaining the status quo, and it is no different in the case of sex role stereotypes. If, for instance, females do not prepare to enter previously masculine fields, such fields will remain male-dominated, allowing another generation of counselors to assure girls that females can't work in them. In addition, it is questionable whether counselors' notions of "reality" in fact keep pace with reality. There is undoubtedly a lag between expanding opportunities and changing sex role definitions on the one hand, and counselors' awareness of these phenomena on the other.

Teachers themselves express sex role stereotypes, according to the findings of two students, Pam Maye and Sara McMillan, in a study of kindergarten and first- second- and third-grade teachers in the San Antonio, Texas, area. Over 90 percent of teachers sampled were female, and over two thirds were married; all were college graduates. About one in three of the female teachers at least occasionally, if not more often, felt personally "compelled to act less knowledgeable than they are to impress a man." More striking are some of the findings presented in Table 3.3. Forty percent of the teachers felt that aggression is a biologically innate trait of males but not females. Males were also considered more capable than females of abstract reasoning, whether because of biology or culture. Conversely, over one third felt that females but not males are innately compassionate and sentimental, and even greater percentages felt that "intuitiveness" is a characteristic innate to females alone. Eighteen percent stated that females are innately "followers" and "idealistic," while very few stated that with reference to males. It is also interesting to note that the majority of teachers perceived differences between the genders in most of the traits, regardless of the reasons that would account for this.

TABLE 3.3

CHARACTERISTICS ASSIGNED MALES AND FEMALES BY GRADE SCHOOL TEACHERS

| Characteristic | Biologically Innate to: | | No Difference | Cultural Trait of: | | Total N* |
	Males	Females		Males	Females	
Aggressive	40%	6%	26%	26%	1%	147
Practical, objective	15	15	34	20	15	116
Compassionate, sentimental	3	39	26	1	30	148
Idealistic	3	19	48	5	25	151
Verbal ability	8	11	54	16	11	149
Follower	4	18	31	1	45	144
Moral, trustworthy	3	13	67	5	13	150
Intuitive	3	41	33	2	21	150
Abstract reasoning ability	16	10	47	20	6	152

*Totals vary because "no responses" were omitted.

Other findings of interest from this study include the fact that at least two in three teachers agreed at least to some extent with the assertion that "Most women have only themselves to blame for not doing better in life" (more will be said on that topic in the next chapter). About one quarter agreed at least slightly with the false-hood that "women are usually less reliable on the job than men"; more than one in three were at least somewhat inclined to agree with the empirically false statement that "children of working mothers tend to be less well adjusted than children of unemployed women"; finally, one in four felt that women may "best achieve full self-devel-opment" by being "good wives and mothers." Assuming that the behavior of teachers more or less reflects these views, there can be little doubt that they too contribute to reinforcing cultural stereo-types of masculinity and femininity.

Adolescence: A Time for "Adjustment"

In analyzing the impact of the media and schools on sex role learning, it should be recalled that the media directed to adolescents, whether popular songs, magazines and underground papers, TV, or school texts, have been found to strongly reinforce sex role stereo-types. In addition, junior and senior high school curricula, counsel-ing, and extracurricular activities tend to segregate the genders and encourage them to think, behave, and plan in different (stereotyped) ways. A few costs of such procedures for adolescents have already been suggested, including premarital pregnancies for girls and delin-quency for boys.

In any consideration of adolescents, two related concepts appear repeatedly: "identity crisis" and "anxiety." From puberty until they complete school and enter their adult statuses both males and females in contemporary American society are thought to undergo more or less severe emotional crises centered around questions of who they are and what they will become. Questions concerning sex role identi-ties contribute mightily to such problems, although they are broader than this alone. It is during the years following the onset of puberty that both males and females are faced with making major decisions that will usually influence the manner in which they live the rest of their lives. Such decisions are most often made within the boundaries of sex role stereotypes. Boys are generally urged into courses of action preparatory to some occupational commitment, girls into behaviors designed to ultimately attract a suitable mate.

The impact of peers on behavior and thought is probably never greater than at this period of life when, as young adults, they strive to establish their independence by breaking ties with their parents. The strong gender segregation characteristic of younger peer groups begins to break down somewhat during adolescence, with dating. However, all-male and all-female friendship groups or cliques persist, as indeed they do in adulthood. Moreover, peer groups become relatively more important in influencing the behaviors and attitudes of young adults. They also play a major role in determining the chances of their members for success with the opposite sex.

As a general rule, all-male groups determine the relative status and prestige of the various individual males within them. Such prestige is a function of how well the adolescent boy fulfills the norms of the group. Thus, in middle-class peer groups boys are often expected to be good (but not *too* good) students and active in a number of extracurricular activities, which function as modes of preparation for college and a high-status career. They are also expected to maintain athletic competence and achieve considerable independence from their families. Working and lower-class peer groups usually place heaviest emphasis on independence, physical courage, and adventuresomeness, sometimes as tested in illegal ventures. These groups generally deemphasize and even denigrate school success. Those who manage to achieve high status within such all-male groups attract the most numerous and attractive females from among class and ethnic equals. In turn, status within all-female groups is largely contingent upon the status of the males the girl is able to attract as dates or "steadies." In other words, female peer groups at this stage of the life cycle (and probably thereafter) base their internal prestige structure on their members' relative abilities to do best that which society commands: attract (potential) outstanding mates.

Note that in the case of female groups there are no differences by socioeconomic class (see Flora, 1971, for a related argument). Male groups also base their internal structure on that which society suggests is appropriate to the gender, but class variations do exist. Females of all classes are enjoined to find mates as their primary responsibility. Males of all classes are enjoined to be physically coordinated and aggressive, and to acquire an occupation. However, the occupational roles anticipated by working- and lower-class youths are generally not of a nature where school performance will be very relevant. Thus, in these peer groups, other aspects of the stereotype become overwhelmingly dominant. Middle-class males, for whom school performance is relevant to future occupational expectations, develop norms by which these other characteristics share importance with academic success.

In examining the pressures exerted on adolescents and the ways in which they contribute to "anxieties" arising from "identity crises," it should be noted that whether or not the female has conformed previously to stereotypical notions of femininity (and substantial numbers of "tomboys" have not), the pressure by peers and parents to do so in adolescence becomes substantial (Freeman, 1970, pp. 38–39). At this point in her life, preparation for the search for a "mate" and the search itself begin in earnest, and that is presumably the one crucial fact of her entire future existence and identity. Girls perform substantially better than boys in the earlier years of school, probably out of a "feminine" desire to please the teacher. Suddenly in high school and, especially, college their performance declines noticeably, while that of males, particularly those in the middle class, improves markedly in preparation for a career. Adolescent girls are enjoined to "play dumb and weak" in order to "boost male egos" and thereby attract and hold a suitable mate whose identity they can then assume. In a now-famous series of experiments conducted among female college students, Matina Horner (1969) demonstrated that females actually fear achievement and success (also see Gornick, 1972). The bright, dynamic, adolescent Jane, the one who is planning a career, or the good athlete either "plays dumb and weak" and lives a frustrating lie, or she pursues her interests as a relative outcast, dateless and low in prestige among her peers, wondering bitterly and anxiously why she isn't more "feminine." This will continue and increase in college, in graduate school, and even throughout life. Many finally conclude that they cannot have both a fulfilling life in terms of their own interests and aspirations and a satisfactory relationship with a male. Whichever goes by the wayside, life will be less rich as a result of the phony choice offered by society and beginning most noticeably in adolescence.

Nor is the girl who opts for "femininity" at the expense of her individual needs and inclinations any better off later, as the material cited in the last chapter demonstrates. In their quest for identity through an attachment to a male, many adolescent females find themselves pressured into sexual relationships in an attempt to attract, please, or "hold" boyfriends. This may be particularly true for less attractive girls. Such relationships often result in out-of-wedlock pregnancies, "shotgun" marriages, adjudication as "delinquent," or serious emotional problems for those who have been trained to consider sex outside of marriage as "evil" or "sinful." In any case, such sexual experiences, *when engaged in for those kinds of reasons,* often develop into unpleasant situations, fraught with problems of every variety and hardly beneficial to the development of a positive identity. In this context I am not addressing myself to all premarital sexual relations but only those engaged in out of a desire on the part of the female to please the male, regardless of her own personal needs and feelings at the time. In their quest for identity through attachment to a male, all too many young women leave themselves open to crass sexual exploitation and, as we shall see, most males are pressured into taking advantage of such situations.

Dick, too, is facing his share of problems at this stage. Where Jane at least has the option, however unpleasant the consequences may eventually become, of taking a future mate's identity as her own with no further ado, Dick must work out his own in an increasingly complex and incomprehensible world. First and foremost, especially if Dick is middle class, that identity will be in terms of his occupation, and beginning in high school he must seriously begin to decide what he "wants to be when he grows up." The decision to become a minister rather than a professional soldier, for instance, is based on rather different notions about oneself and the world, and these must first be sorted out. In addition, if his potential occupational talents and personal predilections run in certain tabooed directions, such as art, literature, or music, he will face ridicule from his peers for being something less than "masculine"; likewise, in many cases, if he takes his studies "too seriously."

While engaged in these decisions, he must nonetheless maintain some demonstration of his "physical prowess" and "bravery." That may not present too much of a problem if he happens to be 6' tall,

180 pounds, and coordinated, but what of all those who are 5'6" and 115 pounds? Those who, in the old Charles Atlas ads, got sand kicked in their faces, the sensitive souls who cannot bear to inflict pain on others, the boys who lack coordination, are all subject to severe doubts about their masculine identity. Such "shortcomings" can be particularly anxiety-producing for working- and lower-class youth, although they will obviously affect the middle-class male as well.

Equally important to adolescent boys is the need for independence, sometimes financial and almost always in terms of freedom from adult supervision. However, in a society where, increasingly, males remain in school under adult supervision and out of the labor force well into their twenties, such independence becomes problematic. Told to "act like a man" but often constrained to "beg" his parents for money, use of the car, and other "necessities," adolescent males sometimes find it difficult to live up to the social prescriptions and so begin to doubt their very "masculinity." Dick finds himself in need of emotional support from people who accept him as he is, with all his weaknesses, shortcomings, and insecurities. Yet he is trying to break away from emotional dependence on his family, about the only people who might accept him unconditionally. The world of adolescent males has little mercy on the boy who never managed to make the break from a too close identification with and attachment to mother.

Left with residual doubts about his masculinity from childhood (if we accept Lynn's analysis), faced with making important career decisions, encouraged to be independent and physically and emotionally strong while also constrained from these things by his inexperience, student status, and need for emotional support, the adolescent male faces a tough time in developing a sense of himself. Finally, while he is not pressured into seeking a mate at this point (except by adolescent females), he is expected by his peers to "prove his masculinity" by revealing his "prowess" with the girls. As they brag to one another about their sexual exploits, some unfortunate lads actually believe what they hear (or say). A vicious cycle of anxiety and lies is often the result. The inexperienced (namely, most boys) lie about their conquests to cover their felt inferiority, listen to others do the same, believe them, and feel yet more anxiety about their masculinity. At its worst, this eventuates in sexual exploitation of girls who allow themselves to be used in an attempt to establish their own feminine identity.

This brings us finally to the subject of the nature of the relationship between adolescent males and females. It is, first and foremost, broadly sexual in nature and based around "dating." For the boy or girl who is not interested in this or who matures late physically, relationships with the opposite sex are almost nonexistent, and prestige with the same sex is low. We are all quite familiar with the pattern: the female more or less passively awaits an invitation from a male, after taking the greatest pains to appear "attractive" by whatever are the standards of the day; the boy will usually try to "get as much" as he can from her sexually; she, as repository of "sexual morality," is responsible for not allowing sexual play to "get out of hand." She has been fed (and believes) a diet of "romantic" notions about love and sex which puts her at a disadvantage in relationship to boys, who are usually substantially less devoted to the ideal of romance. While she bases her existence on his attentions, he has a variety of other, often more important, matters to attend to. The game that ensues makes honest communication and affection between two human beings difficult, if not impossible. Moreover, in many ways this process comprises the worst possible preparation for a satisfactory marriage for either. Indeed, as Margaret Mead (1970, chap. 14) first pointed out nearly three decades ago, dating is really oriented toward gaining prestige among the peers of one's own gender, and it is thus quite impersonal. More recently the process has been viewed as a failure "because it does not assist couples in learning how to develop and maintain vital and meaningful relationships" (Olson, 1972, p. 16).

Other Bulwarks of Sex Role Stereotypes

It should be clear by now that in the normal course of events most children rather completely internalize socially defined roles, including sex roles, at a young age. However, no society can afford to rest on the assumption that the socialization process alone, as conducted rather informally by parents, teachers, and peers, will ensure substantial compliance or conformity. Therefore, in every human group there are a variety of "reinforcers" and social control mechanisms constantly at work to more or less subtly pressure individuals into conformity with social expectations. Some of these have already been examined, including the media, Madison Avenue's commercial use of the media (see Andreas, 1971, pp. 87–91), and the schools. The next chapter will consider the ways in which the political, legal, economic, and advanced educational institutions function to support sex role stereotypes. Here two types of idea systems, religion and science, that strongly support the status quo in a variety of ways, including the one in question, will be briefly examined. These two ideological structures constitute potent forces in the thinking of most Americans.

Religion

Virtually all major religions of the world include strong commandments to the two genders to act in a manner consistent with traditional patriarchal social arrangements (Andreas, 1971, pp. 68–77). Since the United States is overwhelmingly a Judeo-Christian society, the two Testaments can be taken as the religious basis of our society. However, it should be noted that certain tenets of various other faiths, including traditional Hindu practices such as *suttee* (widow suicide by burning) and Confucian injunctions to wives to distrust themselves and obey their husbands, are even more traditional in their treatment of the genders as separate and unequal than contemporary Judeo-Christian practice and theology is.

God is a male to most Americans who visualize a deity; so is His son Jesus. In Genesis, that male God single-handedly created a male human. Then, in further opposition to all the laws of nature, he is said to have had that first male symbolically give birth to a female to function as his helpmate. It seems, in fact, that the mythology of much of the ancient civilized world included a major male deity giving birth to offspring in a manner that makes him in fact a "mother" (Stannard, 1970, pp. 25–26). The concept of "womb envy" discussed in Chapter 1 might help explain such a widespread phenomenon. At any rate, after creating Adam and Eve, the Bible makes gullible Eve the chief instigator of evil and the human agent responsible for their departure from earthly paradise. As punishment Eve and her female descendants will have to birth future generations painfully and submit to the will of Adam's future male descendants who, in turn, are enjoined to work hard for little return. A good woman, henceforth, is a faithful and submissive one. The stage is set for rationalizing patriarchy. In fact, very early versions of the Old Testament depict God creating a male (Adam) and a female (Lilith) at the same time. When Lilith demanded treatment as Adam's equal, difficulties arose, and she went into exile. Later mythology depicted her as a demon, and the story of Eve came to replace the original version of the creation in Judaic tradition (Rivlin, 1972).

Various laws and traditions in the Old Testament rather clearly establish male primacy. For instance, only a male could divorce a spouse. A girl who was not a virgin upon marriage could be stoned to death. A man who raped a virgin, however, had merely to pay indemnity to her father and marry her. If a woman made a vow, her father or husband could void it. Polygamy was frequent in the Old Testament, polyandry nonexistent. Females were frequently bought from their parents by men wanting wives, such as the purchase of Rebecca by Isaac. While a few females, such as Deborah, Bathsheba, and Jezebel, had *de facto* political influence, leadership and power were essentially male prerogatives. Only one Old Testament book, Ruth, is devoted specifically to a woman. Males are frequently found making misogynic comments such as that in Ecclesiastics: "And I find more bitter than death the woman, whose heart is snares and nets, and her hands as bands; whoso pleaseth God shall escape from her; but the sinner shall be taken by her." Women worked hard and had important economic functions tending flocks, working wool and flax, planting vineyards, cooking, minding children, and so on. Husbands of such hard-working wives are often pictured sitting around talking with the elders. To this day an Orthodox male Jew begins each day with a prayer thanking God for not making him a woman. Until very recently the Jewish scholar (rabbi) was virtually excused from any economic duties. Since rabbis were always male, these duties fell to their wives. In fact, it was only in May 1972 that the first female rabbi was ordained.

The advent of Jesus was a mixed blessing for females. Sexual intercourse becomes a rather nasty thing in Christianity, presumably because women are somehow "dirty." Jesus was supposedly born without benefit of it, and to this day the Catholic Church grants legitimacy to sexuality only inasmuch as offspring may result. The Virgin Mary is practically deified and has high status in the New Testament and Church dogma. However, this status rests only on the fact that she is the mother of the Savior and not on any real accomplishments of her own; after all, Jesus is the son of a male God, not really Mary. Jesus himself did not seem to make any distinctions between the genders, although it is curious that all of his disciples were male. He raised the prostitute Mary Magdalene to respectability; Mary of Bethany is portrayed in theological disputes with males; it is females, not even the disciples, who stand by Him at the crucifixion and discover the empty tomb. However, it was the Apostle Paul who chiefly shaped the early church, and his pronouncements included such statements as "the husband is supreme over his wife," "wives, be obedient to your husbands," and "But woman reflects the glory of man; for man was not created . . . for woman's sake, but woman was created for man's sake." In these statements Paul was reflecting his times and the patriarchal structure of classical Roman and Hebrew society. That he was a product of his sociocultural milieu is also clear in his assertion that "It is a disgraceful thing for a woman to speak in a church meeting." If a female wants to know something, she is enjoined by Paul to ask her husband at home. The various Christian churches have not generally treated females as equals. The Catholic Church still does not have female clergy, and only very recently have various Protestant denominations and sects allowed women to assume that role. Moreover, only recently has "cherish" been substituted for "obey" in the traditional marriage vows made by the female.

Science

Although religious affiliation and attendance have increased in recent decades, it is probably the case that most Americans are taking traditional theology less seriously than in the past and are relating to their religious institutions in a more secular manner (Herberg, 1960, pp. 1–4). "Science" has become our national theology, although this may be changing somewhat, especially among the young. However, science is not value-free on the issue of sex roles or, for that matter, any other topic. A few of the sex role biases that creep into medical science have already been mentioned. Those disciplines that deal more directly with human behavior, especially sociology and psychology, have in recent decades contributed substantially to reinforcing sex role stereotypes under the guise of "scientific truth."

From World War II until very recently sociology has been dominated by that theoretical approach known as functionalism, which is associated primarily with Talcott Parsons. Perhaps nowhere has the influence of this orientation been greater than in the field of marriage and the family, in which it has remained dominant even while the rest of the discipline is increasingly questioning it. Marriage and family courses are probably taken by more undergraduate students, including majors from virtually every discipline, than any other sociology courses, except possibly the introductory course. It is most frequently taken by college women as a "practical" course preparatory for marriage. It is, therefore, of utmost importance to consider the kinds of things students are learning in such classes and will very likely attempt to practice someday in their own lives.

A basic criticism of the functional approach is that it tends to confuse description with prescription; what is with what ought to be. In very simplified terms and at the risk of some distortion, functional sociology may be said to be concerned with those social structures and processes that contribute to the maintenance of "equilibrium." In turn, many modern functionalists tend to equate equilibrium with existing social structures and processes, namely, the status quo. Forces that encourage change in the status quo, including conflict of any variety, are often viewed as "deviant" or "pathological." Given this approach, the implicit if not explicit approach to social arrangements is "if it exists, it is good." Stated otherwise, starting with the (questionable) assumption that our society is in a "state of equilibrium," namely, functioning in a basically satisfactory manner, the various social arrangements characteristic of the society are considered to be mostly functional for maintaining equilibrium. From this theoretical perspective, major changes in social institutions will usually result in "disequilibrium," which is implicitly bad.

In terms of an analysis of marriage and the family, this approach leads to the inevitable conclusion that many aspects of traditional sex role stereotypes are inviolate, but for social, not necessarily biological, reasons. Utilizing Robert Bales' (1950) analysis of "expressive" and "instrumental" role functions in all human groups, functionalists conclude that females do (and implicitly ought to) fulfill the former functions, and males the latter. Since groups, including families, presumably cannot survive without such functions being fulfilled, and since in contemporary American society there exists a division of labor between the genders in their fulfillment, therefore (so the argument goes), the "normal" family will consist of an expressive female and an instrumental male. Quite simply, students are told in scientific jargon that males accomplish the instrumental goal of working and making money, and females fulfill the expressive function of soothing feelings and caring for husband and offspring. Moreover, to disrupt this pattern is "pathological" and will eventuate in the probable failure of the family to persist. In this scheme the individual carries the burden of adjusting to social reality, that is, the status quo. Most of the popular marriage and family texts utilize this approach. It is exemplified in the following quotes from a typical family text (Martinson, 1970); any number of other books could be used to demonstrate the same thing.

> Systems which endure over a period of time are characterized by the fact that roles within the system become differentiated from each other. . . . A major part of the way of life of any family that lasts over a period of years is made up of expectations specifying how each member of the family should behave. . . .
> . . . Father and mother in a nuclear family tend to constitute a leadership coalition, but they also enact roles differentiated from each other. . . . The two basic problems of the family system—adapting to other social systems and integrating inside activities—call for different kinds of leadership. . . . The outside activities in large measure determine how the family survives in the community;

the inside activities are concerned with integrating the group behavior that arises out of the external system and reacts upon it. . . .

The function of bearing and giving early care to children estab-
lishes a strong presumptive primacy for the mother as integrative-
emotional leader in the family. She becomes the focus of gratification
as the source of security and comfort not only for the newborn but
for all members of the family. . . . Her support of her husband becomes a critical condition of the stability of the family. . . .

. . . his primary function in the family is to supply an income (pp.
112–3).

Or again:

In marriage the wife is supportive of the husband's tasks. . . . He
carries an instrumental role—that is, he is responsible for the
family's standard of living and sets the pace of upward mobility.
Ideally, he has the interest, moral support, and appreciation of his
wife (pp. 116–17).

Carol Ehrlich's (1971) study of six widely used marriage and
family texts demonstrates that this approach is endemic to the field.
Moreover, the fact that they strongly reinforce sex role stereotypes
has not been lost to feminists. Betty Friedan (1963, chap. 6) and
Kate Millett (1970, pp. 220–33) mount scathing attacks on the
functional school of sociology (and anthropology). Addressing themselves to such biases, increasing numbers of students and faculty are
demanding less stereotyped academic consideration of the roles of
males and females in contemporary society. Such pressure has
resulted in the creation of new courses entitled "Sex Roles," "The
Sociology of Women," and so forth. However, changing notions of
sex role behavior do not appear to have seriously permeated "Marriage and Family Life" courses, where they logically belong in most
curricula. Rather, side by side with the new courses, traditional
marriage and family classes continue to teach traditional views as
"scientific truths."

Functional sociology has drawn rather heavily on neo-Freudian
theory, as have many areas of psychology, psychiatry, and social
work. Freud's ideas pertaining to psychosexual development were
discussed briefly in Chapter 1. As they have been interpreted and
popularized by several generations of his followers, Freud's ideas

have become potent bulwarks for traditional notions about sex roles, and they have been thoroughly criticized by feminists (Friedan, 1963, chap. 5; Firestone, 1970, chap. 3; Greer, 1970, pp. 82–91; Millett, 1970, pp. 176–220; Weisstein, 1970). They, too, have long been disseminated as scientific truth in academe, in the offices of the "helping professions" such as clinical psychology, social work, and psychiatry, and through literally thousands of popular "advice" columns, articles, and books. Indeed, Phyllis Chesler (1971, p. 746) views psychotherapy as a "major socially approved institution" for white middle-class women through which they may gain "salvation" with the aid of "an understanding and benevolent (male) authority." Even more than functional sociology, neo-Freudian notions of masculinity and femininity have shaped our concepts of "mental health" and "normal" behavior. Those who fail to conform are not merely "deviant"; they are labeled "sick," "neurotic," and so forth. Moreover, objections to this theoretical framework are usually taken by its proponents as further evidence of just how "sick" the objector is. This type of approach constitutes a truly potent social control mechanism.

Material critical of Freudian and neo-Freudian theory is widely available. The phrase often used to summarize this school of thought is "Biology is destiny." Freud himself may have been at least somewhat more sensitive than many of his later followers to the crucial impact of society, via the inputs of parents, on psychosexual development. Even granted this, however, it is clear in many of his writings that he thought that females are by nature designed to rear as well as bear children and not to compete in the world of work; that they are passive and masochistic, and to be otherwise is "neurotic." Conversely, he viewed the male as an active agent, creative in all areas of endeavor save childbirth and rearing and equipped with a well-developed conscience (superego). Females emerge in his writings as defective males missing that most crucial of all appendages, the penis. Males appear as perpetually frightened lest they lose that presumably glorious tool. In short, the two genders are depicted as distinctly different:

> . . . women are different beings—we will not say lesser, rather the opposite—from men. . . . Nature has determined woman's destiny

through beauty, charm and sweetness. Law and custom have much to give women that has been withheld from them, but the position of women will surely be what it is: in youth an adored darling and in mature years a loved wife (Jones, 1961, p. 118).

Freud and his followers saw their neurotic female patients as basically in need of sexual fulfillment. This, in turn, could result only from an acceptance of their passive feminine role (as then defined in Western society) and a rejection of their "masculinity complex." Translated by popularizers and practitioners alike, this came to mean that an ambitious woman who sought independence and career and/or rejected domesticity and child rearing was by definition neurotic and incapable of sexual fulfillment. She had never overcome her childhood "penis envy," which in "normal" females is presumably translated into a desire for babies. Moreover, if she enters the masculine world of work, she is defined as a "castrating female," desexing not merely herself but the males around her. Males, by comparison, are presumed by Freud and his followers to have a substantially greater "libido." It is through the "sublimation" of this, required in working through their "Oedipal complex" and overcoming "castration anxiety," that males gain their vastly superior creative energy upon which civilizations are built. Relatedly, gender differences in libido mean that males are naturally much more aggressive and females passive, even masochistic. In Freud's own words:

> Women represent the interests of the family and the sexual life; the work of civilization has become more and more men's business; it confronts them with ever harder tasks, compels them to sublimations of instinct which women are not easily able to achieve. Since man has not an unlimited amount of mental energy at his disposal, he must accomplish his tasks by distributing his libido to the best advantage. What he employs for cultural purposes he withdraws to a great extent from women and his sexual life; his constant association with men and his dependence on his relations with them even estrange him from his duties as husband and father. Woman finds herself thus forced into the background by the claims of culture, and she adopts an inimical attitude towards it (1930, p. 73).

Here, as with functional sociology, "science" has come to the rescue of the sex role status quo, offering powerful "reasons" why males must persevere in work even at the expense of their personal lives, and females must confine themselves to home and children regardless of personal inclinations—why the former must be aggressive, the latter passive. The influence of such thought remains persuasive. Indeed, even contemporary sex manuals, written after medical science had discovered females' ability to achieve multiple orgasms, continue to stress the passive role of the female *vis-à-vis* the male (Gordon and Shankweiler, 1971). Research concerning the content of recent gynecology texts further demonstrates pervasive sex role stereotyping in "science" (Scully and Bart, 1973).

Dick and Jane go to Sunday (or Saturday) school and learn their religious heritage. They go to public school and college and learn the latest that science has "discovered." They look to scientific specialists to solve their personal problems. The notions they have learned more or less informally from parents, peers, the media, and school personnel are constantly being reinforced, explained, justified, and rationalized. Against the combined weight of all these factors, it is difficult to argue.

Postscript

By now readers should be wondering why it is that many if not most people they know do not appear to be nearly as stereotypically "masculine" or "feminine" as the last two chapters depict. I have been concerned to this point with a discussion of the forces that reinforce any social arrangement and predispose systems to maintain the status quo. Socialization and social control are two of the most potent such forces. Similar effects from a number of other institutional networks will be discussed in the next chapter. However, there are mechanisms at work that are encouraging change in the sex role status quo. Even as I write, recent changes are already making my description of current sex roles somewhat obsolete. A careful reader might have picked up hints of such changes in the discussions to this point. The nature and roots of changes in sex role stereotypes will be analyzed more fully in the final chapter.

References

Andreas, Carol. *Sex and Caste in America.* Englewood Cliffs, N.J.: Prentice-Hall, 1971.

Baumrind, Diana. "From Each According to Her Ability." *School Review* 80 (February 1972): 161–95.

Bales, Robert F. *Interaction Process Analysis.* Reading, Mass.: Addison-Wesley Press, 1950.

Booth, Alan. "Sex and Social Participation." *American Sociological Review* 37 (April 1972): 183–93.

Chesler, Phyllis. "Women as Psychiatric and Psychotherapeutic Patients." *Journal of Marriage and the Family* 33 (November 1971): 746–59.

Cooley, Charles H. *Social Organization.* New York: Scribners, 1909.

De Beauvoir, Simone. *The Second Sex.* Translated by H. M. Parshey. New York: Alfred A. Knopf, 1953; first published in 1949.

Ehrlich, Carol. "The Male Sociologists' Burden: The Place of Women in Marriage and Family Texts." *Journal of Marriage and the Family* 33 (August 1971): 421–30.

Firestone, Shulamith. *The Dialectic of Sex.* New York: Bantam Books, 1970.

Flora, Cornelia Butler. "The Passive Female: Her Comparative Image by Class and Culture in Women's Magazine Fiction." *Journal of Marriage and the Family* 33 (August 1971): 435–44.

Freeman, Jo. "Growing Up Girlish," *Trans-Action* 8 (November–December 1970), pp. 36–43.

Friedan, Betty. *The Feminine Mystique.* New York: Dell Publishing Co., 1963.

Freud, Sigmund. *Civilization and its Discontents.* London: Hogarth Press, 1930.

Gordon, Michael, and Shankweiler, Penelope J. "Different Equals Less: Female Sexuality in Recent Marriage Manuals." *Journal of Marriage and the Family* 33 (August 1971): 459–66.

Gornick, Vivian. "Why Women Fear Success," *Ms.* (Spring 1972): 50–53.

Greer, Germaine. *The Female Eunuch.* New York: McGraw-Hill Book Co., 1970.

Herberg, Will. *Protestant, Catholic, Jew.* Garden City, N.Y.: Anchor Books, 1960.

Herschberger, Ruth. *Adam's Rib.* New York: Harper and Row, 1954, first published 1948.

Horner, Matina. "Fail: Bright Women." *Psychology Today* 3 (1969): 36.

Howe, Florence. "Sexual Stereotypes Start Early." *Saturday Review,* October 16, 1971.

Jones, Ernest. *The Life and Work of Sigmund Freud.* Abridged by Lionel Trilling and Steven Marcus. New York: Basic Books, 1961.

Lewis, Michael. "Culture and Gender Roles: There's No Unisex in the Nursery." *Psychology Today,* May 1972, pp. 54–57.

Lynn, David B. *Parental and Sex Role Identification: A Theoretical Formulation.* Berkeley, Calif.: McCutchan Publishing Corp., 1969.

Maccoby, Eleanor (ed.). *The Development of Sex Differences.* Stanford, Calif.: Stanford University Press, 1966.

Martinson, Floyd Mansfield. *Family in Society.* New York: Dodd, Mead & Co., 1970.

Mead, George Herbert. *Mind, Self, and Society.* Chicago: University of Chicago Press, 1934.

Mead, Margaret. *Male and Female: A Study of the Sexes in a Changing World.* New York: Dell Publishing Co., 1970; first published 1949.

Merton, Robert K. *Social Theory and Social Structure.* 2nd ed. Glencoe, Ill.: Free Press, 1957.

Millett, Kate. *Sexual Politics.* Garden City, N.Y.: Doubleday & Co., 1970.

Millett, Kate, and Swift, Casey. "De-sexing the English Language," *Ms.* (Spring 1972): 7.

Olson, David. "Marriage of the Future: Revolutionary or Evolutionary Change?" In Marion Sussman (ed.), *Non-Traditional Family Forms in the 1970's.* Minneapolis, Minn.: National Council on Family Relations, 1972, pp. 15–25.

Piaget, Jean. *The Moral Judgement of the Child.* Translated by Marjorie Gabain. New York: Harcourt, Brace, 1932.

Progrebin, Letty Cottin. "Down with Sexist Upbringing." *Ms.* (Spring 1972): 18, 20, 25–30.

Rivlin, Lilly. "Lilith." *Ms.* (December 1972): 92–97 and 114–115.

Scully, Diana, and Bart, Pauline. "A Funny Thing Happened on the Way to the Orifice: Women in Gynecology Textbooks." *American Journal of Sociology* 78 (January 1973): 1045–50.

Stannard, Una. "Adam's Rib, or the Woman Within." *Trans-Action* 8 (November–December, 1972): 24–35.

Thomas, W. I. *The Unadjusted Girl.* Boston: Little, Brown & Co., 1923.

Weisstein, Naomi. " 'Kinder, Kuche, Kirche' as Scientific Law: Psychology Constructs the Female." In Robin Morgan (ed.) *Sisterhood Is Powerful*, pp. 205–20. New York: Vintage Books, 1970.

Weitzman, Lenore J.; Eifles, Deborah; Hokada, Elizabeth; and Ross, Catherine. "Sex Role Socialization in Picture Books for Preschool Children." *American Journal of Sociology* 72 (May 1972): 1125–50.

Women on Words and Images. *Dick and Jane as Victims: Sex Stereotyping in Children's Readers.* Princeton, N.J., 1972.

Chapter 4

The Bringing Down of Jane

In our society, as well as in most others, the genders are not only different but unequal. This has become so obvious that some students of sex role phenomena (Andreas, 1971; Hacker, 1951) view the relationship between males and females in terms of the stratification concept of caste. In all known human societies, people rank one another hierarchically on a continuum from "superior" to "inferior." Individuals or groups are generally ranked according to how well they embody key societal values. Since such values differ, the nature of ranking or stratification systems varies from one society to another.

Among the many types of variations in the way people rank one another, one is particularly important in the sociology of sex roles: Stratification levels may be more or less permeable. This variable relates to the degree to which movement up or down the hierarchy is possible for individuals. A caste society is one in which groups of people are assigned superior or inferior positions in the stratification hierarchy on the basis of some common ascribed characteristic. Because the basis of that assignment is ascriptive (an unchangeable, often physically identifiable characteristic with which individuals are born), there is virtually no vertical mobility between castes; they are, for all practical purposes, impermeable. The classic caste society was India, but the concept has been widely used with considerable justification to refer to the stratification of races in American society. It may be fruitful to look at the genders in the same conceptual light. Patriarchy is caste. It implies the superiority of one group of individuals—males—over another—females. Moreover, gender is an ascribed and, except for very few individuals, unchangeable characteristic. Patriarchy is probably the oldest form of exploitation and subjugation of one part of a population by another. It probably has also served as the model for all other forms of relegation, be they on the basis of race, ethnicity, religion, or class. Once such a system is established, those in high-caste positions, in this case males, develop a vested interest in the maintenance of the basic structure and their own advantaged status. Moreover, caste considerations pervade the major (and even minor) institutions of a society, so that they also have a vested interest in the maintenance of the caste status quo. Thus the short-run interests of males as males and, perhaps more importantly, as leaders of political, legal, economic, and educational institutions are best served by maintaining and reinforcing traditional sex roles. It is the task of this chapter to document this assertion.

The Female Caste

Discussion in the first three chapters has often shown that the sexes are not merely different but, in many ways, unequal in contemporary society. When the stereotypes developed by students were reviewed, it was obvious that, numerically, many more negative attributes were attached to the feminine sex role than to the masculine one. Similarly, when language was discussed, males emerged as the basic norm, females as "the other." Science and religion were noted as being strongly supportive of male dominance over females. In short, prejudgment, as defined in Chapter 2, is, in fact, antifeminine prejudice. The question now is whether antifeminine prejudice is operationally translated into discrimination.

A few words of clarification are needed at this point. To say that males comprise a higher caste than females and that it is in their direct self-interest to maintain the sex role status quo is not to imply a number of things:

1. It is not saying that very real "costs" are not involved in the masculine role. The opposite has already been shown to be the case.
2. It does not mean that many *individual* males will not favor basic changes in the sex role status quo and perceive that their own *long-range* interests are, in fact, better served through such changes.
3. There is no implication that all females are of an equal status to one another, or all are lower than all males. As Jessie Bernard (1971, chap. 1) cogently points out, the differences among females are often as great as those between males and females.

Stratification hierarchies, be they in the form of a caste or of any other type, are based on specifiable attributes prized by society. In industrial societies, the single most important such trait is generally occupational prestige, although such considerations as amount of income and education, life style or consumption level and habits, and power are also relevant. These usually correlate highly with one another, especially with occupational prestige. The difficulty in conceptualizing the genders as being in a castelike relationship arises from two related facts. First, until recently most females were not gainfully employed (that is, employed for wages outside of the household), and even today slightly more than half of all adult American females are not. Thus, as traditionally defined, occupational prestige is difficult, if not impossible, to assign to females. Second, largely because of this, the status of an adult female is assumed both by society and by those who study stratification phenomena to be that of her husband (and the status of children of both genders is that of their father). Typically, studies of social stratification are studies of male samples. Of course, this very difficulty may be a function of the fact that students of social stratification have been overwhelmingly male. Whatever the reason, the fact is that the available conceptual apparatus does not easily lend itself to an attempt to look at females as well as males in terms of a unitary stratification hierarchy (Acker, 1973).

To accomplish this the first step would involve ruling out any consideration of status accruing to a female solely on the basis of her relationship to a male. This approach would be generally unacceptable to women who function as homemakers for high-status husbands. Be that as it may, let us begin with the assumption that our society tends to place highest value on the accomplishment of instrumental ends. Specifically, Americans value activities that involve the creation of new techniques and their application to changing the physical and social environment. In short, society values the kinds of things that we have already seen are very much part and parcel of the masculine stereotype. Moreover, the more "mental" and less "physical" the endeavor, the more this society generally prizes it; and the more authority exercised over others, the greater its value. The engineer who designs a machine stands higher in the stratification hierarchy than the worker who bolts it together; the mayor of a city is esteemed more than a city councilor. Money or income is the primary, but not sole, indicator of the degree to which American society believes particular activities contribute to these values. In turn, the amount of income accruing to an activity becomes a value in itself, and we come to grant prestige to a job because it provides a high remuneration.

To the extent that these comprise the key values underlying the American prestige structure, we can ask of all adults, female as well as male, a number of questions:

1. To what extent do their daily activities (not "occupations") involve the creation and application of new techniques?
2. To what extent are their daily activities mental rather than physical?
3. How much authority over others do they exercise in their daily activities?
4. How much money do they receive in return for their activities?

The answers to these questions, combined in some sort of a scale, could make it possible to stratify the entire adult American population without incorporating a biased notion of occupation based primarily on the male experience. It should be noted, however, that this approach presupposes the dominant American value system, which is probably defined largely by social elites. These, in turn, are overwhelmingly male (as well as white).

Approached from this perspective, it becomes clear that females in general comprise a lower caste group. This is true despite the facts that there are often marked differences between them and some females will have higher status than some males. Most adult males are probably engaged in some occupation that directly or indirectly creates or applies new technologies in changing the environment. They vary rather markedly in the degree to which their activities are mental rather than physical, the extent of their authority over others, and the amount of income received for their work. They can thus be ranked from the "highest" (e.g., a physician who alters human existence by developing new techniques that vastly increase life span; is essentially engaged in intellectual work; exercises authority over patients, nurses, and others; and may earn $100,000 a year) to the "lowest" (e.g., a ditch digger who breaks his back for $1.65 an hour digging holes for a new highway and has no subordinates). That half or so of the female population employed outside the home can be similarly ranked. When this is done however, females generally fall toward the lower end of such a hierarchy, as I shall discuss more fully below.

But what of the other half of the female population, the home-makers? First of all, they are paid nothing for their work. Any money the housewife receives is granted for "expenses," or out of "kindness" as an "allowance"; it is not considered *rightful* remu-neration for her activities. Whether her spouse receives $20,000 or $5,000, is generous or stingy, she will do the same basic work. In short, whatever funds she receives are not pegged to *her* toil. Her work is very heavily, although not exclusively, manual and repetitive in nature (scrubbing floors, ironing, polishing, laundering, chauffeur-ing, etc.). Differences in their spouses' income may mean that some homemakers and not others are able to afford machinery or help to reduce the arduous nature of housekeeping, but almost all are engaged in substantial manual work. Her nonmanual work, more-over, is chiefly "expressive" and is thus not held in very high regard in this instrumentally oriented society. The only people over whom she generally exercises authority are her children, and only while they are young. Finally, the degree to which she functions to create new techniques or apply them to alter the environment is relatively minimal. She cooks but does not contribute to the creation of the stove or even, usually, the food. Nor has she constructed the house she lives in and cares for (although she may have decorated it), written the books she reads her children, built their toys, and so forth. Perhaps the homemaker's major contribution to changing the human environment is an indirect one that arises from her role as chief consumer of her family; her choices presumably affect the decisions of producers, although even that is questionable in our contemporary oligopolistic economy. Moreover, Americans usually juxtapose consumption with production and have traditionally placed considerably more value on the latter (a phenomenon in the process of change, recently). Media romanticization of homemaking notwithstanding, the person who hires out to do these chores (a "maid") is the lowest paid of all the low-paid workers, which should tell us something about society's view of the activity. If they are shorn of the considerations of luxury arising from their spouses' positions, even homemakers for wealthy husbands (and most are not that fortunate) are situated toward the bottom of the stratification hierarchy from the perspective of our most cherished social values. With about half the adult female population so placed and, as we shall see, the other half tending to fall toward the bottom of the "normal" occupational hierarchy, females may indeed be said to comprise a group of low status based on the ascribed characteristic of gender; in short, they are a low caste.

If it is true that regardless of the occupation, income, and power of their husbands, housewives comprise part of a low caste group, why do many, if not most, fail to perceive themselves in these terms? Every institution in American society is geared toward defining the wife in terms of her husband's identity, as we have had ample opportunity to note. Particularly for those males in the upper reaches of the stratification hierarchy, but also for all those who can conceivably afford it, wives, along with children and household goods, provide displays of what Thorstein Veblen labeled three quarters of a century ago "conspicuous consumption" and "conspicuous leisure" (Veblen, 1953). To the degree that the male's dependents appear pampered, surrounded by goods and services, and relieved of the necessity of being "productive," his personal status is enhanced. Moreover, although American housewives usually work very hard, from any perspective other than middle-class America's they are often surrounded by an incredible luxury of goods and services and relieved of the absolute necessity of regular productivity. Auspicious and noncompulsive use of these goods and services can potentially result in rather large quantities of leisure, although as often as not they are not used to accomplish this purpose. All of this is hardly geared to create in the housewife an awareness of her own *personal* low-caste position. Just as the liveried servants (and even many slaves) of the 19th-century "gentlemen" vicariously basked in the reflected glory of their masters, so too does today's housewife. They are all examples of what Karl Marx labeled "false class consciousness" (see Amundsen, 1971, p. 21).

Patriarchy, or the sexual caste system, has been with us at least since the dawn of civilized society. It predates current institutional arrangements, be they capitalism or socialism in the economic sphere, democracy or totalitarianism in the political arena, and so forth. The key institutions in current society thus arose after a well-established system of super-subordinate relationships between the genders had been established, and they can be expected to rather fully reflect this fact. Stated otherwise, the institutional arrangements of society support the sexual caste system or what contemporary feminists label sexism, and that system, in turn, feeds back and supports current institutional arrangements. In the remainder of this chapter, four key American institutional networks will be examined from this perspective: the economy, higher education, the law, and politics.

The Economy

So much has been written recently on the position of females in the economy that a thorough analysis would comprise several volumes. The facts, figures, and anecdotes of job, pay, and promotion discrimination in contemporary America are widely available and will only be mentioned here as needed. For more detailed analyses, see

Amundsen (1971); Bernard (1971); Bird (1968); Epstein, (1970); Knudsen (1969); and Mead and Kaplan (1965).

In the past, most females participated to a large extent in the production activities of their societies. From at least the inception of settled agrarian communities until a mere century or less ago, women and even children worked beside men in the fields, in the barn, and in the household, producing almost all the goods and services needed to sustain their lives. Since about 90 percent of all families in preindustrial societies were agrarian, it is clear that the overwhelming proportion of humans spent the bulk of their lives in active production activities.

As the household economy gave way to factory-centered production with the advent of the Industrial Revolution, this pattern began to alter. At first the wives and children of the poor continued to engage in production, side by side with males, although they were hideously exploited as "cheap labor" until laws at the close of the 19th century came somewhat to their rescue. The secular trend during the past half century or more has been toward an ever-increasing standard of living which has permitted more and more wives to choose to absent themselves from production activities. Homemaking, like virtually all other tasks, has become a specialized activity. It is important to realize, however, that the phenomenon of a large proportion of women devoting many years or all of their adult existence to child rearing, housekeeping, and consumption is new in history. While many more females are "employed" in official terms today than in the past, most of those who were not technically "working" in earlier times were probably in fact functioning as producers. Until a half century or so ago only a tiny minority of the wealthy and the aristocratic had the luxury of orienting their lives to nonproductive activities.

Two other related economic phenomena have been occurring in what is increasingly being labeled "postindustrial" societies. Expanding production techniques brought an undreamed opulence of goods and a general prosperity to most workers. As an increasing number of women were relieved of engaging in productive work in order to acquire family necessities, the economy *as structured* was coming to rely more and more heavily on very high levels of consumption to maintain growth and prosperity. Moreover, production of goods was becoming less labor intensive, and a relatively smaller proportion of the population was needed to run the machines (although the labor force has grown through the increase of service industries). What better support for a postindustrial, particularly a capitalistic, economy could there be than a definition of sex roles that bound males to continued efforts to produce and most females, at least in the middle classes, to continued efforts to stay home and consume for much of their lives, if not the entirety? Such a circumstance would ensure, if nothing else, good profits for industry. In addition, the more babies middle-class women, in particular, could be induced to have, the more consumption would be increased in the present as well as the indefinite future.

If and when the labor market was in need of more people, the conditions and definitions could always be altered enough to bring some of those women back into the labor force, a phenomenon most evident in wartime. After the emergency they could be sent home again, as was done after World War II, when the number of women in the labor force declined by more than two million between 1944 and 1946, despite the fact that polls revealed most women in the wartime economy wanted to continue employment after the end of hostilities (Trey, 1972). Females have thus comprised a "reserve" labor force to be manipulated as the economy needs them. They are truly the last hired and first fired. Males, too, have been manipulated, in this case into an overwhelming devotion to productive labor (the "Protestant work ethic"). Only now, as our productive capacity is beginning to outstrip even the female's ability to consume, is the male being enjoined by the media to add consumption to his definition of "masculinity." Males are now informed that all kinds of cosmetics, hair products, deodorants and so on will add stature to their masculine image.

Males in Postindustrial Economies

The ramifications of these processes are many and varied. First, let us briefly explore their meaning for the "upper caste" males. Regardless of personal preference, males are enjoined from childhood to plan on working in the economy for virtually their entire adult existence. The upper caste creates its own trap. However, as we saw when discussing the economic relevance of sex role stereotypes in Chapter 2 and again in Chapter 3, relative to females they are generally well equipped from youth with the personality attributes and social skills that contribute to success in the occupational realm. This is particularly true if their family origin was middle class.

Essentially, one of two things can happen in the occupational lives of males. Most do not become what Americans would call very "successful" on the job. The majority are manual workers or low-level white-collar employees earning modest to poor wages. Many spend the bulk of their waking hours five days a week doing mindless, alienating, and sometimes backbreaking work. In return, they are only capable of supporting their families in what, by American standards (and by contrast with the "ideal" exemplified in the media), is a more or less minimal fashion. Such men often suffer feelings of indequacy and may even desert their families to avoid such feelings (see the analysis of poor black males in Liebow, 1967; also see Grønseth, 1971–72). Countless others feel inadequate as males because their wives go to work to supplement their meager incomes, while still others take second jobs, thereby sacrificing virtually all other activities.

But what of the substantial numbers of males, particularly those in nonmanual occupations, who are "successful" in career terms? In an excellent analysis of the modern work environment, Myron Brenton (1966, chap. 1) argues that the nature of jobs today is such that most males will be frustrated regardless of how high they may rise in the prestige hierarchy. Having learned the stereotypical notions of masculine prowess, activity, aggressiveness, and competitiveness, the increasingly bureaucratic setting of most work creates for males the problem of

> How to reconcile the sedentary, overrefined present, which is marked by an extreme lack of physical challenges, with the age-old image of the male as hunter, builder, hewer of wood, and drawer of water —a male who, in short, establishes a primitive contact between himself and his surroundings (Brenton, 1966, p. 18).

Since William H. Whyte's analysis of the "organization man" nearly two decades ago, the modern middle-class male has frequently been viewed as primarily seeking security and orderly progression up the bureaucratic ladder. To accomplish this in the face of numerous others seeking the same goals means competition, but not the overt, "invigorating" competition that spurs "a man to give the very best he has . . ." (Brenton, 1966, p. 35). Rather, confined by the "social ethic" (Whyte, 1956, p. 13), modern man engages in a "frantic, paralyzing kind" of competition, always under pressure to "succeed" (Brenton, 1966, p. 35).

Regardless of these costs, males in our society have been encouraged to view themselves as active, responsible people endowed with both brains and brawn superior to that of females, which most certainly entitles them to better jobs with better pay. In addition, the male generally has a wife, and this is no minor consideration in occupational achievement (Papanek, 1973). A recent paper by Judy Syfers (1972) depicts the advantages of having a wife (simply substitute "job" for "school" and "work" for "study"):

> I would like to go back to school so that I can become economically independent, support myself, and, if need be, support those dependent upon me. I want a wife who will work and send me to school. . . . I want a wife who takes care of the children when they are sick, a wife who arranges to be around when the children need special care, because, of course, I cannot miss classes at school. . . .
>
> I want a wife who will care for *my* physical needs. I want a wife who will keep my house clean. A wife who will pick up after me. . . . I want a wife who cooks the meals, . . . a wife who will plan the menus, do the necessary shopping, prepare the meals, serve them pleasantly, and then do the cleaning up while I do my studying. . . .
>
> I want a wife to go along when our family takes a vacation so that someone can continue to care for me and my children when I need a rest and change of scene.
>
> . . . I want a wife who will listen to me explain a rather difficult point I have come across in my course of studies. . . .
>
> I want a wife who will take care of the details of my social life. . . . When I meet people at school that I like and want to entertain, I want a wife who will have the house clean, will prepare a special meal, serve it to me and my friends, and not interrupt when I talk about the things that interest me and my friends.

"Wives" allow husbands to concentrate their major attention on their work and not clutter their minds with the myriad details of daily living. Moreover, husbands and fathers suffer little loss of prestige if they perform these roles poorly; not much is socially expected of males in terms of family commitments. For the male competing to move up the organizational structure, what could be more convenient? Females trying to make that same move have no "wives" to help them. Indeed, they usually *are* also wives; as such, they are held responsible by society for being "good wives and mothers," regardless of other commitments.

Females in the World of Work

This brings us to a discussion of the role and status of females in the economy. Most females in our society marry at some time in their lives. Most also work at some point. Indeed, 31 million adult females are employed, comprising 40 percent of the total work force (Amundsen, 1971, p. 8). The effects on their job opportunities of the fact that women marry and work cannot be overstated. One of the most important is the problem of role conflict. The term "role conflict" refers to two phenomena: a conflict of expectations arising from two or more roles that an individual holds simultaneously, and a conflict of expectations built into a single role. Employed females, especially but not solely if they are married and have children, are subject to both.

It has been noted that the mere fact that males have wives is important in helping to advance career aspirations. More than two thirds of all American wives are employed outside the home at some time in their married life, and nearly 40 percent of all married women in 1968 were working wives (Amundsen, 1971, pp. 15 and 31). Such women are trying to fulfill two separate roles, each of which makes strong (and often conflicting) demands on time, energy, and attention. Wives and mothers who work outside their homes (and even about one in three mothers of young children are employed) are not excused by society, nor do they excuse themselves (Paloma & Garland, 1971) from the many time-consuming activities involved in these family roles. When daughter Jane has the flu, Mother is somehow expected to arrange her work day to get daughter to the doctor. The ironing and vacuuming get done at night or on Saturday, but they are expected to be done by the wife (few employed wives can afford the services of even part-time household help). An "understanding" husband-father may, out of "the goodness of his heart" "help" his wife by drying the dishes; he may even "babysit" while his wife attends an important evening or Saturday meeting (but have you ever heard of a mother "babysitting" for her own children while father is out?). However, he is always a "helpmate," and the responsibility remains hers.

The working wife ends up working at two full-time jobs, and the time and energy commitments of these must necessarily conflict, as well as exhaust her. Since the husband and father roles specify so little by way of actual, expected tasks at home, few such conflicts are apt to arise for the male. In short, most work roles are currently structured for people whose main, indeed sole, important task is that of "provider" and who have little else to divert their attention. Wives and mothers are simply not by social and personal definition in that situation.

The work role, then, is structured by our economy for males (which is perhaps the real meaning of "sexism"). It is hardly likely that a research scientist, a lawyer, an artist, an administrator, or anyone else can compete for excellence in their chosen field, and the promotions and raises that result, if they are diverted constantly by worries about what to defrost for dinner, running noses, dry cleaning, the plumbing, and so forth. This is especially the case if the competitors are freed from such concerns. In addition, many women lose valuable years of work and experience on the dubious assumption, reinforced by media and "scientific" experts such as Dr. Benjamin Spock, that newborns need the constant presence and attention of their mothers. This, too, puts them at a competitive disadvantage. Indeed, a number of organizations which have routinely granted leaves to males for the discharge of military obligations, guaranteeing their jobs on return, have no parallel policy for pregnancy leave. This virtually forces females to quit work when pregnant, only to have to begin again from the bottom when they return to the labor market.

The problems faced by women who are both wives and employees exemplify one kind of role conflict, namely, interrole conflict. Females are also handicapped by the other type: intrarole conflict. This second type of conflict exists for female workers regardless of marital status and may even be somewhat worse for the unmarried. The modern work environment in postindustrial societies is heavily bureaucratic and administrative. A premium is placed on brains rather than brawn, since few jobs today require a degree of physical strength greater than that probably possessed by all healthy adults. Thus females today should be in an infinitely better position to compete in the economy than previously, when physical strength was a more important component of most work. The fact that this is not the case results from the values instilled in females by the kind of upbringing documented in the preceding chapter and strongly reinforced by male-dominated media, science, and religion.

Females are trained to be sensitive, emotional, intuitive, passive, unaggressive, and so forth, but the modern work environment increasingly requires rational, logical, aggressive, ambitious, competitive, and mechanical traits. It has, in fact, a "masculine" orientation. On the one hand "feminine" females lose out in the job market because they lack the requisite mental habits to function in any but the most menial jobs. On the other, females who enter the world of work at higher levels, unlike males, are forced to behave in one way on the job and another with dates and families. Moreover, if they exhibit too strongly those "masculine" traits that enable success, they are labeled "bitches" or "castrating females" and shunned by male colleagues, to both their personal and professional detriment (Rossi, 1970). Females in more responsible positions are thus faced with a "catch 22." They must maneuver on a narrow balance beam between the contradictory traits that on the one side would win them admiration as females and on the other would enable them to function professionally. The psychic costs and waste of valuable energy are immeasurable, and the result again is a strong competitive disadvantage with males.

Several other considerations make matters worse for women in the world of work. Faced with psychologically distressing and physically exhausting role conflicts, females who compete for good jobs find their male "peers" expect little of them—after all, they're "only" females. If she performs as well as a mediocre male a woman will often find herself loudly praised, and when she does poorly it's dismissed with a "Well, what did you expect of a woman?" These kinds of responses come to constitute self-fulfilling prophecies and hardly comprise the kind of spur that promotes excellence (Epstein, 1970, p. 131).

When a woman finds herself discouraged at work, as everyone, regardless of gender, does from time to time, she will know that she can quit without suffering social criticism. Indeed, she will generally be praised for leaving career behind and devoting herself full time to home and family. She must, therefore, constantly recommit herself to work. By comparison, males are rarely free to leave the world of work and are thus, ironically, freed from the psychological stress entailed in worrying about whether or not to remain employed. From youth she has been encouraged by schools, parents, and peers to view work in terms of "contingency plans" in case she "has to work," and she has been told to leave enough options open to avoid conflict with the career needs of whatever male she eventually marries (Husbands, 1972). As a result, many females find themselves in fields they dislike but have chosen because they can practice them anywhere their husbands might go. They only too eagerly give them up when possible, or at least they approach their jobs with something less than enthusiasm.

Finally, "victimized" people, whether black or female, tend to suffer from a lack of self-confidence, or an inferiority complex. The feminine stereotype explicitly encourages such a self-concept in regard to males, and males are taught from an early age that they are indeed "superior" to females. These attitudes will hardly benefit a female in pressing for the acceptance of her ideas or in any aspect of job competition with males. Indeed, most employed females have had the experience of finding themselves virtually "invisible" to their male colleagues—their ideas ignored or stolen—and incapable of asserting themselves in response.

Job Discrimination Against Women

These competitive disadvantages rooted in the feminine sex role are strengthened by overt, as well as more subtle, forms of discrimination on the part of employers, who are overwhelmingly male. Rationalizing on the basis of a series of myths, employers still blatantly disregard the law, refusing to hire females for a large number of high-status and well-paid positions, failing to promote them, and paying them less than males engaged in the same work. As of the 1964 Civil Rights Act and a number of subsequent executive orders, discrimination on the basis of gender is illegal. It is noteworthy that this stipulation was added by Senator Harry Byrd as a "joke," in an effort to block passage of a law designed chiefly to end racial discrimination.

Let us consider first some of the more subtle forms of discrimination. To a large extent, policy is formed, "deals" are closed, contacts are made, and information is exchanged in male-only clubs, bars, and such lofty sites as men's rooms and locker rooms. When feminists picket men's grills or such an establishment as the all-male Detroit Economic Club they are not engaged in a trivial exercise. Among other things, they are asking that the key sites for important business dealings be made accessible to females—how else can they hope to achieve anything in the business world, even if they manage to reach positions with grandiose titles? The "protégé" or apprentice system, especially in academia and other professions, constitutes another subtle form of discrimination (Epstein, 1970, pp. 169–73). Top positions in many fields are filled by an informal process in which the potential employer calls around to his (male) friends and asks whom they recommend. They recommend their protégés, who, given the sponsors' own prejudices, are rarely female. Only open advertising of all openings can avoid this type of discrimination, a major demand of many professional women's groups. There is, finally, what Cynthia Epstein (1970, pp. 87–90) refers to as "status-set typing." This "occurs when a class of persons shares statuses (that is, certain statuses tend to cluster) *and when it is considered appropriate that they do so*" (p. 87). For instance, most top-level administrators of large corporations also share other statuses in common, namely, they are white, Protestant, and male. Although these other statuses are theoretically irrelevant to their functioning as corporate administrators, people who do not share the cluster make the others "uncomfortable"; something doesn't seem to "fit." The irrelevant statuses then become the most salient ones to the individual as well as to colleagues, in the process obscuring the chief status, which in this case is that of corporate administrator. Under these circumstances the individual will find it difficult to function effectively. Virtually all economic positions of much prestige have as part of their status-set the attribute of maleness.

Discrimination scarcely ends with these subtle forms. On the basis of a series of myths and half-truths, employers often outspokenly defend their "right" to grant males preferential treatment in job considerations.

Myth 1: Females are only working for "pin money." The idea behind this myth is that since their husbands are supporting them, females do not need as much income as males. One thing is certain, females do not *receive* as much pay as males, even those in the same positions. In 1972 full-time employed females earned 60 percent of the males' average income; the median female income was $5,323, compared to $8,966 for males (*Time,* March 20, 1972, p. 81). Where in 1969 13 percent of all employed males earned in excess of $10,000, the corresponding percentage for females was 1.4. The median wages of white females are considerably below those of black males, and the doubly discriminated-against black females are at the very bottom of the salary scale (Bird, 1968, p. 3; Amundsen, 1971, p. 32). Moreover, college-educated women earn about the equivalent of a male with an eighth-grade education (Bird, 1968, p. 64; Amundsen, 1971, p. 36). Females in sales positions earn only 42 percent of the salary of males in sales; those in the census category "professional, technical and kindred," about 68 percent; craftsmen and foremen, 58 percent; clerical personnel, 68 percent, and so on (Sexton, 1969, p. 148). Finally, females have an unemployment rate that is double that of males (Amundsen, 1971, p. 44).

The "result" of this myth is obvious; the only problem is that the "cause," namely, the lesser need for income, is simply not true. Five and a half million American families are headed by females—single, widowed, divorced, or separated—and in 1969 their median income amounted to a mere $4,000. It should therefore come as no shock to learn that 2.4 million of those families live below the poverty line, accounting for 4.5 million dependent children (Amundsen, 1971, pp. 26–27). The divorce rate has been rising so sharply that no female can assume any longer that she will be supported for the rest of her life. Those husbands who are supposed by many to be supporting their estranged wives in luxury averaged a mere $12 per week in support payments a few years ago (Amundsen, 1971, p. 28). But what about working wives with husbands present and employed? The simple truth is that the bulk of employed wives are married to men who do not earn very much, and it is often their wages that maintain the family above the poverty line (Suelzle, 1970, pp. 55–56). In short, women who work are generally either the sole support of self, and frequently family, or they provide much-needed income to maintain life above the poverty line. Salaries are scarcely "pin money" to these millions. Salary discrepancies are also not irrelevant to businesses. A recent newspaper report (*Houston Chronicle*) estimated that if females were paid at the same rate as males, the annual national payroll would have to be increased by $59 billion! Exploitation is only too profitable.

Myth 2: The wealth of our nation is mainly in the hands of females. Females comprise only one third of the top wealthholders in this country and about half of the adult, individual stockholders. Moreover, they acquire their wealth at a much later age than males, primarily through widowhood. Of the younger women in this group, much of their wealth is largely a matter of assets assigned them in name only by husbands and fathers for tax purposes. In any case, *de facto* control of wealth usually remains in male hands, be it father, husband, or a trustee in the form of a lawyer, banker, or broker (Amundsen, 1971, pp. 52, 93–95). Kristen Amundsen concludes that "The implications of these findings are quite clear: Women wealth-holders are not likely to have the expertise, the experience, or the opportunity for putting their resources to use in an attempt to influence the trend and shape of the economy" (p. 94).

Myth 3: Women aren't worth hiring where any training or investment is involved, since they just get married or pregnant and quit. Females do indeed quit jobs more often than males, and frequently they give family-related reasons. However, when occupational level and income are held constant, males and females do not differ significantly in turnover rates (Mead and Kaplan, 1965, p. 52). What does this mean? Females are more frequently hired for menial, routinized, duller jobs than males. Moreover, they are often "overeducated" for them. The college-educated female working as a receptionist or clerk-typist (while supposedly "proving" she is worthy of more serious consideration) is no rarity. Among all such jobs turnover rates are very high; the overwhelmingly male, but dull, routinized auto-assembly industry is plagued with the highest job turnover rate of any. Where females and males in the *same* job and income categories are compared, little difference is found.

It is only because of their differential distribution within the occupational structure that females have a higher turnover rate. Thus, for instance, 14 percent of all male workers but only 4 percent of females are in proprietary or managerial positions; the corresponding figures for craftsmen are 20 and 1. These are relatively interesting and well-paid jobs. Looking at the more routinized, poorly paid occupations, 42 percent of the employed females are clerks or sales workers (mainly retailing the less expensive items for poor wages), compared to 13 percent of the males (mainly wholesaling industrial products or retailing expensive items on commission); 6 percent of the females and less than 1 percent of the males are household workers (servants); and the corresponding percentages for service workers are 16 and 7.

Myth 4: Women are weak and frequently sick, thus missing too many days of work. This is seen as a justification for not giving them much responsibility. The facts are that females miss more days due to acute health conditions than males, but males miss more for chronic conditions. In total, females average 5.3 and males 5.4 sick days in the course of a year (Suelzle, 1970, p. 55).

Myth 5: No one wants a woman boss. This is really not a myth; most employees of both genders seem to resent the idea of a female superior. Given our notions of "masculinity" and "femininity," it would be surprising if this were not the case. But most whites resent a black boss, and that is no longer considered a legitimate reason for not having them. When faced with the reality of a superior who is black or female, most employees manage to adjust quite readily.

Myth 6: Women don't want the responsibility entailed in many high-status jobs. Given the upbringing of most females, again it might be a shock to find any who do want the responsibility, but there are in fact many. And again, to assume that a particular Jane does not want responsibility because most females do not want it is nothing less than discrimination. At any rate, it is clear that females are not to be found in substantial numbers in decision-making positions. For instance, in the federal Civil Service, where discrimination is supposedly nonexistent, only 4 percent of the top-level bureaucrats are female. In the predominantly female field of social work, where almost all workers have about the same educational accomplishments, 58 percent of the males but only 43 percent of the females function in any kind of administrative capacity. Moreover, the very top positions in social work agencies and departments are almost all filled by males (Stamm, 1969, pp. 41–42; also see Chafetz, 1972). A similar phenomenon is evident in two other "female" fields: nursing and public school teaching. In 1966 46 percent of all male nurses but only 32 percent of the females were functioning in an administrative capacity (Grimm and Stern, 1972). It is also clear that males are disproportionately promoted to principalships and school district administrative positions. Thus, where 90 percent of the elementary school teachers are female, only 50 percent of the principals of elementary schools are, and this proportion is declining (Lewis, 1968, p. 134).

As virtually all semiprofessional and professional fields have become more bureaucratic and "scientific" in recent years, the few "havens" for ambitious women that existed in such traditionally female occupations as library science, social work, nursing, and public school teaching are being taken over at the top levels by males (the converse has not happened to traditionally male fields). The female professions in the past represented something of an extension of traditional female duties within the home. It was considered "legitimate" and "feminine" to be employed teaching children, nursing the sick, and caring for the needy—all activities females normally do for free as housewives. Because it was "only" females who were engaged in such activities, salaries and prestige were uniformly low in the "feminine professions" (Chafetz, 1972). As they changed somewhat in character, males entered them and salaries gradually increased (although which came first is unclear). The result is that the female social worker or teacher who might readily have worked her way into an administrative role years ago has less chance today, since the newly entering males are preferred for such jobs.

Myth 7: Females lack the physical strength for many highly skilled and well-paid manual jobs, especially in the crafts. Unions are often guilty of perpetuating this myth. Given current machinery, most such jobs rarely entail more physical exertion than that involved in carrying a 60-pound child or transporting a desk typewriter from one office to another—both tasks done frequently by a large number of the "weaker sex." In any event, recalling the discussion of overlapping normal curves in Chapter 2, it is clear that some males are physically weaker than most females, while some females are stronger than most males.

Myth 8: Well, anyway, a woman who is really *ambitious and qualified* can *get ahead and acquire an interesting, responsible job.* True. If she has somehow managed to avoid the tremendous pressure to conform to stereotypical "femininity"; and if she has put up with many years of drudgery, poor pay, and discouragement from everyone; and if she still has energy, creativity, and ambition left, *then,* when she reaches middle age, she may be in a position commensurate with that of a male 15 years her junior who has less experience, ability, and frequently less by way of formal credentials. Personal "horror stories" abound among working women to document this. Typically, Jane was graduated from college and headed for the "big city." There, at office after office, she was administered a typing test while classmate Dick took an aptitude test. Finally, she settled for a secretarial job at under $100 a week on the promise that "if things work out" she would be promoted to research, editing, copywriting, administration, or whatever. Meanwhile, Dick was hired at $8,000 as a management trainee. She worked overtime and Saturdays (without extra pay) and gradually took over many of the duties assigned to her $20,000-per-year boss. If she was lucky, five or so years later her boss was promoted or quit, and she moved up to his job (which she had been doing all along)—for less than half his pay and a new, less official-sounding title. The bigger the company, the more apt this scenario is to be played. Even with all this, her advancement opportunities were not infrequently tied to sexual favors granted to various levels of bosses, or at least the willingness to play flattering "alter ego."

Myth 9: "I don't know what American women today are complaining about; they are much better off than ever before." (You know, "you've come a long way, baby.") Those who espouse this myth also maintain that American women are much better off than their sisters in other nations and that it takes time to change things, but "we're getting there." Nothing could be more incorrect than these assertions. In a now-classic article written in 1969, Dean Knudsen documented the declining status of females in American society from 1940 to 1966. He concluded that:

> . . . women have experienced a gradual but persistent decline in status as measured by occupation, income, and education. The sources of the lowered status include diminished efforts by women and institutionalized discrimination, both of which derive from a normative definition of sex roles based upon functionalist assumptions and presuppositions about the nature of society and reality. Thus, given the conviction that women should not pursue occupations in competition with men, women and employers together develop a self-fulfilling prophecy (1969, p. 192).

Taking a closer look at some of these trends, where in 1940 41.6 percent of those in professional and technical jobs were female, in 1966 this figure had declined to 37.9 percent; among those in routine jobs like clerical positions the proportion of females rose sharply from 53.9 to 71.3 percent; even the proportion of private household workers who were female increased from 94.4 to 98.0 percent, and service workers jumped from 38.4 to 55.0 percent (Knudsen, 1969, p. 186). More specifically, and with reference to professional occupations, the proportion of females in college teaching and administration dropped from 32 percent in 1930 to 19 percent in 1960; dentistry from 3.2 percent in 1920 to 2.1 percent in 1960; science, from 11.4 percent in 1950 to 9.9 percent in 1960; mathematics, from 38.0 percent in 1950 to 26.4 percent in 1960, and so on (Epstein, 1970, p. 7). In short, even as women began increasing their numbers as a proportion of the job market from the fifties to the present, their proportion in high-status fields declined; they were and are entering the labor market at the lowest levels and remaining there. The income gap, too, has widened in many cases. In 1939 female managers and proprietors earned 57.3 percent of the income of similarly employed males, in 1966, only 54.0 percent. Between 1939 and 1966, clerical females went from 78.5 percent of the income of their male counterparts to 66.5 percent; in sales, from 51.3 to 41.0 percent; craftsmen and foremen, from 63.7 to 60.4 percent; and service workers, from 59.6 to 55.4 percent. In virtually no case was the gap decreased (Knudsen, 1969, p. 187; also see Sullerot, 1971, p. 122). As with blacks, females' salaries have increased, but nowhere near as rapidly as those of white males. This places females in a position that is *relatively* worse as years pass.

Females in our society are no better off than many other places in the world and are in a worse relative position than women in some nations. Females in the United States comprise 6 percent of the medical doctors, where in Sweden they represent 13 percent; India and Japan, 9 percent; France, 22 percent; Great Britain, 25 percent; and the U.S.S.R., 76 percent (Epstein, 1970, p. 12; Sullerot, 1971, p. 151). In 1960 over 40 percent of the medical students in China were female (Cohen, 1970, p. 417). Of all U.S. lawyers, 3½ percent are female, a figure considerably below that for France, Denmark, Sweden, Germany, Poland, and the Soviet Union, where females comprise 38 percent of the lawyers (Epstein, 1970, p. 11; Sullerot, 1971, p. 152). Comparative figures reveal similar findings with reference to engineering, science, university-level education, judgeships, and so forth. Clearly, many European societies are somewhat ahead of the United States in opening the professions to women, and the Soviet Union is very far ahead. It is true that some of these professions are less prestigeful and less well paid abroad than here, especially medicine (which in the U.S.S.R. is considered a "woman's occupation," as grammar school teaching or social work is here), but the fact remains that interesting, responsible positions are more open to women in many nations than in America.

When relative income is considered, females in this country seem to fare about the same as their counterparts abroad. Women in France earn about 70 percent of males' income, somewhat better than in this country, but in Great Britain the figure is about 50 percent, or somewhat below ours. In no case does it seem to approach real equality (Sullerot, 1971, pp. 125–27). However, in a number of nations, including Austria, Denmark, France, Germany, Italy, Spain, Sweden, and Yugoslavia, postnatal maternity leave varying from four to ten weeks is a right granted by law, and in many instances such leave is either with partial pay or accompanied by governmental allowances (Sullerot, 1971, p. 241).

In addition to these common myths, two other factors have a strong bearing on the job prospects of females—age and "looks." Quite bluntly, male employers often look at female employees as sex objects, and "good looks" are for women an important consideration in acquiring many jobs; the unattractive female, regardless of qualifications, is seriously handicapped. This is compounded by the fact that our society generally has as its model of feminine pulchritude the looks of an attractive 20 year old. In contrast, good looks are far less important for males in the labor market. The model of an attractive male is also taken to be the successful, middle-aged man, graying slightly at the temples, and having "character" in his face (those "unsightly lines" in females). A quick check of advertising in television or magazines will verify this difference. A female is thus considered "old" about the time a male is considered to be in his "prime" (Bell, 1970; Moss, 1970).

The implications of this emphasis on looks and age are very important for women. Females are most frequently in the labor market at two times in their life cycle: for a few years before marriage and childbearing, and for a much greater number of years after age 35. Today most females have had their last child by about age 30, and this child is in school full time by the time the mother is in her mid or late thirties. Since females now have a life expectancy of about 75 years, increasing numbers are looking to the job market to provide a functional role for the many years after the main child-rearing tasks have been completed. However, by that age they are already considered "old" and "unattractive," and therefore unsuitable for many jobs. Thus, for instance, in 1965 between 40 and 50 percent of the women in the labor force aged 45 and over were officially unemployed (Bell, 1970, p. 78). In a study of want ads Inge Bell (1970, pp. 79–82) found that 97 percent of all advertisements for females asked for a "girl" or a "gal," compared to a mere 2 out of 2,272 male listings requesting a "boy." When asked what these terms meant, employment agencies explained that employers were seeking females generally under 30, or 35 at the outside. When females over 35 were sought, the term "mature" was employed. In addition, ads for females, but almost never for males, frequently employed descriptive adjectives such as "attractive."

Room at the Top

I will conclude this section on the economy with a brief discussion of some findings from an unpublished study by Janet Chafetz and Barbara Polk of those few females who have "made it to the top" and gained positions that place them in the national "elite." The criterion used for determining "elite" status was listing in *Who's Who in America* for 1965. A simple random sample of 100 was drawn. Females comprised a mere 4.5 percent of all listings in the 1965 *Who's Who,* down from 8.5 percent in 1925.

The primary bases for elite standing for females differed in some very important ways from those characteristic for males, a sample of 100 of which was also drawn for comparison on this variable alone. These differences can be seen in the data presented in Table 4.1. Females who gained national recognition overwhelmingly did so outside of the realm of the private sector of the economy; where only four women were noted for their business role, over one third of the males were. Women were also totally unrepresented in religion and considerably less well represented than males in the professions. The two institutional sectors in which the genders were similarly represented were education and government service. In those areas that were least dependent on male-dominated, formal institutions, namely, the arts and philanthropic–social action organizations, females strongly outnumbered males. It is also notable that 28 females compared to only 8 males were eminent because of roles that did not require absence from the home—family connections and two of the arts, plastic arts and writing. Over time there has been a considerable change in the proportion of females fulfilling such roles: in a similar 1925 sample substantially more than half of the elite Ameri-

TABLE 4.1

PRIMARY BASES FOR ELITE MEMBERSHIP, BY GENDER (1965)

Bases for Elite Membership	Females	Males
Family of birth or marriage	1	0
Activity in philanthropic and/or social action organization	9	0
Religion	0	3
Government service	12	11
Business	4	38
The arts	38	8
Education and education administration	27	24
Professions	12	20
Totals*	103	104

*Totals come to more than 100 because some of the subjects had two primary activities for which they were noted.

can females functioned in the three roles that did not require their absence from the home.

Considering other characteristics of the 1965 sample, one in three of all elite females were single and had never married. This is a very high proportion, considering that less than 10 percent of Americans of both genders fail to marry at some time in their lives, a figure probably more typical of elite males (for similar findings by occupation see Epstein, 1970, p. 97). The educational level of the single female elites was considerably higher than that of those who had ever been married: 97 percent of the former had university or specialized training, compared to only 73 percent of the latter. This finding suggests the possibility that, on the one hand, marriage and, on the other, substantial education with a resulting profession may to some degree have served as functional alternatives for females of the generation represented in the 1965 sample, namely, those born between 1890 and 1920. Thus, if a female was willing to sacrifice marriage and concentrate her attention on acquiring a superior education, she had a better chance of achieving in socially valued contexts. Such a choice is not, however, forced on males (Havens, 1973).

Educational Institutions

In postindustrial societies where the economy is dependent on technology and rational administration, education is the key to higher status positions. This is not to say that education guarantees a high-status or well-paid job. It does not. Moreover, it particularly fails to serve as such a guarantee to those who are lower caste, including females and blacks. As noted in the preceding section, females are frequently "overeducated" for their jobs, and they earn the equivalent of males with substantially less education. However, it is also clear that without the "credentials" supplied by higher education there is little chance for anyone to enter such positions. Therefore, if females in fact comprise a lower caste in our society, this should be reflected in our educational institutions, which in turn feed into the economic realm.

In public school education, as noted in Chapter 3, school personnel separate the genders and treat them differently, urging students to uphold stereotyped notions of masculinity and femininity and plan their lives accordingly. The substance of many of the courses taught both at that level and in the universities supports the current sex role status quo. The concern now centers on the extent of discrimination in higher education which is being increasingly well documented by female academics in a wide variety of fields.

When the relative proportion of male and female students is examined, "The rule is a simple one: the higher the fewer" (Harris, 1970, p. 284). More females than males complete high school, although the proportion of high school graduates who are female has declined steadily since 1900, when 60 percent were female, to the mid sixties, when it was about 51 percent (Epstein, 1970, p. 57). Fewer females than males enter college (43 and 64 percent of female and male high school graduates, respectively) and, naturally, fewer graduate. Only a little over 40 percent of all bachelors' degrees in 1965 were granted to women (Epstein, 1970, pp. 57 and 139). Proportionately even fewer females earn more advanced degrees. In 1966 only one third of the masters and slightly more than 10 percent of the doctorates were awarded to women, and these figures represented a decline from earlier in the century. Thus, for instance, in 1930 40 percent of the masters and 15 percent of the doctorates were earned by women (Epstein, 1970, p. 58; also see Roby, 1972).

How much of this is due to overt, antifemale discrimination and how much to a lack of interest in higher education on the part of those socialized to be "feminine"? Both factors are undoubtedly influential, and no figures are available that demonstrate the relative effects of one or the other. However, it is not difficult to document overt discrimination. Several institutions have admissions quotas: Stanford requires a 60 percent male class, Princeton three males for every female, Harvard 25 percent female. Females generally need much higher grades to get into college. They also receive substantially less in scholarship money: $518 per annum is the average for women, $760 for men (*Time,* March 20, 1972, p. 91). This fact is especially important when we consider that parents are more willing to make financial sacrifices to send their sons to college than to do so for their daughters (Roby, 1972, p. 123).

Prejudice and discrimination against female graduate students is even more severe. Thus, in one year 34 percent of the females entering graduate school at the University of Chicago had at least an A minus average, compared to only 27 percent of the males. Conversely, 41 percent of the males had a B average or below, compared to only 30 percent of the females (Harris, 1970, p. 287). Some medical schools have even established a combined quota for "minorities," that is, females, blacks, and browns, thus setting them in direct competition with one another, without hindering the opportunities for white males to gain entrance (Harris, 1970, p. 288). Moreover, the more prestigious the school, the more they discriminate at all levels. In short, females must be better qualified than males to get into a less prestigious school (Roby, 1972, pp. 122–23).

Faculty and administration prejudice against females is rampant. Harris quotes a number of statements "garnered from various institutions," including such gems as the following:

> I know you're competent and your thesis advisor knows you're competent. The question in our minds is are you *really serious* about what you're doing.
>
> The admissions committee didn't do their job. There is not one good-looking girl in the entering class.

A pretty girl like you will certainly get married; why don't you stop with an M.A.?

You're so cute. I can't see you as a professor of anything.

[Professor to student looking for a job] You've no business looking for work with a child that age.

We expect women who come here to be competent, good students, but we don't expect them to be brilliant or original.

Why don't you find a rich husband and give all this up?

[From Bryn Mawr, a woman's university] Our general admissions policy has been, if the body is warm and male, take it; if it's female, make sure it's an A—.

Somehow I can never take women in this field seriously (1970, p. 285).

A few years ago the president of Harvard, Nathan Pusey, was quoted as saying, with regard to the effects of the draft on applications to graduate school, "We shall be left with the blind, the lame, and the women" (Harris, 1970, p. 283). Upon assuming the presidency of Sarah Lawrence, a woman's college, Charles de Carlo said "feminine instincts are characterized by caring qualities, concern for beauty and form, reverence for life, empathy in human relations, and a demand that men be better than they are" (Harris, 1970, p. 284).

All of the myths explored earlier about females being less "dedicated" than males, more apt to drop out, and less capable appear as justifications for discrimination in education. As graduate students I and other females were informed that we should feel very fortunate to receive assistantships, since we would probably get married and drop out of the labor market. The same logic was used to deny such assistance to countless others. The truth of the matter is that 90 percent of the female Ph.D's are still employed ten years after their degree is completed, a figure comparable to that for males (Harris, 1970, p. 284). Another fairly common phenomenon arises when graduate assistantships and fellowships, which are not generally granted on the basis of financial need, are revoked when a female marries, on the grounds that her husband can now support her. No such issue is ever raised with reference to married male students whose wives are working. Such practices serve to make the myths about female students self-fulfilling since, in the first instance, they have an uphill battle merely to gain the credentials.

Academia's own record of employment practices is also dismal. The 1964 Civil Rights Act did not cover universities; until it was expanded in the fall of 1972, it was not *illegal* for them to practice job discrimination. However, since virtually all colleges and universities were dependent on monies from the federal Department of Health, Education, and Welfare, and since by earlier executive order federal monies could not go to discriminatory institutions, academic females have been active in forcing their institutions to end discrimination by threat of having these funds withdrawn. In the process, their research has unveiled solid facts and figures, discipline by discipline, school by school, to document discrimination. It is in no way dissimilar to the job situation outside of universities: females are hired less frequently and by less prestigious institutions, they are not promoted, and they are paid substantially less than their male colleagues (Roby, 1972, pp. 123–30). Moreover, over the past 30 or so years the position and numbers of female academicians have steadily deteriorated. The nepotism rules extant in most schools, by which members of the same family cannot be employed by the same institution, serve in practice to keep qualified females either unemployed, exploited as part-time instructors, or working in positions far below the level for which they are trained.

The importance of this is probably somewhat greater than similar discrimination in other areas of the economy. As we saw in the preceding chapter, young women are usually discouraged from thinking in terms of a career commitment. In addition, most children of both genders rarely see females in any but a small number of roles outside the home. By the time they reach college, many female students have never known or even seen a female engaged in any occupation other than teacher in a public school, librarian, nurse, secretary, saleswoman, or totally menial types of jobs. In more technical terms, they have had few, if any, role models for other than stereotypically feminine positions. Speaking from personal experience, a female professor can, simply by existing, be a formidable influence on a female student. By occupying a position in a "man's field," she sets an example that says "it can be done." Conversely, the absence of such role models implies the opposite, and to a large extent that is the situation at most American colleges and universities in all but a few "feminine" fields, such as home economics, education, nursing, and such. It is even increasingly the case at women's schools where in recent decades males have been preferentially hired as faculty and administrators (the converse has not taken place at men's institutions).

To sum up, females are denied truly equal access to educational opportunities and discouraged systematically from using those available. This denial is based on the assumption that they will not adequately utilize their expensive educations in the work world and, therefore, scarce resources are better spent on males—even less qualified ones. This becomes self-fulfilling, since ill-equipped workers, as well as qualified ones who are assumed to lack dedication, will find only dull, poorly paid jobs which they will readily quit. Just in case a few stubborn women stick it out, male-dominated media, science, religion, and so on will be there to further encourage them to depart the "masculine world" of work and competition. Males *as a group* profit much by a situation that relieves them from having to worry about competition in these important realms from fully half the human race.

The Law

So females are kept down in the economy and in our educational institutions. But, some say this is surely the result of a tradition which our laws will sooner or later change. The fact is that gender caste and stereotypical notions of both sex roles are strongly reflected in and supported by our present legal system in a myriad of ways (Schulder, 1970). It is virtually impossible to review the entire legal system of our society, consisting as it does of laws on the federal, state, and lesser political levels, as well as judicial precedents on a number of different levels. What follows is therefore designed only to suggest some of the most salient ways by which laws reflect and reinforce tradition in this area. Leo Kanowitz's book on the subject, *Women and the Law* (1969), is an excellent reference.

Before reviewing some of the relevant laws, a note of qualification needs to be stated. At this writing, the Equal Rights Amendment to the Constitution of the United States is in the hands of state legislatures for ratification. At that level it is facing increasing opposition, and its future is becoming problematic. The amendment was introduced during every congressional session since 1923 and was finally passed by both houses in March 1972. It was passed without the various crippling amendments that had been suggested by many; if ratified, it makes virtually all laws that arbitrarily differentiate between the genders unconstitutional. In short, it would accomplish for the genders what the 14th Amendment theoretically did for the races 100 years ago. However, even if ratified it would not take effect until after 1975, and even after that it would undoubtedly take decades of court battles to wipe most of the discriminatory laws off the books.

Why is such an amendment needed? The 5th and 14th amendments, which extend "equal protection of the law," supposedly, to "all," have repeatedly (and even recently) been held by the Supreme Court to be inapplicable to females (Kanowitz, 1969, chap. 6). The only *right* females are explicitly guaranteed is the right to vote, won in 1920. Because of this the vast number of criminal and civil laws that treat the genders in different and unequal ways could only be removed by legislative action on all the various political levels. As we shall see in the next section, males, who usually profit most by such laws, comprise almost the entirety of all the various legislative branches. Under the circumstances, legislative action which would radically undercut the legislators' own caste position is unlikely.

With the exception of eight states (Arizona, California, Idaho, Louisiana, Nevada, New Mexico, Texas, and Washington), the legal system of our society is based directly on English common law; those eight are called community property states and their legal system derives from Continental Europe. However, in practice, although not theory, their laws as they pertain to the subject at hand are quite similar in their effects to those of the other 42 states.

Originally, under English common law, upon marriage a female ceased to be a person in the eyes of the law. This is called the doctrine of "coverture," under which she and her husband became one entity legally. This was meant quite literally; the "one," of course, was the male. The female lost all her property upon marriage, as well as her name, her right to select a domicile, to enter contracts, to keep any income earned during the marriage, and so forth (Kano-witz, 1969, chap. 3). During the 19th century, in a series of acts known collectively as the Married Women's Property Acts, the British gradually granted many of these rights to females. There is no direct parallel in this country, however, meaning that such changes as have been made have occurred piecemeal and vary widely from state to state.

Most states today still do not permit a married woman to retain her "maiden name" (curious term!) unless she petitions the courts for special dispensation. In such cases, the husband's permission is usually required. As recently as the summer of 1972 a Maryland woman had her driver's license revoked because she had not used her married name in acquiring it. For females who have, for instance, built a professional reputation before marriage, the required name change can be costly. It is interesting to note, also, that although married females in many states cannot change their names without their husband's permission, males are bound by no such restriction. More-over, in some states a divorced woman must keep her former hus-band's name if she is the defendant ("guilty party") in divorce proceedings (Kanowitz, 1969, pp. 43–44). In 32 states a married woman's legal domicile is that of her husband, regardless of where she actually resides. This can pose real problems for women who might be employed somewhere other than where their husbands live (and there are an increasing number of them). They must vote, pay taxes, and conduct all other legal business on the basis of their hus-band's residence (Kanowitz, 1969, p. 47). Moreover, on this legal basis, at many state universities if a female student who was a resi-dent of that state marries a nonresident, she must subsequently pay nonresident tuition. The same does not apply where the student is male and the nonresident spouse is female. In some states if a wife dies intestate the husband inherits the entire estate; if the husband leaves no will, the widow receives only half of his estate. For women who would start a business, in at least 11 states there are legal restrictions on the right of a married female to enter contracts; in many cases her husband must be a co-signer (Kanowitz, 1969, p. 52 ff.). In some states married women are restricted in their rights to engage in a separate business enterprise altogether; in some their independent right to sue is limited; in some they cannot serve in positions of legal trust, and so on and on and on.

Such restrictions on married women are paralleled by laws making the male legally responsible for the entire family. Thus, in most states the husband alone is liable to creditors. This law (and, in its absence, tradition) leads most creditors, including banks and retail stores, to deny married women credit in their own names, even if they are employed. A disastrous situation occurs if there is a divorce, since the woman then has no credit rating. Husbands are also legally responsible for the financial support of wife and, especially, children, whether or not they remain married. Indeed, the entire justification for the legal restrictions placed on wives is based on the legal responsibility of the husband to function as provider and head of household. Thus our family laws lock the male firmly into the stereotyped sex role requirement that he support the family. That "jail," however, usually becomes obvious and unpleasant for males only if and when they get a divorce and find themselves paying child support and perhaps alimony. Usually such laws provide a distinct advantage to the male. Conversely, they seriously limit the ability of wives, many of whom will again be unmarried some day, to compete in the economy. Over and above the actual obstacles placed in their way there is the more subtle, psychological effect of a legal system that defines women in terms of their husbands, thus reinforcing the cultural stereotype of dependent "femininity."

Family law is but one small part of our entire legal system. There are numerous other parts that serve to reinforce stereotypical notions of the sex roles and the sexual caste system. On the surface many such laws appear to be, and are, strongly disadvantageous to males; underlying these disadvantages, however, is the presumption that males, unlike females, are responsible human adults. To mention but a few (some of which have very recently been changed):

1. Spouses cannot be tried for conspiracy in some states due to the doctrine of "presumed coercion," by which the wife is released from responsibility for crimes committed in the husband's presence (Kanowitz, p. 88 ff.). The implication is that the wife is not a responsible, independent human being; only the husband is.

2. In some states female criminals have been treated like minors,

given indefinite sentences to "reforming" institutions called something other than "prisons;" such terms can turn out to be far longer
than a formal jail sentence given a male for the same crime (Kanowitz, p. 167 ff.).

3. Many laws exist making it illegal for a male (only) to use "vul-
gar," "obscene" or "abusive" language in the presence of children
and females. Again there is an implication that females are not quite
mature adults (Kanowitz, p. 175 ff.).

4. In the recent past, medical examinations for venereal disease in
some states were required of males only upon application for a marriage license, reflecting the double standard by which females only
were assumed to be virgins.

5. Prostitution is defined in such a way that it is legally impossible
for a male to be one. Normally, moreover, only the prostitute, not
the male client (without whom there would be no prostitution) is
punished by law (Kanowitz, p. 16).

6. Conversely, statutory rape, or sexual intercourse with someone
deemed legally too young, is defined in such a way that only a male
can commit the crime. There is, according to law, either no such
thing as a male too young for sex or no possibility that an older
female might "seduce" a juvenile male. In either case, the sexual
double standard is assumed.

7. The so-called "unwritten law" defense, which has actually been
written in New Mexico, Utah, and Texas, allows that a husband who
kills his wife found in the act of adulterous intercourse has committed justifiable homicide and is guilty of no crime. The wife who performs in the same manner is guilty of murder. The law again strongly
supports the sexual double standard and holds that it is "proper, if
not inevitable, for husbands to be more outraged by the adultery of
their wives than wives are expected to be in the reverse situation"
(Kanowitz, p. 93).

8. Until the Supreme Court decision in January 1973, abortion
was about the only specific medical treatment with which the law
concerned itself. Until that time, in most states a woman was not
legally free to decide not to bear an unwanted child unless she could
show that it would seriously jeopardize her life. In the absence of a
court decision, these laws would undoubtedly remain extant, regard-

less of the fact that it is her body and hers alone that bears the physical burden and consequences of pregnancy or abortion, and in spite of the fact that more women die from childbirth than from abortions done under proper medical auspices. Indeed, until recently some states also banned contraceptives (e.g., Connecticut) thus totally denying the female the right to control her own reproductivity. Such laws were particularly harmful since, regardless of legalities, women will abort unwanted fetuses (estimates have placed illegal abortions at about one million per year in recent years), and when forced to do so illegally they face grave dangers to their lives. In 1969, 8,000 women died from illegal abortions, and over a quarter of a million required hospitalization. Moreover, such laws discriminated most stringently against the poor, since if a woman had the money to travel she could easily acquire a safe, legal abortion somewhere.

9. In 39 states the law allows females to marry at a younger age than males, with and without parental permission. The implications of this are very interesting. Denied the right to consent to any number of other things allowed males, this stipulation looks curious, at least until we stop to consider the assumptions involved.

> Recognizing that early marriage impedes preparation for meaningful extrafamily activities, society has decreed that males should not be permitted this digression from life's important business at too early an age. Since women's participation in meaningful activities outside the home was until recently socially inconceivable, no great harm was seen in permitting females to follow their biological inclination and to marry earlier than males (Kanowitz, 1969, p. 11).

10. As recently as 1966 three states denied females the right to serve on juries, and they still are granted some kinds of exemptions not available to males in a large number of states. In a few states females must volunteer if they wish to serve, where males are required to do so unless specifically exempted (Mead and Kaplan, 1965, pp. 67–68; Kanowitz, 1969, pp. 28–31). The implication of second-class citizenship is evident.

11. Males, but not females, were, until the draft was abolished in January 1973, liable to be drafted into the armed services. The implication was that females do not owe society the same duties as males. Regardless of how one feels about the draft, the implication

of second-class citizenship exemplified by such a distinction is unpleasant.

12. All kinds of "protective laws" pertaining to the conditions of work exist throughout the nation and serve today, although perhaps not originally, to "protect" females out of a number of usually well-paid jobs. Laws specifying maximum numbers of hours females (only) can work per day or week (as low as 40 in South Carolina) "protect" women from time-and-a-half overtime pay, as do laws in 12 states specifying that women cannot work at night. These also serve as excuses for employers not to hire females at all for many jobs. They are particularly obnoxious given the fact that housewives, who are not paid at all for their work, average over 90 hours per week of work (Scott, 1972, p. 56). Laws specifying the maximum weight females can lift (in one case as little as 10 pounds!) also "protect" them from getting all kinds of especially skilled manual jobs, as do laws specifying that a job must be located within a certain proximity to a "ladies' room." In a number of states specific, often lucrative occupations are legally barred to females, including mining, bartending and the retail sales of liquor, and working around moving machinery. Many such laws have recently been declared illegal under the 1964 Civil Rights Act. The courts now require that an employer prove that a job has a "bona fide occupational qualification" on the basis of gender in order to discriminate (e.g., actor for a male role). However, many such restrictions are still in force (Bernikow, 1972).

The issue of "protective laws" has often set middle- and working-class women's liberation proponents in opposition to one another, with the latter fearing that they will be more exploited economically if such laws are abolished (see Jordan, 1970). It seems to me that "progress" entails extending those laws that appear legitimate to cover all, regardless of gender, and doing away with the rest. If toilets are needed nearby for females they are no less needed for males. No one should have to lift weights that are too much (whatever precisely that means), but there is no reason to assume *a priori* that all females can lift less than all males; there are, after all, strong females and weak males. If a job entails strength, the strong should do it—be they male or female. There is no reason why anyone should have a maximum number of work hours specified, although a law stating that no employee can be forced to work past some maximum might be useful for both genders. I can see no useful purpose in legally barring any particular occupation to people simply on the basis of gender.

13. Finally, laws pertaining to welfare also function in fact to discriminate against females (Tillmon, 1970). Ninety-nine percent of the families on Aid to Families with Dependent Children (AFDC) are headed by females, which is scarcely surprising since the law in most states stipulates that a family cannot receive these funds if there is an "able-bodied" male in the household. Thus, millions of husbands and fathers are virtually forced to desert the families they cannot support. As Johnnie Tillmon, a welfare rights activist, puts it: "The truth is that A.F.D.C. is like a super-sexist marriage. You trade *a* man for *the* man. But you can't divorce him if he treats you bad. He can divorce you, of course, cut you off anytime he wants. But in that case, *he* keeps the kids, not you" (1972, p. 111; see also Glassman, 1970).

Welfare departments are notorious for the humiliating regulations they establish, which often involve serious invasions of privacy. In essence, the system provides absolutely minimum sustenance to females who, even if they could find employment and were provided child-care facilities, would scarcely be able to earn enough to support their families. In return, it asks these women to forego a sexual life, accept a myriad of restrictions on their lives, and bow meekly in the face of humiliation heaped upon them by society and politicians. In remaining home to care for their children, indeed in having children, they are doing nothing more or less than that which our society so heartily and repetitiously recommends for all females. It is only their poverty that sets them apart for abuse. Given the high divorce rate, the inequities of our economic and educational institutions, and the law itself, Tillmon is perfectly correct when she warns all females: "Inform yourself on welfare. You may have to live on it sooner or later. Because you're a woman."

Political Institutions

In the final analysis any group of people who find themselves in a lower caste position do so because they lack power. Females are virtually excluded from the major power centers of our society, including the most important ones—the political institutions that govern the society. Political power in America is integrally tied to control of economic resources (Domhoff, 1967) and to a somewhat lesser extent to elite status within such other important institutional realms as the military, the universities, labor unions, and so on (Keller, 1968). We have already had occasion to note that the wealth of this nation is controlled by males, and some indication that they control other institutional realms as well.

In short, females are generally lacking in those resources that can be "traded in" for political influence. About the only such resource they possess is superior numbers. However, without any consciousness that they do indeed comprise a lower caste with common interests that are different from, and often in opposition to, those of males ("caste-consciousness"), these numbers are meaningless; they are not translated into politically relevant terms. The recently formed national and state Women's Political Caucus organizations represent the first beginnings of translating numbers into power, but they obviously have a long way to go to gain broad support and thus power.

Females actively participate in the political processes of this country. They vote, work for candidates, sometimes contribute funds, and occasionally even run for office. They do so, however, primarily within a context defined and controlled by males. The issues that concern them, far from being directed to their own caste interests, are generally those defined by the male leadership of political and other institutions. Indeed, the current feminist movement (as well as that in the 19th century) arose when a few politically active females finally became aware of and fed up with this phenomenon. In the mid sixties radical women working in the so-called Civil Rights and Peace movements began to understand that *as females* they were being "put down," ignored, left with the typing and coffee making and out of the policy making. They began to resent the mentality, widespread in these supposedly "radical" and "humanitarian" movements, so aptly expressed by Stokeley Carmichael's quip: "The only position for a woman in this movement is prone." In short, this relatively small number of females began to become politicized to their own caste interests and became a major nucleus of what is now a rapidly growing social movement. We will return to a discussion of this movement in the final chapter. For now, let us briefly examine the manner in which most females today continue to relate to the political power structure of our society.

Females are virtually absent from executive positions in this country. We have never had a female president or vice-president; in all our history only three have been governors, and they were all wives or widows of past governors. Females are drastically underrepresented in the legislative branches of our various governments. On the national level only a few women (ten) have ever been senators, and the proportion in the House of Representatives is normally about 2 percent. In the 1969–70 Congress there was 1 female senator and a mere 10 out of 435 members of the House. Moreover, most of the women who have ever been elected to Congress (75 in all) were widows of former members. Females, who comprise over half the adult population and 53.3 percent of the registered voters, are as numerous in the legislature as blacks, who comprise about 15 percent of the population (Amundsen, 1971, chap. 4; also see Mead and Kaplan, 1965, p. 72). Moreover, even those females who managed to be elected to Congress have been relatively powerless. In a legislative system where the acquisition of power rests largely on the seniority principle, over a third of the elected females served only one term, and only about a third served four or more terms. Thus, chairs of important committees are, almost never held by females (Amundsen, 1971, pp. 69–70). On the state level in 1967, females held only 318 of the 7,700 legislative seats, a mere 4 percent (Amundsen, 1971, p. 78). On the local level, although 100 mayors in 1966 were female, none governed major cities. Their representation on city councils and other municipal legislative bodies is about the same as it is at the state and federal levels. Even on school boards they amount to only about 10 percent (Amundsen, 1971, pp. 79–80).

They fare no better in other top-level government positions. Only two women have ever served in cabinet posts; none do now. A mere 1.5 percent of the civil servants at grade 16 and above are female; in fact, they comprise only about 5 percent of those at grade 13 or higher. Only ten women served as ambassadors between 1920 and

1970 (Amundsen, 1971, pp. 23–24). There has never been a female on the Supreme Court, and only a couple have made it to any of the higher federal courts. Only three females are to be found sitting on all the various state supreme courts. In total only about 3 percent of all the nation's judges are female (Amundsen, 1971, p. 77).

Further light can be shed on the political status of American females by examining comparable figures on officeholding from some other societies. Two nations today have female chief executives: Israel and "backward" India. Between 1960 and 1966, 15 percent of the Finnish, 11 percent of the Danish, and 9 percent of the Norwegian parliaments, as well as 14 percent of the Swedish lower chamber of Parliament, were female (Haavio-Mannila, 1972, pp. 161–62). France, Britain, Germany, and Italy have far fewer female legislators than the Scandinavian countries, but in all four cases the proportion is at least double ours (Sullerot, 1971, pp. 222–25). Even in China, where women have traditionally been excluded from all aspects of public life, 8 percent of the Communist Party's Central Committee was female in 1969 (Cohen, 1970, p. 416).

American females are seldom rewarded for their political participation with any power, yet without their participation our political parties could scarcely function. Because of their economic situation, females are not often in a position where they are able to contribute any substantial sums to the party coffers independently of their husbands. Without their extensive *volunteer* services, however, the machinery of politics would fall apart. Females in vast numbers run the typewriters and mimeos, stuff envelopes, and canvass the voters by phone and on foot. In short, they do all the dull, routine tasks that must get done but which males will not bother with because they are too busy doing "important" things (like deciding strategy and policy), and they do most of them for no return in monetary or power terms. Finally, as wives of politicians females do all the laborious tasks involved in campaigning plus their housekeeping and child-rearing tasks, often in the frequent and prolonged absence of their husbands. It is little wonder that the divorce rate among these women is rapidly rising. Since 1971 at least six prominent members of Congress have been divorced or separated from their wives, an act almost unheard of ten years ago.

If women are active in the political process but not generally on behalf of their own caste interests, then what do they support? First, there is no evidence to reenforce the myth that females vote for "sexy" candidates (*Time,* March 20, 1972, p. 33). Women vote in about equal proportions to men, except among the rural population and those with less than an eighth-grade education (Steinem, 1972, p. 48). Moreover, most research has shown that more than three quarters of all married couples vote the same, although few are willing any more to conclude from this that the wife is voting like her husband rather than vice versa. There are some noticeable gender differences, however, in the political attitudes of males and females. Females tend to be somewhat less racist than males (and thus supported Wallace less frequently); they are more sensitive to issues of poverty, more opposed to capital punishment, more in favor of gun-control legislation (Steinem, 1972, pp. 49–50). In short, as underdogs themselves they tend to empathize more with others in the same position. Their views on "women's liberation" are ambiguous. Perhaps most women reject the title and refuse to formally associate themselves with the movement. Moreover, as recently as 1971 one study found that males were somewhat more frequently sympathetic to issues such as equal pay for females. However, during the course of the past year or two females have begun to rapidly outnumber males in their support of many of the issues raised by the movement. One of the most striking and important differences between the genders is the fact that females are, and have long been, noticeably more opposed than males to institutional violence, especially war. On this basis they tended to support Nixon less and McGovern more than did males (see Ellsberg, 1972; Starr and Cutler, 1972; Steinem, 1972; *Time,* March 22, 1972, p. 33).

Women's liberation advocate Gloria Steinem (1972) concluded from these facts that in most ways women are more "liberal" than men; *Time* magazine (March 20, 1972), considering the same phenomena, concluded that "women seem to prefer the safe-and-sound candidate, the one least likely to embark on war or some other hazardous undertaking." These two different conclusions point up a very serious phenomenon that results largely from the fact that our key institutions, especially the political ones, are so lopsidedly masculine. To *Time* war is simply a "hazardous undertaking," and those who do not support it are accused of taking a "safe-and-sound" approach. This is patently a masculine view that grows directly out of that sex role stereotype. This is not to suggest that females do not often support and condone violence; the opposite is only too obvious in a number of circumstances. However, females engage in and support violence primarily when they perceive it as a matter of self-defense. It is much more a masculine phenomenon to condone and participate in violence for the sake of "honor," face saving, or territorial expansion (Steinem, 1972, p. 50). When Nixon (and before him Johnson and Kennedy) proclaimed that he would not preside over this nation's first "defeat," or that we would not be "bullied" by other nations, he was the voice of the "masculine mystique." "Peace with honor" is clearly more important than human lives in such a world view. "Real men" can't appear "chicken" (Stone, 1972). I. F. Stone's analysis of both the United States and the Soviet Union during the Cuban missile crisis and in Vietnam revolves around precisely this view: "Their calculus of political expediency rests on the existence within each nation's boundaries of a sizable population of small boy mentalities and primitives who still see war as a test of their virility" (1972, p. 13).

Recent social-psychological research (Pruitt, 1971) has shown that when people make decisions in a group the outcomes are either more cautious or more risky than those that would be made by the individuals comprising the group acting alone. Stated otherwise, there is a tendency for groups to shift their orientation toward one extreme or the other. Which direction those decisions assume—greater risk or caution—is a function of the prior values held by group members, especially those who emerge as group leaders. It is evident by now that the masculine stereotype encourages adventuresomeness or risk taking far more than the feminine. To the extent that political decision-making groups are comprised overwhelmingly of males, the implication is that decisions arising from such groups will tend to be far more risky than might be the case if they were made either by individuals or by groups comprised of more females. Therefore, to the extent that war is a "risky undertaking," it would arise more frequently from male-dominated councils than it might otherwise.

Taking this kind of analysis one step further, it is possible that not merely is war frequently the result of the fact that our political institutions are male dominated, but the rape of our environment also results in part from this same fact, coupled with male dominance of the economic sphere. The overwhelming emphasis in the masculine sex role stereotype on "instrumental" behavior or competitive productivity at the expense or neglect of other aspects of life has very likely contributed substantially to those decisions that have yielded the present environmental crisis.

Conclusions

Females *qua* females are devalued in this and most other societies. Thus the things females do are devalued, and devalued activities are left for females to do. Wherever you find any type of activity done largely by females, you will find it has low prestige and little or no pay, be it medicine in the Soviet Union, grammar-school teaching or secretarial work in the United States, or child-rearing and housekeeping almost everywhere. Every institution in society is more or less geared to maintaining females in a lower caste position, thus guaranteeing that females will do the less prestigeful and more poorly paid tasks. In so doing males *qua* males and as heads of the key institutions benefit enormously. Housewives do $250 billion worth of unpaid work per annum, and this arduous and necessary labor is not even counted as part of the almighty gross national product (Scott, 1972). Billions more are saved by industry by underpaying employed females. The ego-gratifying rewards of power and prestige are also left primarily to males. In short, males need not compete with more than 50 percent of the population in dividing up the scarce, valued rewards of society.

The most insidious aspect of this caste system is the psychological effect it has on most females. For many it serves as a self-fulfilling prophecy, rendering them virtually unfit to assume anything other than the passive, dependent role for which they have been programmed. For countless others it entails perpetual anxiety and guilt over what they are and do versus what they "ought to be," according to society. But for some, and especially those who "make it" in the males' world, it entails assuming the values of the upper caste and denigrating all aspects of femaleness. It is not uncommon to discover in "successful" career women a deep-seated antipathy to females, to the feminist movement, and to all things "feminine" (see Decter, 1972, for a good example). These are the ones who staunchly argue that females have only themselves to blame for their problems. They maintain that there is really not much discrimination —at least, that since they overcame it, everyone who really wants to can do so. Such women regard females, as a rule, as dull people with whom they would rather not associate (ever notice how many women pride themselves on not liking women and how seldom any male is ever heard to make analogous statements about his entire gender?). In short, they believe that with a few "exceptions" (like themselves), males are the superior gender. Such group "self-hatred" is not unusual among lower caste peoples, but it is surely one of the most hideous results of subjugation. These women, and especially those who are professionals, might function to provide much-needed role models for the young and to question the sexist assumptions in the practices and theories of their own institutions and society in general. Instead, the "self-hatred" exacted as the price for their success has led them to side with the upper caste in helping to maintain the sex role status quo, and in so doing to keep their sisters down.

References

Acker, Joan. "Women and Social Stratification: A Case of Intellectual Sexism." *American Journal of Sociology* 78 (January 1973): 936–45.

Amundsen, Kristen. *The Silenced Majority.* Englewood Cliffs, N.J.: Prentice-Hall, 1971.

Andreas, Carol. *Sex and Caste in America.* Englewood Cliffs, N.J.: Prentice-Hall, 1971.

Bell, Inge Powell. "The Double Standard." *Trans-Action* 8 (November–December 1970): 75–80.

Bernard, Jessie. *Women and the Public Interest.* New York: Aldine Atherton, 1971.

Bernikow, Louise. "Heaven Won't Protect the Working Girl." *Ms.* (Spring 1972): 123–25.

Bird, Caroline. *Born Female: The High Cost of Keeping Women Down.* New York: David McKay Co., 1968.

Brenton, Myron. *The American Male.* Greenwich, Conn.: Fawcett Publications, Inc., 1966.

Chafetz, Janet Saltzman. "Women in Social Work." *Social Work* 17 (September 1972): 12–18.

Chafetz, Janet Saltzman, and Polk, Barbara Bovee. "Female Elites in the U.S. and Great Britain and the Early Woman's Rights Movement: A Trend Analysis," unpublished manuscript, University of Houston, 1971.

Cohen, Charlotte Bonny. "Women in China." In Robin Morgan (ed.), *Sisterhood Is Powerful,* pp. 385–417. New York: Vintage Books, 1970.

Decter, Midge. *The New Chastity and Other Arguments against Women's Liberation.* New York: Coward, McCann and Geoghegan, 1972.

Domhoff, G. William. *Who Rules America.* Englewood Cliffs, N.J.: Prentice-Hall, 1967.

Ellsberg, Daniel. "Daniel Ellsberg Talks about Women and War." *Ms.* (Spring 1972): 36–39.

Epstein, Cynthia Fuchs. *Woman's Place.* Berkeley, Calif.: University of California Press, 1970.

Glassman, Carol, "Women and the Welfare System." In Robin Morgan (ed.), *Sisterhood Is Powerful,* pp. 102–15. New York: Vintage Books, 1970.

Grimm, James, and Stern, Robert. "Sex Roles and Professional Labor Markets: Intra-Occupational Structuring," paper delivered at the annual meeting of the Southwestern Social Science Association, San Antonio, Texas, March 30–April 1, 1972.

Grønseth, Erik. "The Husband Provider Role and Its Dysfunctional Consequences." *Sociological Focus* 5 (Winter 1971–72): 10–18.

Haavio-Mannila, Elina. "Sex Roles in Politics." In Constantina Saflios-

Rothschild (ed.), *Toward a Sociology of Women,* pp. 154–72. Lexington, Mass.: Xerox College Publishing Co., 1972.

Hacker, Helen M. "Women as a Minority Group." *Social Forces* 30 (1951): 60–69.

Harris, Ann Sutherland. "The Second Sex in Academe." *AAUP Bulletin,* Fall 1970, pp. 283–96.

Havens, Elizabeth. "Women, Work, and Wedlock: A Note on Female Marital Patterns in the United States." *American Journal of Sociology* 78 (January 1973): 852–72.

Husbands, Sandra Acker. "Woman's Place in Higher Education?" *School Review,* 80 (February 1972): 261–74.

Jordan, Joan. "Comment: Working Women and the Equal Rights Amendment." *Trans-Action* 8 (November–December 1970): 16–22.

Kanowitz, Leo. *Women and the Law: The Unfinished Revolution.* Albuquerque, N.M.: University of New Mexico Press, 1969.

Keller, Suzanne. *Beyond the Ruling Class.* New York: Random House, 1968.

Knudsen, Dean. "The Declining Status of Women: Popular Myths and the Failure of Functionalist Thought." *Social Forces* 48 (December 1969): 183–93.

Lewis, Edwin C. *Developing Woman's Potential.* Ames, Iowa: Iowa State University Press, 1968.

Liebow, Elliott. *Tally's Corner.* Boston, Mass.: Little, Brown & Co., 1967.

Mead, Margaret, and Kaplan, Frances Balgley (eds.). *American Women: The Report of the President's Commission on the Status of Women.* New York: Charles Scribner's Sons, 1965.

Moss, Zoe. "It Hurts to be Alive and Obsolete: The Aging Woman." In Robin Morgan (ed.), *Sisterhood Is Powerful,* pp. 170–75. New York: Vintage Books, 1970.

Paloma, Margaret M., and Garland, T. Neal. "The Married Professional Woman: A Study in the Tolerance of Domestication." *Journal of Marriage and the Family* 33 (August 1971): 531–40.

Papanek, Hanna. "Men, Women and Work: Reflections on the Two-Person Career." *American Journal of Sociology* 78 (January 1973): 852–72.

Pruitt, Dean. "Toward an Understanding of Choice Shifts in Group Discussion." *Journal of Personality and Social Psychology* 20 (December 1971): 495–510.

Roby, Pamela. "Structural and Internalized Barriers to Women in Higher Education." In Constantina Saflios-Rothschild (ed.), *Toward a Sociology of Women*, pp. 121–140. Lexington, Mass.: Xerox College Publishing Co., 1972.

Rossi, Alice S. "Job Discrimination and What Women Can Do About It." *Atlantic Monthly*, March 1970, pp. 99–103.

Schulder, Diane. "Does the Law Oppress Women?" In Robin Morgan (ed.), *Sisterhood Is Powerful*, pp. 139–57. New York: Vintage Books, 1970.

Scott, Ann Crittenden. "The Value of Housework: For Love or Money?" *Ms.* (July 1972): 56–59.

Sexton, Patricia Cayo. *The Feminized Male.* New York: Vintage Books division of Random House, 1969.

Stamm, Alfred M. "NASW Membership: Characteristics, Deployment and Salaries." *Personnel Information, NASW,* 12 (May 1969): 34–45.

Starr, Jerold, and Cutler, Neal. "Sex Role and Attitudes toward Institutional Violence among College Youth: The Impact of Sex-Role Identification, Parental Socialization, and Socio-Cultural Milieu." Paper given at the 67th meeting of the American Sociological Association, August, 1972.

Steinem, Gloria. "Women Voters Can't Be Trusted." *Ms.* (July 1972): 47–51, and 131.

Stone, I. F. "The Offensive: Machismo in Washington." *The New York Review of Books,* May 18, 1972, pp. 13–14.

Suelzle, Marijean. "Women in Labor." *Trans-Action* 8 (November–December 1970): 50–58.

Sullerot, Evelyne. *Women, Society and Change.* Translated by Margaret Scotford Archer. New York: McGraw-Hill Book Co., 1971.

Syfers, Judy. "I Want a Wife," *Ms.* (Spring 1972): 56.

Tillmon, Johnnie. "Welfare Is a Woman's Issue." *Ms.* (Spring 1972): 111–16.

Time magazine staff, special edition on the American woman, March 20, 1972.

Trey, J. E. "Women in the War Economy—World War II." *The Review of Radical Political Economics*, 4 (July, 1972): 1–17.

Veblen, Thorstein. *The Theory of the Leisure Class*. New York: Mentor Books, 1953, first published 1899.

Whyte, William H., Jr. *The Organization Man*. Garden City, N.Y.: Anchor Books, 1956.

Chapter 5

Personal Relationships and Sex Role Playing

The intimate relationships of most people with other humans are among the most important aspects of their lives, if not the single most important one. Such relationships are undoubtedly colored strongly by sex roles, yet, ironically, this is precisely the subject about which social science has the least unbiased relevant research information available. Nonetheless, no discussion of sex roles can ignore their impact on interpersonal relationships. This chapter is an attempt to explore the issues, despite the relative paucity of relevant data. The basic question is: To the extent that males and females fulfill their respective sex role stereotypes, what are the implications for a variety of types of relationships?

Because few people of either gender "live up to" their stereotypes totally, the relationships discussed in the following pages will necessarily be exaggerated. The issue is not how many people really behave in these ways. Rather, we can more profitably ask what aspects of our relationships reflect, however dimly, the processes hypothesized as resulting from the pressures exerted by sex role stereotypes. Beyond that more cannot be said, in the absence of research evidence.

Theories of Human Relations

Dick and Jane interact with a myriad of people of both genders, and they do so in a variety of ways. Human relationships have long been categorized as falling into one of two broad types: primary and secondary. Secondary relations are those ritualized interactions between two or more individuals playing specific roles who come into contact for a limited purpose. The interactions that normally occur between salesclerk and customer, teacher and student, doctor and patient, are all examples of secondary relations. One can rather easily predict the content of such exchanges, since they are generally prepatterned to a substantial degree, the behaviors are limited in scope, and emotional responses are minimal. Primary relations are exactly the opposite. They consist of interactions among people in a broad spectrum of ways and settings in which some degree of emotional commitment is usually present. Relationships between lovers and/or spouses, friends, and children and parents, are all primary in nature. Naturally, the line between the two types is not clear-cut: many secondary relations shade into primary ones, while in some circumstances primary relations partake of secondary elements. The focus in this chapter is chiefly on primary relationships among adults.

The same individual is never precisely the same in relationship to a number of other individuals, although there is a tendency toward consistency. We have all experienced the feeling that the Dick or Jane we know is "not the same person" as that same Dick or Jane is to someone else. The stoical, silent Dick we know is loquacious, sensitive Dick to someone else; scatterbrained outgoing Jane to someone else is that bright but somewhat shy Jane we know. Are Jane and Dick hypocrites, hiding their "true selves" from us, someone else, or both? Probably not; they are merely performing in response to different circumstances, as well as differing perceptions and expectations of themselves. Stated in another way, we all have a very large repertoire of behaviors; other people elicit some elements of it, but not all. It is probably the case that no one person ever elicits the entire range of behaviors from another, regardless of how close the two may be or how long they have known one another. In primary relations, however, a substantial proportion of that repertoire is often revealed. Sooner or later there will still come that time when we scratch our heads and wonder why Jane or Dick "acted out of character," i.e., showed us some part of their behavior repertoire we had not seen before.

Sex role playing constitutes one among several important factors that influence the behaviors an individual will exhibit in a given relationship. As a feminine person, Jane will tend to display somewhat different behaviors to males who might be romantic partners than to females or even to other categories of males. Some of this difference may be a conscious effort to fulfill certain assumed expectations; for example, she may "play dumb" to attract a certain male whom she believes feels threatened by bright females. This is called "impression management" (Goffman, 1959). More important, however, are those behaviors she does not consciously manipulate. She may actually *be* rather dependent *vis-à-vis* a given male, while fairly independent with her female friends. This results from the fact that she has somewhat different self-concepts when she is with that male and with her friends which developed because she was sanctioned differentially by them; she was "punished"—rebuffed or affection withdrawn—when she acted in an independent manner with her potential mate, but "rewarded" for the same efforts with her friends. Because the "definition of the situation" differed in the two instances, the behaviors rewarded differed, and the situations came to constitute self-fulfilling prophecies. The key is the nature of these situational definitions, and the point is that they are more or less strongly influenced by sex role stereotypes.

There are a number of other social-psychological theories dealing with human interaction which may help us understand the possible effects of sex role stereotypes on various human relationships. People who remain in a close primary relationship either originally agree on most issues deemed important by those involved or evolve into such agreement over time. Stated another way, individuals who continue to participate in a close relationship feel the same way about most fundamental things (Newcomb, 1961). Thus, for instance, a female who rejects the traditional feminine role (or a war, or a political ideology) is not apt to be found in a stable, long-term relationship with a male who accepts that role as appropriate; sooner or later the "imbalance" will become too uncomfortable or "dissonant," and if neither changes, the relationship will usually terminate. Thus, there are basically two possibilities when a fundamental lack of agreement exists: the relationship may end, or one or both individuals' attitudes may change. Indeed, the feminine sex role encourages women not to become too committed to any attitudes that may conflict with those of a mate, that is, women are encouraged to defer to a male's opinion. Thus there is a built-in tendency for this kind of circumstance not to reach the point of real conflict in that particular type of relationship.

Which of these two possibilities in fact occurs in the face of conflict depends in large measure on the quantity and quality of other satisfactions being derived from a relationship. Exchange theory (Homans, 1961; Thibault and Kelly, 1959) postulates that in any human interaction the participants receive certain "rewards" and pay certain "costs." For an interaction to continue, the rewards must be equal to or greater than the costs for the parties involved. According to this approach, the motivation for people to remain in a relationship exists when there is a "net profit" or, minimally, no loss. The only exception is when individuals who are experiencing a loss nonetheless remain in a relationship because the alternatives appear even more costly (Thibault and Kelly, 1959). For instance, a wife who is quite unhappy in her marital relationship may fail to seek a separation or divorce if she thinks that the resultant loneliness, lack of father-presence, and so forth will be worse (more costly) than her current misery.

The key to this approach resides in what people define as rewarding and what as costly. Such definitions are undoubtedly strongly influenced by sex role stereotyping. Females are systematically taught that one of the most important rewards they can receive is an overt display of warmth and affection; the withdrawal of this constitutes a cost. Past a very early age, males are not taught to value overt affection and, indeed, may even be taught it is "unmanly." It is not surprising that they are frequently embarrassed by, or at least oblivious to, the little signs of affection deemed so important by most females. One might say that giving these signs constitutes a cost for many males. Our folklore is full of jokes which center on precisely this phenomenon: husband forgets wife's birthday, their anniversary, the morning goodbye kiss, to compliment her new dress or a new recipe she has tried. Marriage manuals routinely contain advice to the male not to forget "afterplay" in sex, namely, a display of affection and warmth that is no longer explicitly directed at sexual fulfillment. Females are also taught to value dependency—psychological and financial—*vis-à-vis* males, for whom support may well come to constitute a cost.

Males, on the other hand, are systematically taught to value more concrete rewards, such as money or service, as well as power or dominance and prestige. Using the marital relationship as an example, Dick's rewards consist of such things as an orderly and well-kept home (children quiet, dinner ready, socks clean), an ear that will listen, a mouth that will compliment, and, perhaps more importantly, an overall impression that he is dominant (Laws, 1971, p. 507). Conversely, all these things may be said to constitute costs for many wives. Our folklore reflects this as well, with endless stories about the wife who manipulates her spouse while making it appear that he is dominant and competent.

This chapter analyzes the ways in which people seek to have their needs met by others and the effects that sex role stereotypes have on this process. Fulfillment of such needs certainly constitutes a reward, but it might well entail a cost for the interaction partner. The thesis to be developed is that sex role stereotypes tend to decrease the ability of individuals to achieve need satisfaction (rewards) and increase the costs of granting such satisfaction to others. In short, sex roles encourage the dissolution of a variety of types of interpersonal relationships.

Interpersonal Relations Between the Genders

In our society there is an ever-present tendency for relationships between a male and a female to either become "romantic" (i.e., sexual in the broadest sense of the word) or to dissipate; platonic or nonromantic relationships are seemingly very unstable. This phenomenon results from a limited and limiting view of love fostered by Hollywood, television, true-romance-type magazines, and indeed, our entire culture. Before male-female relationships of any type can be understood, it is crucial to examine our culturally accepted notion of this emotion.

Our language has but one word to cover a multitude of different emotional states: "love." We must then add adjectives to distinguish between the love parents and children have for one another from the love that is characteristic of close friends or romantic love, or, in some instances, forego the use of the word. We further distinguish between "infatuation," as a supposedly temporary, totally sexually based kind of romantic love; "liking," which is nonsexual love; and "TRUE LOVE," which is held out as the highest pinnacle of human emotion and sexuality and excuses all sins we may commit in its name.

Perhaps because we basically have only one word for all these various emotions, we tend to treat love as a zero-sum game. A zero-sum game is any situation in which one person's gain automatically entails another's loss. If, for instance, one gains to the hypothetical value of $+1$, the "opponent" loses to the value of -1, totaling zero when summed. In terms of love, this means the following. We begin with the very dubious assumption, rarely made explicit, that each person has a fixed, finite quantity of that emotion available to give. TRUE LOVE is assumed to take virtually all of it. Thus, if a person also "loves" someone else (not to mention many others), be it child, friend, or another romantic partner, he or she is automatically assumed to be giving less to the "legitimate" recipient. The result is a feeling called jealousy which is generally excused by society unless it is manifested in a fashion that is too dangerous (e.g., murder). Even then, as we saw in the preceding chapter, it is often excused. We frequently hear about the "problems" a new father experiences as his wife "withdraws" some of her love to focus it on the new child. It is not unusual for people to be jealous of a spouse's or lover's same-sexed friends. Mother-in-law "problems," about which so many jokes abound, are often reflecting the same phenomenon. Most serious are the problems that develop around one spouse's sexual and/or emotional "unfaithfulness" to the other. Why do we say that a married person who engages in sexual intercourse with another to whom she or he is not married is "cheating"? The very word carries the connotation that the "cheating" spouse is taking something that rightfully belongs to the cheated-upon person; one's gain constitutes the other's loss.

The emotion we call love is not a zero-sum game. We are just not that limited in our emotional energies. Humans are capable of loving many others at the same time as well as serially (and, in fact, often do so). Indeed, it is unlikely that any one individual can ever fill all of another person's emotional needs. To gain a full life and have a variety of their needs met, humans must develop deep emotional commitments to more than one individual and in more than one way.

Platonic Relationships

The widespread if subtle acceptance of a zero-sum concept of love helps to ensure that many loving relationships, especially platonic love for a member of the opposite sex, will be less rewarding and long-lived than they might otherwise be. Most Americans suspect that platonic relationships between a male and a female are something other than they appear. Husbands or male lovers, even more than their female counterparts, are apt to react to such relationships on the part of their mates with suspicion and jealousy. They are apt, in other words, to interpret such a friendship in terms of an increase in the cost of the relationship and a diminution of the rewards, thus creating an element of instability in both relationships. According to tradition and the masculine mystique, wives and female lovers are property not to be shared with others. Any hint of such sharing places the male in particular in an extremely embarrassing situation among his peers and undercuts his own feelings of masculinity. In most societies few insults are worse than accusing a man of being cuckolded by his wife or girl-friend; it is grounds for divorce in virtually every state even when no other grounds exist, although adultery is not always automatic grounds for a wife seeking divorce. Moreover, jealousy and a zero-sum concept of love (i.e., strict monogamy) cannot possibly be inherent in our species, given all the societies in which polygamy and polyandry have functioned.

Thus any attempt at a close platonic relationship between a male and a female will elicit suspicions if either is romantically committed to someone else. If, however, they are not committed to others, such a relationship will create ungrounded assumptions arising from stereotyped notions of how the sexes "ought" to relate to one another. Both male and female sex role stereotypes encourage individuals to define members of the opposite gender in broadly sexual terms. Females are taught to view males primarily as potential mates or husbands, namely, the objects of TRUE LOVE. Males learn to view females primarily as sex objects to be exploited if possible, married if necessary.

Indeed, it is not altogether unfair to view our cultural notions pertaining to sex, especially for males, in terms of war. Sex is often used as a method of proving dominance rather than a means of communication and mutual pleasure. In extreme cases we call this "rape," but the same general mentality exists in much of what passes for "normal" sexual activity, especially for males (Millett, 1970, p. 44). For many men the way to end an argument is to initiate sex. Our slang terms relating to sexual intercourse also generally reflect this attitude. "Screwing" refers both to copulation and exploitation, and one can be "laid" in bed or "laid out" in a fight; "balled" in love or "balled out" in punishment; "fucked" sexually or in terms of being "taken" or exploited; "banged" in bed or with a gun. The male sexual organ is also characterized by slang expressions emphasizing dominance: a "cock" is a fighting bird; a "prick" is something that produces pain.

In short, the one way in which neither sex is taught to view the other is as potential friends and peers. Thus in any platonic relationship there is a built-in dynamic encouraging one or both participants to redefine the situation by "falling in love." Generally, either both do, in which case TRUE LOVE results, or one alone does, in which case the relationship becomes uncomfortable and is usually abruptly terminated.

Even though platonic relationships between males and females tend to be short-lived and unstable, they cast a very interesting light on contemporary sex role phenomena. Typically, the relationship begins with the male approaching a female he knows in order to confide something and/or seek advice. Or he asks her for a date and they then discover that, although they are not sexually attracted, they do like one another. In either case the stereotypical prerogative of male initiation of cross-gender interaction is maintained, even when the purpose is clearly not sexual or romantic. Many males confide things to female friends they would never broach with other males. Basically the masculine stereotype discourages males from speaking openly with one another about their fears, anxieties, or weaknesses. It fosters intellectualizing, bravado and competitiveness among males, all of which are directly antithetical to more intimate personal exchanges. As a result, males often seek the ear of a non-threatening female for such purposes. But notice how strongly the two sex role stereotypes are reflected in this. His expectation is that she will function basically as a compassionate, even ego-boosting listener and make few such demands in return; she usually supports such expectations. If, perchance, she attempts to elicit the same attention from him that she gives to him, she will often find a bored expression, an attempt to change the subject, or a quick excuse for leaving. His rewards in the relationship are obvious, his costs few. Her motivations are more difficult to comprehend. Probably she remains in it because her ego is boosted simply by virtue of the fact that a member of the superior caste has "chosen" her—for whatever purpose. Moreover, she is being given the opportunity to perform the kinds of expressive functions she has been taught to value so highly.

Romantic Relationships

However influential sex roles are in shaping platonic relationships, they are that much more powerful in their effects on romantic male-female interactions. It is probably the case that truly open and honest communication, mutual respect, and the concomitant emotions of warmth and deep affection can only result from interaction among equals (O'Neill and O'Neill, 1972). Yet the genders are anything but equal in this society and most others. To put it bluntly, in most such relationships the male has considerably more power, resulting from his provider function, from those myriad personality differences instilled in the two genders by socialization and, if need be, from his superior physical strength. Sexual attraction, protectiveness, dependency, and a host of other emotions can all develop among people who are unequal (even masters and slaves in times past sometimes held such feelings for one another), but not the TRUE LOVE or the equalitarian, companionate marriages lauded in the media and found so rarely in reality (Gillespie, 1971; Safilios-Rothschild, 1972). As long as our culture maintains two different and unequal sex role stereotypes that enable people to explore a mere half of their human potential, interpersonal relations, and most especially those between males and females, will fall far short of our ideal norms concerning love relationships (Firestone, 1970, chap. 6).

Compounding the inequality of the genders is the fact that our sex role stereotypes have left virtually the entire realm of emotional expression and human caring to femininity. It is difficult to imagine a genuine loving relationship involving the stoical, unemotional, instrumentally oriented, dominating, aggressive, and competitive creature of the masculine stereotype. Moreover, both males and females view a husband's primary function as that of provider; there is no socially defined and sanctioned expectation that he confide, comfort, or share, and without these there is scarcely "love." It is, of course, equally difficult to imagine a male developing deep respect for the scatterbrained, passive, dependent, vain creature who would be "feminine."

Regardless of how contradictory sex roles are to establishing a love relationship, when Dick and Jane come together they generally share many, if not most, of the stereotypical notions of masculinity and femininity. In turn, these shape their expectations of one another and themselves. On the one hand, if they live up to these expectations, their behavior will often prove costly to one another because of the types of considerations discussed above. On the other hand, if either one fails to live up to these expectations, that failure may be defined as a cost or a diminution of rewards by the other. Dick may have a very real need to express his emotions, maybe even to cry; he may have dependency needs and a whole host of other traits that belie his masculinity. And Jane really may not be all that passive; moreover, she might be a straight A student and very competitive and aggressive. As their relationship deepens and a broader range of their behavior repertoires is revealed (often long after marriage), they begin to see signs of these unexpected traits in one another.

From that point the relationship may go in a number of directions. It may simply end as one or both find that the costs of having their expectations unmet is too high. When this occurs people later look back and wonder what it was they ever saw in him or her. Such a response usually results only if the pair has not yet made a binding commitment to one another, but the relatively high divorce rate today attests to the fact that it may occur even after such a commitment has been made. If, however, the mutual "profits" derived from other aspects of the relationship are great enough, the couple may grope toward redefining those expectations and ultimately rejecting society's stereotypes. Although this solution may bring with it real human growth and a more satisfying relationship, it is painful, and because of this, it is perhaps not too widespread. Probably the most common solution if the two are married, and especially if they have children, is the sort of compromise that eventually shatters whatever emotional ties may have existed: they simply attempt to ignore the discrepancies and work around them.

Let us explore this last option more closely. Dick and Jane are unwilling or unable to reject the stereotypes they have internalized and strike out as "deviants" in relatively uncharted directions; they are also unwilling to separate (because of "the children," the new house, their religion, whatever). At this point they turn to manipulation, play-acting, withdrawal, and a variety of means of displacement in an attempt to have their needs and expectations met. Let us suppose that Jane is really a very aggressive and competitive person. She cannot directly manifest these traits and still appear "feminine" to herself and her mate. What she can and does do, often quite unconsciously, is express these personality attributes by nagging, flattering, and manipulating Dick; she uses "feminine wiles" to get her way (Hacker, 1951, p. 65). She nags him to do better on the job, pushing him ever harder to "succeed" while belittling his efforts. She does this not so much because of the new car she claims to want as for the vicarious thrill of experiencing competition and success through him.

Hanna Papanek (1973) has recently coined the term "two-person career" in examining the vicarious ways in which wives share their husbands' occupational fortunes. Were she out competing in the world herself, she would have no need to displace her needs by badgering her husband. Or maybe Jane likes to dominate. She cannot go out and obtain a position of power; moreover, Dick refuses to be directly dominated. Her response is to develop timely "headaches" when he wants to engage in sex; she openly flirts with his best friend at a party; she belittles him in public or gives away the punch line to the joke he is telling. In short, those unpleasant qualities of nagging, whining, manipulating, perhaps even frigidity attributed so often to wives result largely from the fact that in trying to conform to their sex role stereotype many Janes find that they are left without direct expression of much of their personality (Greer, 1970, especially pp. 281–89). Ironically, the state of being married, to which they have devoted so much of their attention since youth, is a highly disadvantageous one for most females, who nonetheless spend their lives thinking "if only (I was different, he was different, etc.) life would be bliss." Research has repeatedly shown that wives are more unhappy in their marriages than husbands (Bernard, 1971).

What is Dick doing in response to Jane's behavior and to his own unsatisfied needs? In the first place, unlike Jane, Dick never expected his entire life to revolve around the marital relationship. Thus he is psychologically in a position to use both her behavior and his needs as a justification for various forms of withdrawal. He withdraws affection from her; spends his time at home glued to the TV, a book, the newspaper, a hobby; stays late at work or takes a second job. All of these can be forms of withdrawal from an unpleasant relationship. Ultimately he spends less and less time at home and more time with "the guys" or a succession of girl friends who "understand him" and his needs. Another reaction Dick may have is to engage in never-ending "put-downs," denigrating his mate's abilities and intellect and thus her "right" to belittle or even disagree with him. In turn, this behavior feeds back and exacerbates his wife's nagging and whining. It is also not uncommon for him to react to his mate with various degrees of physical violence or threats of violence. This is most frequent among those in the lower classes (Komarovski, 1967, p. 227).

In all of this Dick has one strong advantage over Jane. He, unlike she (if she is a housewife), has the world outside the home in which to seek satisfaction of his needs. Given the current isolated nuclear family structure, if he can't satisfy her needs she has very few options. In the relatively happy circumstance that they "deviate" from their sex roles in congruent fashion—for instance, he by being dependent, she by being domineering—they can switch roles. In doing so, however, they will frequently reap the sneers and scorn of others. Mostly, the war between the sexes goes on in millions of homes, each skirmish helping to ensure that the next will be worse (Jones, 1970). A vicious circle develops in which her unpleasant behavior elicits withdrawal, denigration, or violence from him, which in turn results in worse behavior by her and more reaction by him. Communication, respect, and affection are all casualties of trying to live within the straitjacket of the sex role stereotypes.

While the picture just presented may represent something of an extreme, elements of it are undoubtedly present in a very large proportion of marriages. Given this, one can only view the relatively high divorce rate with optimism. If nothing else, it represents an attempt on the part of millions to opt out of relationships that bring out the worst human traits and seem to grant so little by way of rewards for so many (Scanzoni, 1972, chap. 4). From this point of view divorce is hardly the "failure" it is frequently pictured. Rather, it may represent significant human growth for one or both of the former spouses.

There are also many cases where the partners comfortably conform to the relevant sex role stereotype, and he, she, or they have so strongly internalized them that the kinds of displacements suggested above do not occur. If both have done so, conflict is probably minimal, but so too are genuine sharing and two-way communication; the masculine role particularly, has hardly prepared a male to enter a close, open relationship, nor would the power differential encourage it. The situation in which both sex role stereotypes are conformed to is probably increasingly rare in today's world of flux, although it might possibly have been the norm in more traditional times and places. Such a relationship would tend to be quite stable. If only the female has truly internalized her role, her partner will face different kinds of problems than those already discussed. Instead of a bitchy, nagging, manipulative spouse, he will find himself saddled with a human being who is virtually totally dependent upon him for the fulfillment of all her needs, for making all the decisions, and so on. Moreover, such a wife will be of little help to him in coping with whatever insecurities he may have. What starts out to be an ego trip quickly becomes a heavy burden for many modern men. Few honest males today would deny that such overwhelming responsibility is extremely difficult and unpleasant, as well as constricting to their own lives. If only the male has fully internalized his role, his mate is likely to respond in the manner delineated earlier and become manipulative and nagging in an effort to extract more open affection and attention, as well as more power in the decision-making process.

In general, the less similar the daily activities and interests of the male and female (or of any two people) (i.e., the more stringent the sexual division of labor), the more difficult communication and understanding between the two are likely to be. Perhaps ironically, males have been found to be more willing to engage in household and child-rearing activities than females are willing to allow them to do so, especially as the years go by in a marriage (Safilios-Rothschild, 1972, p. 67). By the time children arrive, most couples have developed a fairly precise and stereotyped division of labor that often serves to encourage further deterioration in the relationship. Wives and mothers jealously guard the only realm of activity that is socially defined as their legitimate preserve, resisting any but the most minimal efforts by their husbands to engage in them ("because they are inept"). After a while the husband who has been ejected from the kitchen and nursery no longer offers his services at all. This provides his harried wife with an excuse to play the "martyr" and proclaim his lack of appreciation for her efforts, and him with the opportunity to complain about the disorganized state of their home. Again, we have come full circle to find her complaining and him withdrawing.

At this point the natural question arises concerning the possibility of a long-term loving relationship between a male and female working out happily. Such a relationship is possible, but probably only if the two are willing to engage in the difficult tasks of overcoming many aspects of the traditional sex role stereotypes and striking out in new directions that allow both to explore their human potential more fully. A first but by no means sole requisite for this is equality between the two parties, and one important road to equality is for the female to be actively engaged in self-fulfilling activities outside the home. Research has consistently indicated that working wives, especially those with a "career" as opposed to a mere "job," have more power in the decision-making process *vis-à-vis* their mates than housewives (Scanzoni, 1972, p. 69). It is reasonable to assume also that such women will find more direct fulfillment of their own personal needs and develop more self-confidence, both of which are necessary to a mature relationship.

The basic fact remains that females and males who attempt to conform to their sex role stereotypes enter romantic relationships with one another based on the supposition that their partner will behave in certain predictable ways. They also assume that such behaviors will serve to fulfill one another's needs. This assumption is largely false, given the fact that feminine needs involve receiving affection, while the masculine stereotype by and large discourages the open expression of emotion. In addition, females expect more personal gratification from a marital relationship than do males, who look more to their work for life satisfaction (Safilios-Rothschild, 1972, p. 67).

It is increasingly unlikely today that either partner truly conforms to these stereotypes and hence to the other's expectations. Nor is our accepted courtship system, as discussed briefly in Chapter 3, likely to reveal many of these disparities until after a binding commitment between the pair has taken place. When you add to this the fact that many males have the opportunity to grow and change in their daily contact with the world, while many females find themselves mentally shrinking in the isolation of their homes and the heavy menial requirements of housework, the probability of any real understanding between the two shrinks even further. The result is millions of families in which frustrated women who feel unappreciated, unloved, and impotent face hostile men who feel exploited as "meal tickets" and react by withdrawing psychically and physically from the relationship. As often as not, they maintain this way of life for the dubious "sake of the children."

Parents and Children

Soon after an American couple marries, pressure by parents and friends to produce children begins, to become a clamor within a few years. As Ellen Peck puts it, people don't ask *if* you are planning to have children, they ask *when* (1971, p. 171). The childless couple is almost as socially deviant as the husbandless woman. Couples who choose not to ever have children are labeled selfish, immature, immoral, or just plain peculiar. Most, of course, desire children; even if the husband does not, his wife has learned to view this as her primary mission in life. Among those who don't, most eventually succumb to the pressure and have them anyway.

Once a couple conforms in this respect, the same society that encouraged their parenthood and prides itself on being so child-centered proceeds to do very little by way of manifesting any further interest in the child. Unlike most European societies, we have no children's allowance (except the humiliating A.F.D.C.); few inexpensive, well-run child-care centers; little provision for ensuring adequate health care for children; and a penchant for turning down school bond issues. In short, once a couple has had a child it becomes solely their responsibility and, in reality, *hers.* This is not an irrelevant fact, given estimates that for a family to raise two children, send them to college, and forego the wife's potential income costs between $80,000 and $150,000! Before the society will intervene in any way the parents must abuse the child to the point of near murder, a not infrequent and rapidly increasing occurrence.

Most couples probably need to make less adjustments to marriage than they do to parenthood (Lopata, 1971, chap. 4). Husband-wife roles may flow fairly smoothly from the girl friend–boyfriend ones. This is especially true if, as is typically the case today, the female continues to work or go to school and if the couple lives in an apartment where housekeeping chores are relatively minimal. The assumption of father and mother roles, however, is usually a completely new experience, and it often entails radical adjustments in both of their individual lives as well as in the nature of their interaction. For those who planned the pregnancy, the news is often greeted with euphoria. The husband becomes extremely attentive to his spouse and to her "mystical" condition. Indeed, females often desire pregnancy precisely to elicit such attention. Very soon after the birth, if not somewhat before, this starts changing. He begins to resent the intrusion of the newcomer on his previously exclusive "turf"; she generally ceases employment (at precisely the time expenses have increased) and begins to perceive the realm of the house and child as more or less exclusively hers—in short, it is at this juncture that she turns into the traditional housewife (Gavron, 1966, p. 135). All of the problems enumerated in the preceding section either surface at this time or are exacerbated if they were manifested previously. Far from "bringing a couple closer together," as myth would have it, the arrival of a child strains any but the most solid relationships between parents (Peck, 1971, pp. 15–16 and 20 ff.).

Mother-Child Relations

Young Jane begins learning the mother role when she receives her first doll at about age 2 or 3. If she has a younger sibling, she is probably encouraged to aid in its care. As just about the single most important aspect of the total feminine role complex, motherhood is romanticized and taught to a greater or lesser extent from early youth (Peck, 1971, p. 18 ff.). MOTHERHOOD IS FULFILLMENT! shout the media, the "helping professions," Madison Avenue, and the corporations which see babies as consumers and a high birth rate as a business bonanza. As a social role motherhood is relatively precisely defined, and its obligations are broadly agreed upon by members of the many diverse subcultures that comprise American society. Mother is expected to be responsible for the daily physical and health care of the child from birth until at least adolescence. She is responsible for monitoring the child's emotional and intellectual development. She is expected to function as the chief mediator between the family on the one hand, and school, church, and the families of the child's friends on the other. Particularly during the preschool years, she is chiefly responsible for amusing the child or seeing to it that someone else does. Above all, mother is held to be the major emotional mainstay of the child: the constant provider of unconditional affection, understanding, and moral support. These things are expected of mothers regardless of their education, social class, interests, abilities, mental health, and so forth.

The theoretical basis of these social expectations is the simple fact that, usually, it was the woman's body that carried and eventually gave birth to the child. Myth has it that the process of being pregnant and giving birth magically results in instant "mother love," namely, an overwhelming desire to nurture and care for all the needs of her offspring for the next 15 or 20 years of life (Lopata, 1971, p. 35). If, indeed, "nature" provided such an urge we could scarcely account for the large numbers of mothers who neglect, abuse, and abandon their children, not to mention the even larger number who perform their maternal tasks poorly. Nor could we account for the deep "maternal" love people of both genders often develop for children they did not physically conceive. The fact of the matter is that a *social* injunction is placed on virtually all females to be mothers, to do the required types of things and develop the "appropriate" emotions, as outlined above (Peck, 1971, chap. 5). The context in which the role of motherhood is normally played in contemporary America is that of the small, isolated nuclear family with only two or three children. When grandparents are present in middle-class, white families, they tend to be excluded from serious participation in family life. Moreover, most "experts" and public opinion maintain that the only way in which one can adequately play the mother role, especially when children are young, is for the specific woman who is the mother to be constantly accessible, that is, not employed outside the home. This again is enjoined without regard to the particular mother's interests or abilities, unless she is poor.

The ramifications of these circumstances for children and for mother-child relations (not to mention the mothers themselves) are relatively disastrous. Until quite recently in history most people lived in extended families consisting usually of at least three generations, a number of adults of both sexes, and a number of children of various ages and both genders. A child was reared in a microcosm of the world in which it would probably live as an adult. It had a variety of role models and a variety of inputs to its developing behaviors and attitudes. With a number of adults and older children to share the responsibility, a young child was not an overwhelming burden to any one individual; its many needs could be easily met because there were many people to meet them. If the biological mother lacked in any way the interest or ability to fulfill the many and varied responsibilities entailed in child rearing, there were always others to make up for the deficiency. Larger families precluded concentrating close attention and scrutiny on every move of the child; they discouraged an intense, all-consuming interest in any one individual. In this way they encouraged cooperativeness and discouraged extreme ego-centeredness. Moreover, they necessitated active contributions on the part of all but the very youngest, thus giving all family members functional roles and a concomitant sense of importance. In fact, the very concept of "childhood" as a distinct stage during which individuals are treated in a markedly different manner from adults is only a few centuries old at most (Firestone, 1970, chap. 4).

By contrast, the modern middle-class mother has little choice but to lavish attention on her few children, and she is strongly encouraged by society to focus on the most minor details of their daily existence. Barraged by a constant stream of "expert" opinions on child development, she scrutinizes every aspect of the child's life, apprehensive lest she damage its psyche or fail to recognize and correct some "abnormality." Ironically, in the process she works harder than her predecessors, with their larger families and lack of modern conveniences. The children, in turn, have few other adults present during their waking hours to turn to or emulate. They exist, by and large, in a world of children their own age and even sex which bears little resemblance to that which lies outside the home, and they have few if any functional roles to fulfill to give them a sense of worth. Young mothers, bound to children during virtually all their waking hours and almost alone responsible for fulfilling all their needs (as well as performing all the other household duties) quite frequently find themselves harried, exhausted, and frustrated. They periodically explode with anger for minor infractions of rules by their offspring and subsequently feel guilty at their own reactions. Survey the mid-afternoon or late-morning scene at any supermarket and you will see this drama endlessly played. Years later, these same mothers are reluctant to allow their children the independence that spells the end of their only major functional role in life.

But the problem only begins here for many women. The same aggressive, dominant, ambitious wife who must live vicariously through her husband because she is prohibited by her sex role from direct and constructive expression of these traits will do the same to her children—and especially her male offspring. If she can dominate no one else, she can at least wield power over her young (Sexton, 1969, chap. 3). Little Dick *must* be the best athlete, get top grades, be most popular, in short, *succeed;* little Jane *must* be the prettiest girl in her class with the best wardrobe, best in dancing and piano lessons, have the most dates, and so forth. Mother vests all of her pent-up energies and needs on her two or three children, dragging them from one organized activity to another, lavishing attention on their "progress" that is reminiscent of a horticulturist in a hothouse. She ends up putting incredible pressure on them to be not themselves but some version of her own dreams. Her self-definition becomes that of her offspring (the final insult occurs when her husband begins referring to her as "mother" or "mom"). Dick can't grow up to be a plumber rather than a lawyer, nor can Jane marry the former rather than the latter; it would reflect badly on mother. She comes to expect that the costs in terms of work and "sacrifice" for her children will be repaid in terms of rewards accrued from a vicarious thrill in their successes.

In the past decade middle-class adolescents (and even younger children) have found their own ways of striking back at all this close scrutiny and pressure. They have committed suicide, run away from home, and become juvenile delinquents in unprecedented numbers; they have turned to an escapist drug culture; they have created an entire youth culture designed to flout the most cherished ambitions of the adult world. Far from being the result of a "permissive" upbringing, these phenomena have resulted from a pressure-cooker environment in which they are pressured to perform well a series of nonfunctional activities. Without the daily inputs of a variety of adults, without the independence that can only arise from a studied *lack* of attention to all aspects of their daily existence, without meaningful roles to fulfill during the many years before they finish school, youths have a difficult time trying to develop a clear sense of themselves as self-reliant, independent, responsible human beings with some sense of purpose in life (Friedan, 1963, chap. 12; Grønseth, 1971–72, p. 13).

Motherhood cannot be an all-encompassing activity, for the sake of both the mothers and the offspring. Quantity of attention (past some absolute minimum) is simply not an important consideration in how children "turn out." A few hours a day of intensive, loving, high "quality" attention to a child by a mother who is happily growing and fulfilling herself the rest of the time is worth infinitely more than the never-ending hours of incessant bickering that passes for child rearing in so many homes today. Try as they might, researchers have failed to document any substantial differences in adjustment, happiness, and so forth between children of working mothers and those of housewives. In fact, it seems to be the case that children of nonworking mothers who wish they *were* working suffer the most, and youngsters whose mothers work are generally more self-reliant than others (Bird, 1968, p. 182; Friedan, 1963, p. 186). If mother love means anything, it must involve encouraging a child to fulfill its own potential—not to live the life its mother would have liked to live had she not been bound by social convention. It means raising a child who is capable of functioning without her (by providing a model of an independent person) and then encouraging that offspring to do just that. It is difficult to imagine how our current family structure, combined with our definitions of motherhood and of the feminine sex role, can function to permit that kind of mother love to thrive.

Father-Child Relations

The role of fatherhood is very dissimilar to that of motherhood in three crucial ways. First, it is a very minor part of the total masculine role constellation; it ranks relatively low on the list of priorities a male is likely to have, and he is not strongly sanctioned socially for playing this role either well or poorly. Second, our society does not have a precise, agreed-upon definition of the components of this role, beyond the ever-present obligation to "provide" in economic terms. Finally, almost nothing in the prefatherhood learning of most males is oriented in any way to training them for this role (Brenton, 1966, p. 130 ff.). They are actively discouraged as children from play activities involving baby surrogates, and, except in rare instances of large families with few or no older sisters, they are not usually required to help much in the daily care of younger siblings. In short, a new father has only the vaguest idea of what he is expected to do and how he ought to do it, and often his commitment to the role in the first place is marginal.

Females are prompted in part to have babies because society has continually informed them that their primary function in life is motherhood. Males are under little such direct social pressure to become parents, except as it is exerted through their wives. It is not surprising, then, that males are generally somewhat less enthusiastic about the prospect of parenthood (Peck, 1971, p. 19) and may in fact face it with grave trepidation. They may fear the added financial obligation and the decreased freedom to come and go at will, as well as a decline in attention from their wives. Counterbalancing this is the vague notion, especially within some ethnic subcultures and the lower classes, that to father a child "proves" one's potency, hence one's "masculinity." Indeed, much opposition to vasectomy or male sterilization results from an erroneous confusion (not altogether at the intellectual level) of male fertility and sexual potency. Related to this is the masculine emphasis on "productivity"; fathering children comes to be viewed as a kind of sexual productivity, and later the offspring themselves may be viewed as products more or less "owned" by the father.

In the past fatherhood was a rather more clearly defined role than today. Father was the chief disciplinarian; mother's threat of "wait 'till your father comes home and hears of this" was enough to quell the most obstreperous child. Today mother is more willing and father less so to engage in such tasks; discipline is no longer a critical component of the father role as distinct from parenthood in general. Before the Industrial Revolution, father was also the chief mentor of his sons, passing on his craft or trade through an apprenticeship program begun early in the child's life. In the remote and complex work world of postindustrial society this task has been virtually abandoned, devolving instead on formal institutions, most notably the schools. In simpler times father was the fount of all knowledge, the primary educator of his children. Today his well-educated spouse is usually more available and as well equipped as he to answer children's questions, if indeed anyone in the family is capable of so doing.

In recent decades countless popular articles and books have encouraged father to be a "pal" to his children—especially his sons, who spend their days in a virtually maleless environment. Simultaneously, the "experts" have warned him not to be "*too much* of a pal"—to remain authoritative and, when needed, capable of discipline. He is enjoined to somehow avoid both being an ogre and being "permissive," yet he is given little time or opportunity to learn how to walk this tightrope (Brenton, 1966, pp. 120–21). His major responsibility remains his work, and now he has even greater financial needs than before he had children. For the up-and-coming middle-class businessman or professional, this means that he will rarely even see his young children awake. The working-class father, pressured by financial need to work overtime or at a second job, will also rarely see his children. Yet when such fathers find that their eight-year-old sons are incapable of throwing a ball decently or are too "tied to mother's apron strings," they react with guilt and a sudden burst of attention. Even then they are hampered by their sex role. The "masculine mystique" has discouraged males from learning to relate to people, including children, in a compassionate, warm, open, affectionate manner. The instrumental orientation they have been taught all their lives leads them to praise their children's successes but ill equips them to sympathize with their bumbling errors. They are thus able to offer "conditional affection" only.

Moreover, if father is not very successful at work, he (like his mate) is apt to pressure his children, especially the males, to succeed in order to enjoy a vicarious compensation for the failures and frustrations he has experienced. Caught in the "success ethic" himself, he is likely to stress achievement more strongly than just about anything else (Brenton, 1966, p. 138 ff.), thus perpetuating this component of the masculine mystique. When father proudly proclaims "This is *my* son," he is engaging in that "ego trip" that says, "If I have succeeded in nothing else, look at what I have produced." In the process he forgets that he took little part in the actual upbringing of the child, not to mention the fact that the child was the one who actually accomplished whatever it was that elicited the outburst.

By and large most fathers, especially in the white middle class, probably relate very little to their children during infancy and early childhood, perceiving them as more or less of a nuisance (Peck, 1971, chap. 6). Later, often much to the anger of the mother, they may return slightly from their withdrawal. They take the children (usually the sons) to interesting places and engage them briefly in the kind of exciting play for which the harried and exhausted mother has little time or energy. They buy them special things (not their everyday needs like clothes and school supplies). They occasionally "flirt" with and heap praise upon their dressed-up daughters (one of the few things many fathers actually do with daughters). They teach their sons sports and hobbies. They badger them to succeed in school and in sports and tend to reward them only contingent upon such success. In short, fathers do not actively partake of the petty, daily problems and needs of their offspring; they remain tangential to the intimate lives of their children, involved only in the "special" moments of excitement or disaster. In most cases, fathers refuse to even engage in physical contact with their sons past infancy, preferring the handshake to the kiss. All too often a divorce between the parents reduces the quantity and quality of the father's interaction with his children little, if any (assuming they all remain in the same geographical vicinity), and occasionally even increases it because of the guilt involved.

Motherhood is often said to have a humanizing effect on women because of their intimate daily contact with a developing child, with all its strengths and frailties. To the extent that fathers do not actively engage themselves in their children's daily growth process, in the minor changes in their offsprings' abilities and activities, the experience of paternity will not result in their own human growth. Once again the sex role stereotype is responsible for a vicious and unrewarding circle: ill equipped by the masculine stereotype to deal with children on a deep emotional ("expressive") level, caught in an often all-consuming devotion to work and economic success, the father fails to involve himself in his child's life to the extent necessary to ultimately develop the more humane and compassionate aspects of his personality which might, in turn, make him better able to relate to his offspring. The nature and costs of both sex role stereotypes, combined with the isolated nuclear family structure characteristic of this society, have thus resulted in parent-child relations that fall far short of our cherished social ideals and, in the process, create numerous problems for the next generation of adults.

Same-Sexed Friendships

It might seem that if sex role stereotypes are irrelevant to any type of interpersonal relationship, it would be in friendships between members of the same gender. The fact that this is not the case underlines the all-pervasive quality of such stereotypes in virtually every aspect of human existence.

Male Friendships

From early childhood males are encouraged to form friendship and peer groups with other members of their gender, and to cooperate with other males for the achievement of mutually desired goals, often in competition with other all-male groups. Chapter 3 showed how the play activities of young males foster the formation of such relationships, and they scarcely end at adolescence. "Bonded males," or all-male groups, as Lionel Tiger (1970) argues, persist throughout life, be they for work, war, sport, poker, or "drinking buddies." Moreover, a rudimentary kind of superior "caste consciousness" that begins in childhood encourages males to shun the companionship of females for ordinary friendship purposes. It is not unusual for females to be informed more or less explicitly by male colleagues or fellow students that they have enough (male) friends; what they want is a sexual partner, or nothing. When they find their family life becoming unpleasant, males look to other males even more for companionship, often developing a virtual woman-hating fraternity (Fast, 1971, chap. 2).

The same masculine stereotype that encourages male friendships, however, often seriously limits the scope and content of such relationships (Booth, 1972, p. 186), as suggested in the discussion above of male-female platonic relationships. Male friendships are characterized by a kind of rough-and-ready camaraderie. Males will usually be found *doing* something together (fishing, bowling, tinkering with machinery, working). When they are "merely" talking to one another it will usually be on a "light" subject (sports, some "dish" who works in the office), or they may engage in generalized "bitching" about their mates; other topics are approached in an abstract, intellectualized manner. What they are very rarely found doing is talking to one another on an intimate basis about their deepest needs and insecurities. As one male put it who was attempting to organize a men's consciousness-raising group similar to those existing among feminists:

> A salient observation . . . involved an increasing awareness of how annoying the employment of men's values can be. Among such traits observed were dominating, interrupting, condescension, disrespect, aggression, obsession with sex, ego, intellectualization, put downs, and a lack of empathy, emotion, openness, warmth and contact with persons as human beings rather than as competitors for power and position (Farrell, 1971–72, pp. 21–22).

Two major aspects of the masculine sex role discourage intimacy among American males. First, they are taught it is "unmanly" to show most emotions or to express dependency needs. Second, the aggressiveness and power orientation of the masculine role encourages males to view each other as competitors for status, and one hardly reveals weaknesses to a competitor. "One-upmanship" is primarily a masculine game. A pervasive fear of being labeled "homosexual" that is particularly endemic to American males exacerbates these tendencies further; a male who approaches another male on too intimate a basis fears being interpreted as making an improper "pass" (Fast, 1971, pp. 19 and 104–7).

I recall a very amusing incident nearly ten years ago that helps to highlight this national male phobia. Six people were temporarily traveling together: four males, myself, and another female. We reached a city where cheap hotel space was very scarce, so we decided to spend the night crammed into one room. There were only two double beds, and we drew lots to see who was to sleep on the floor and who was to get which beds. Two male American college students who were traveling together for the entire summer drew the lots that gave them one double bed. We awoke to find both, fully dressed, virtually falling off opposite sides of the bed. The very next evening we had occasion to watch two French males, about the same age and patently not homosexual, share a single bed when other facilities were unavailable. They awoke in their underclothes, tangled around one another, and thought it quite funny.

The old adage that males will talk to one another in quite explicit terms about females they don't care for but say little if anything about those they love is also indicative of the level of communication in all-male groups. Sexual prowess is acceptable conversation, emotional commitment is not; the former grants prestige, the latter, if anything, takes it away. The many hours that males spend in one another's presence are rewarding in that they serve primarily to satisfy their needs for amusement, the accomplishment of instrumental goals, and prestige. Status and prestige, however, are relative; by definition someone is always on the bottom. Those males whose prestige among their peers is low are thus impelled to look to the lower caste to resurrect their bruised egos, a role most females know only too well. At any rate, the nature of males' expectations of one another makes it appear far too costly to attempt to push such relationships to a deeper level (Fasteau, 1972). Thus many are left with unmet emotional needs which, as we have seen, are not easily satisfied in their long-term relationships with females, either.

Female Friendships

Females face almost exactly the opposite problems from males in their friendships. They have a more difficult time forming relationships with members of their own sex and do so with less frequency than males, but when they succeed such friendships are qualitatively deeper and more intimate (Booth, 1972). In a study of the aged,

Marjorie Lowenthal and Clayton Haven (1968) found that females were more likely to have a confidant than males, and that the younger the respondents the more pronounced the differences between males and females in this regard. Moreover, among women husbands were least frequently mentioned as confidants, while among males wives were most frequently designated (p. 28). The nature of such female friendships is strongly rooted in the sex role stereotype.

Girls are not encouraged to participate in games that foster cooperation and camaraderie. More importantly, from adolescence females are taught that their major task is to outshine other members of their gender sufficiently to attract and then hold the best possible mate. In centering the female's self-definition around that of the male she will eventually attract and wed, the feminine sex role encourages a kind of constant competition between all members of the sex; the most important aspect of their entire lives rests directly on a never-ending war of all against all. We have all heard repeatedly that women "hate" other women. Unlike the kind of competition fostered among males, this does not in the least entail group cooperation for the purpose of competing. Indeed, best friends among young females often specifically and explicitly exempt the realm of "boys" from their friendship. Males will usually avoid dating a friend's girl friend, to preclude rejection by peers. Females are bound by no such code. From early childhood females learn to size themselves up relative to other females, especially in appearance and "charm," and this habit becomes lifelong for most (Pogrebin, 1972). Matrons enter a party and, while their spouses eyeball the opposite sex, they scrutinize the "competition," namely, members of their own gender, always insecure lest they lose their mate to a better looking woman. The clothing and cosmetic industries have been extraordinarily successful in extracting huge sums of money from females for constant fashion changes precisely because of this mentality.

The isolation caused by this orientation is further encouraged by the isolation of the daily activities of the housewife. Each little nuclear family lives in its own "cell"—be it a 3-room apartment or a 20-room mansion—and each is more or less self-contained as to the tools and appliances needed for its functioning. Housewives need not cooperate with any other females to accomplish their daily tasks, except perhaps in rare emergencies. The result is that for many the only females they know are the wives of their husband's friends and the mothers of their children's playmates, with whom they may or may not have much in common personally. Tied to their homes and to a heavy, time-consuming schedule of household and child-rearing duties, many women have little opportunity to meet other females who share their own interests and points of view, as distinct from those of other family members. It is here that the female's submergence of her own identity in those of her husband and offspring becomes most evident and most costly.

Against all these odds, most females do get to know other females and form close friendships. Housewives often find that they have a lot in common with their husband's friends' wives and their children's playmates' mothers, if for no other reason than that they are all in the same leaky boat. Especially as children grow older, females get out of the house and join voluntary organizations where they meet others with similar interests. Increasingly they go to school or to work and find friends there. Because the feminine sex role stereotype encourages women to express their emotions, needs, and problems without feeling threatened, when and if they get beyond worrying about competition over appearance and males the way is clear for a deep, intimate association. Females talk to females about the males they love—not about those with whom they have had fleeting and casual relations. They discuss their own dreams and insecurities, their marital and even sexual problems (often to the profound embarrassment of their mates, if they discover it). The kaffeeklatsch, afternoon of shopping, or weekly bridge game is often an excuse to gather and talk rather than an activity for its own sake. The telephone has greatly aided such interaction among isolated housewives and, in the process, has spawned its share of male jokes about the female's presumably excessive use of that instrument.

Ironically, some of those very qualities that handicap females most in the world of work and in interactions with males enable them to experience far richer interactions with others of their own gender. Precisely because of their insecurities and general feelings of inferiority and incompetence, it is possible for power plays, dominance, ego trips and abstracted intellectualizing to be absent from their interactions, while openness, empathy, and compassion can readily flourish. However, all of this is possible only *if and when* they surmount the initial hurdle of competing over appearance and male attention. Nowhere is this more evident than in the relative ease with which the growing numbers of feminist "rap groups" have been able to elicit their members' deepest feelings, compared to the great difficulty experienced by the few male groups that have attempted to do the same.

Sexual "Deviance" and Sex Roles

The term "sexual deviance" covers a multitude of behaviors which share in common only the fact that a particular society at a moment in history defines them as "abnormal," "wrong," and often illegal. According to the laws of contemporary America, about the only nondeviant form of sexual behavior is genital intercourse between a male and female married to one another. Our social mores do not really consider such things as masturbation, adultery, premarital and extramarital intercourse, and oral-genital contact between members of the opposite sexes as "sexually deviant," although some of these are not condoned behaviors, either. Prostitution and pornography are considered "more deviant" and homosexuality, transvestism, sodomy, rape, self-exposure, sadomasochism, and other fetishisms are "very deviant" (Gagnon and Simon, 1967). It is impossible and possibly irrelevant to explore all these varied expressions of human sexuality in the context of a book on the sociology of sex roles. However, some of these types of behaviors are probably strongly affected by sex role stereotypes and warrant discussion here.

There is no such thing as a particular expression of human sexuality that is universally "normal" or "natural"; deviant and nondeviant forms alike are learned behaviors (Marmor, 1971, p. 166). When we speak of "sexual deviance" we do not mean the same thing as when we use the term "pathology." The latter implies that the pathological individual is "sick" or "unnatural," and sick people generally want to be and ought to be "cured" if possible. The former term simply connotes that the deviant is doing something that most people in the society define as bad or wrong; from the vantage point of the deviant that is no reason in and of itself to change. Broadly speaking, American mores (although not yet laws) today accept as "normal" adult sexuality almost any behavior between consenting members of the opposite sexes that does not inflict pain and is not directly sold for money. This is the message taught directly and indirectly to members of our society, and most behave in this manner most of the time. What is problematic is why some do not, and part of the answer lies in the pressures exerted by the two sex role stereotypes, beginning in early childhood.

Males and females share some varieties of sexual deviance, but most types are more or less gender specific. Homosexuality is engaged in by members of both sexes, although it is given a special name, lesbianism, among females. Heterosexual prostitution is primarily a female phenomenon; the male counterpart, the gigolo, is relatively rare, and in most places he is not even engaged in an illegal activity. On the other hand, homosexual prostitution is generally a male phenomenon. Rape is, of course, a male activity and, as mentioned in an earlier chapter, so is transvestism, for all practical purposes. Pornography is more frequently consumed by males, but the subject matter is more often female. Finally, sadomasochism probably most frequently follows the pattern of a male sadist and a female masochist, although the converse is by no means unknown.

Most research and writing pertaining to homosexuality concerns itself with the psychodynamics of the origins of this form of deviance as understood on the basis of clinical samples. Even in this corpus of work, however, there seems to be little agreement. Moreover, virtually all professional attention has been focused on the male. Only in the last couple of years has more material begun to appear about lesbians, and the bulk of this literature consists of personal accounts written by radical feminist homosexuals (Abbott and Love, 1972; Aldrich, 1972; Damon, 1970; Koedt, 1972; Martin and Lyon, 1972a and 1972b; Shelley, 1970 and 1971). It is clear that our society and the professionals it supports react far more strongly to male than female homosexuality. Indeed, there is scarcely any recognition that lesbians exist in any numbers worthy of note. The major reason for this one-sided view of homosexuality probably resides in the fact that society places higher value on masculinity than femininity. Males form a superior caste, and "defections" from masculinity appear less comprehensible and more reprehensible than parallel behavior by females. Moreover, male homosexuality is more public than female, and therefore most of the arrests for this activity are male. In addition, as discussed in Chapter 3, the masculine sex role is learned in such a way that males tend to experience far more insecurity about it than do females about their sex role. Since most professionals who study sexual deviance are male (as are the police who arrest homosexuals), their own insecurities might be responsible for the lopsided attention given to homosexuality among members of their own gender.

Popular imagination depicts the male homosexual as "effete" or "feminine" in appearance and behavior; homosexuality and a limp wrist are almost synonymous to Americans. Many even confuse homosexuality with transvestism or female impersonation. In fact the latter are not usually homosexual at all, while the former more often than not are quite "masculine" in demeanor. Similarly, popular imagination pictures lesbians as "bull dykes" who are very masculine in behavior and appearance. "Queens" and "bull dykes" do exist, but they comprise a relatively small, if conspicuous, proportion of practicing homosexuals. Homosexuals are homosexual because they react more positively, that is, are attracted more, to members of their own gender than to the opposite one. What possible reason would they have for being attracted to an impersonator of the opposite sex rather than a member of it? From the perspective of a sex *role* orientation, homosexuals are drawn to members of their own sex because they find their behavior more appealing, and/or they reject those of the opposite gender because the behaviors and attitudes characteristic of that sex are in some way offensive or repellent to them.

If we may believe lesbians' accounts of their own experiences (Martin and Lyon, 1972a), not infrequently at the outset of a relationship one partner will assume the "butch" or stereotyped masculine role, the other the "femme" or stereotyped feminine role. They do so because they too have learned the stereotypes about lesbians. However, in lasting relationships (often characteristic of lesbians although considerably less so of male homosexuals), such role-playing tends over time to decrease and eventually disappear. Most writers on the subject seem to agree that lesbians, like "straight" females, enter "love" relationships before they find themselves actively engaged in sexual behavior (Hedblom, 1972; Martin and Lyon, 1972b, p. 75; Simon and Gagnon, 1967, p. 251). Indeed, many lesbians are sexually passive, disinterested, even frigid before they find themselves in a close relationship with another female. In short, they have internalized the feminine role injunctions concerning sexuality. From their study of a "small sample" of lesbians, William Simon and John Gagnon conclude:

> Most lesbians, apparently, are not exempt from the constraints and norms that regulate the development of female sexuality in general. This appears to be particularly true of the timing or phasing of entry into active sexual roles, as well as of the quality of relationships required to facilitate the entry (1967, p. 253).

Moreover, these same authors found that entry into lesbianism was rarely contingent upon "seduction" by an older woman. In short, females become lesbians primarily because they find they develop more meaningful emotional attachments to other females than to males, and such relationships eventually come to be expressed in sexual terms. Given the problems endemic to male-female relationships discussed earlier in this chapter, it might be considered surprising that there are not many more lesbians, especially since open communication, emotional expression, an absence of exploitation, and real equality between partners is easier between two females than between a male and a female or two males. Counterbalancing these possible advantages, however, is the social abuse which all homosexuals suffer, as well as our social definition of this behavior as "sick," even "evil." These disadvantages probably function as powerful preventatives for most females in translating friendship into a sexual relationship (Shelley, 1970; Damon, 1970).

If female homosexuality reflects an attempt to fulfill the feminine role injunction to base sexuality on the prior formation of an emotional attachment, its male counterpart reflects the very different injunctions that arise from the masculine stereotype. Unlike lesbians, male homosexuals seem to be considerably less frequently involved in a long-term, loving dyad. Their sexual encounters, like those of "straight" males, are likely to be many, fleeting, and exploitative. The one-night stand resulting from a pick up at a gay bar, or what one author referred to as a "market mentality," is far more typical of male than female homosexuals (Hooker, 1967, pp. 176–77); so too is the seduction of an adolescent by an older man. In general their behavior reflects the masculine emphasis on sex divorced from emotional commitment; sex used for status, dominance, and so forth (Simon and Gagnon, 1970). The male homosexual is often narcissistic, sometimes engaging in long hours of body-building exercises; he is the picture of robust masculinity. In fact, many of the societies in which male homosexuality has been relatively widespread and overt have been those most dedicated to the sexual caste system and a masculine mystique, including ancient Greece (especially warlike Sparta), Imperial Germany, and Imperial Britain in the Victorian era. It is possible too that male homosexuality reflects a need on the part of some males to be the object of sexual desire. Females are trained to suppress such desire, or at least not to demonstrate it overtly. The more narcissistic the male, the more he might experience such a need, and therefore the greater the likelihood that he would turn to homosexuality for its fulfillment.

Male homosexuals who play a more "feminine" role (at the extreme, "queens"), along with transvestites who are not homosexual, are often the recipients of cruelty and exploitation at the hands of the straight male world and even "masculine" homosexuals. These are the real sellouts to their superior caste position. Their behavior may reflect a feeling that only in assuming the outward appearance and mannerisms of females are they free to engage in the kinds of emotional expression barred to "masculine" males. At any rate, they are more visible to the general public, which thus mistakes them for the norm.

Male prostitution is generally homosexual in nature and takes particular advantage of the more "feminine" homosexuals. To be more precise, the patron is homosexual, although the seller or prostitute may not be, indeed usually is not (Reiss, 1967). Typically, the prostitute is a lower class male, often an adolescent, who engages in this activity as a quick, easy way to earn money. He strictly limits his behavior to an active role, refusing to receive sexual pleasure in return. By so doing he is able to maintain a self-identity as heterosexual (Reiss, 1967). Not infrequently such encounters (as portrayed in the movie "The Midnight Cowboy") end in the beating and robbery of the homosexual who, given his inability to call upon the police, is completely defenseless. In behaving this way, the prostitute reaffirms to himself his own "masculinity." This situation arises for male homosexuals but not for their female counterparts primarily because of their "marketplace mentality" concerning sex.

Homosexual rape also casts an interesting light on the masculine sex role. This behavior has grown to nearly epidemic proportions in many of our nation's prisons. A study of this phenomenon in one prison system by Alan Davis (1970) shows that the victims are generally young, relatively small males who have committed minor offenses. Their aggressors are older, larger, and guilty of more major transgressions. Most crucially, the rapist does not define himself as homosexual. Indeed, he does not even see himself as engaging in a homosexual act. The author states that this "seems to be based upon his startlingly primitive view of sexual relationships, one that defines as male whichever partner is aggressive and as homosexual whichever partner is passive" (pp. 122–23).

Male heterosexual prostitution is a very different kind of phenomenon. The male prostitute, or gigolo, is, in the most fundamental sense, betraying the masculine stereotype. He is doing so in two ways: by functioning as an economic dependent of a female and by acting as the sexual object and recipient of a female's initiative. It is likely that few males stand lower in prestige in the masculine world than the gigolo, except in some subcultures where the behavior is defined as a "con" and perceived as an acceptable form of exploitation of females.

Unlike lesbians, female prostitutes have been the subject of much discourse for literally eons. They seem to simultaneously intrigue and disgust members of society, yet no form of "sexual deviance" arises so completely from either sex role as this (Nadle, 1970; Strong, 1970). When mother and Ann Landers tell teen-age Jane that if she "gives" her boyfriend "everything" he will have no "reason" to marry her, they are teaching her, albeit subtly and usually unconsciously, to trade her sexual "favors" for economic support. In a thousand ways females are taught to view themselves as sexual objects and informed that males relate to them in these terms. Moreover, they are seriously handicapped in an effort to earn a decent living in most legitimate occupations. It is hardly surprising, then, that even some well-educated females take the relatively small step of translating these messages into a decision to make a living by being sexual objects, namely, going into prostitution. Whether she is a $100-per-hour call girl or a $10-per-job whore, the prostitute is selling femininity and a willingness to be and do that which their clients are often too afraid to request from their mates. The male purchases not merely a willing and sometimes glamorous body to use as his fantasies dictate but often a "sympathetic" ear to listen to his problems, his hang-ups, his hatreds. The fact that he is usually married underscores the nature of much of what passes for love and communication between spouses. The only disgrace he faces from his peers is the fact that he can't exploit a female in this manner for free.

Many prostitutes are protected from abuse by clients and have clients procured for them by male "pimps." The pimp is financially dependent on the prostitute, with whom he may or may not also have a sexual relationship (not surprisingly, a number of prostitutes are lesbian in personal preference). However, he usually approaches total domination of the life of the female (and sometimes a number of them) and is thus able to maintain his self-definition as masculine. It is not uncommon for prostitutes to be drug addicts; some pimps are able to maintain tremendous power over such women by also serving as the source of their drugs.

If female prostitution reflects the feminine role emphasis on woman as a sexual, exploitable object, so probably does sexual masochism. Females are socially devalued and taught to devalue themselves. In its extreme, the feminine stereotype teaches women that their bodies and their sexuality are dirty; that they exist primarily for the gratification of males; that they have little intrinsic worth. What more crystalline expression for this could there be than receiving sexual gratification through pain? To a greater or lesser degree, most females have masochistic personalities, a characteristic well noted, if poorly explained, by Freud and his followers. Many seem to enjoy playing the martyr role—the sacrificing mother (Mother Portnoy) or wife who claims her "reward" is to be ignored and unloved. Like other suppressed peoples, females tend to turn their frustrations, anger, and hatred not toward those who directly create the problems and who are often members of the superior caste, but inward, upon themselves. Such a trait, common in mild form to perhaps most females, is manifested in its extreme as sexual masochism.

Sadism, or the propensity to derive sexual pleasure by inflicting pain on others, can be viewed as an extreme outgrowth of the masculine sex role. Earlier in this chapter it was mentioned that males tend to view sex, to a greater or lesser degree, as a tool for expressing power and dominance. In its extreme this mentality is manifested in rape. The rape of a stranger may be interpreted as a male's proclamation that he can exercise his will over any member of the female gender he selects, and, therefore, his superiority over the entire sex. Our movies, books, and folklore are filled with stories in which the hero "subdues" an independent, unresponsive heroine by the force of "THE KISS," or a more or less explicit rape. Male fantasy pictures the heroine as melting in response, totally captivated by the hero and henceforth completely attached and subservient to him. The same mentality is reflected in the often-heard statement about an aggressive woman that all she needs is "a good lay."

Raped women frequently report that male police treat them with marked contempt and disrespect, virtually blaming the victim for the crime. Such treatment is sufficiently prevalent that many rapes, if not the majority of them, are never even reported to the police. This attitude toward rape victims has recently been manifested in hideous form in Bangladesh (Goldman, 1972). During the civil war Pakistani soldiers raped nearly a quarter of a million women whose husbands refused after the war to accept the "damaged goods" back. For most of these females, this meant that they were faced with virtual starvation, and many responded by committing suicide.

Combining this general mental orientation toward sex with the masculine emphasis on aggression and even violence, it is not difficult to see how some males would come to depend on producing pain in order to receive sexual gratification. Where members of the subordinate caste impotently turn their fury inward, those in the superordinate caste are in a position to externalize their frustrations and hostilities. Regardless of the source of such feelings, males can, if they choose, vent their fury on the opposite and physically weaker sex, an option not readily available to females. The sex role stereotypes combine to produce the "perfect marriage" between the Marquis de Sade and "O"!

The final form of "sexual deviance" to be discussed, pornography, is not really deviant at all. The primary consumers of pornographic materials have been males, homo and heterosexual alike. Perhaps this, too, results from an orientation to sexuality that is exploitative and basically divorced from considerations of the quality of interpersonal relationships, traits characteristic of the masculine but not the feminine stereotype. However, it could simply be a function of the double standard by which males receive fewer negative sanctions than females (and even some positive ones) for engaging in anything relating to sex. Moreover, until the recent liberalization of laws and mores pertaining to pornography and the concomitant increase in their availability, many males viewed the acquisition of pornographic materials as an illegal "adventure" designed to prove one's "bravery," hence "masculinity."

The subject matter of pornography consists of essentially four types of activities: heterosexual behavior (group or dyadic), lesbian activity, male homosexuality, and masturbation (mostly female). Heterosexual males will consume with equal relish material on heterosexual activity or that concerning females only (alone or in lesbian relationships); they are repulsed (and possibly threatened) by male homosexual material. Material that is devoid of females seems to appeal almost exclusively to male homosexuals. Male heterosexuals are predictably attracted to the female depicted in pornography, regardless of what she is doing or with whom she is doing it. What makes less sense is the fact that heterosexual female consumers also are "turned on" by the female figures. It appears that our cultural definition of females but not males as sex objects is so pervasive that women who would never engage in lesbian activities are sexually stimulated by consuming material depicting such behavior. In short, our culture has conditioned all of us, females as well as males (except homosexuals), to perceive the female form in terms of a stimulating sexual object.

Conclusions

This depressing litany of the effects of sex role stereotyping on a wide variety of primary relationships and on human sexual expression is somewhat exaggerated. This has been done in part as a response to the pervasive romanticization of such relationships. However, there can be little doubt that to varying degrees we all relate to other humans in a much constricted manner because of those cultural definitions of masculinity and femininity which have been emphasized and reinforced throughout our lives. We are none of us free to develop truly multifaceted personalities and behavior repertoires in relationship to a number of significant others. Nor are we free to develop our full potential as humans *vis-à-vis* other humans. Another conclusion may also be drawn from this discussion. It would appear that where femininity exacts a high price in the realm of functioning in instrumental roles outside the context of the home, masculinity extracts its greatest toll in the development of rewarding interpersonal relationships within and outside of the family. Were this book written a decade ago, it may well have ended on this bleak note. However, a number of recent developments encourage hope that the heavy burdens of the sex role status quo are beginning to decrease. In the next and final chapter these happy portents of change will be discussed.

References

Abbott, Sidney, and Love, Barbara. *Sappho Was a Right-on Woman: A Liberated View of Lesbianism.* New York: Stein and Day, 1972.

Aldrich, Ann. *Take a Lesbian to Lunch.* New York: MacFadden Bartell, 1972.

Bernard, Jessie. "The Paradox of the Happy Marriage." In Vivian Gornick and Barbara Moran, *Woman in Sexist Society,* pp. 145–62. New York: Signet Books, 1971.

Bird, Caroline. *Born Female: The High Cost of Keeping Women Down.* New York: David McKay Co., 1968.

Booth, Alan. "Sex and Social Participation." *American Sociological Review* 37 (April 1972): 183–93.

Brenton, Myron. *The American Male*. Greenwich, Conn.: Fawcett Publications, Inc. 1966.

Damon, Gene. "The Least of These: The Minority Whose Screams Haven't Yet Been Heard." In Robin Morgan (ed.), *Sisterhood Is Powerful,* pp. 279–306. New York: Vintage Books, 1970.

Davis, Alan. "Sexual Assaults in the Philadelphia Prison System." In John Gagnon and William Simon (eds.), *The Sexual Scene,* pp. 107–24. Chicago: Aldine Publishing Co., 1970.

Farrell, Warren T. "Male Consciousness-Raising from a Sociological and Political Perspective." *Sociological Focus* 5 (Winter 1971–72): 19–28.

Fast, Julius. *The Incompatibility of Men and Women*. New York: Avon Books, 1971.

Fasteau, Marc. "Men: Why Aren't We Talking?" *Ms.* (July, 1972): 16.

Firestone, Shulamith. *The Dialectic of Sex*. New York: Bantam Books, 1970.

Friedan, Betty. *The Feminine Mystique*. New York: Dell Publishing, 1963.

Gagnon, John, and Simon, William. "Introduction: Deviant Behavior and Sexual Deviance." In Gagnon and Simon (eds.), *Sexual Deviance,* pp. 1–12. New York: Harper and Row, 1967.

Gavron, Hannah. *The Captive Wife: Conflicts of Housebound Mothers*. London: Routledge and Kegan Paul. 1966.

Gillespie, Dair L. "Who Has the Power? The Marital Struggle," *Journal of Marriage and the Family* 33 (August 1971): 445–58.

Goldman, Joyce. "Women of Bangladesh." *Ms.* (August, 1972): 84–88.

Goffman, Erving. *The Presentation of Self in Everyday Life*. Garden City, N.Y.: Doubleday Anchor Books, 1959.

Greer, Germaine. *The Female Eunuch*. New York: McGraw-Hill Book Co., 1970.

Grønseth, Erik. "The Husband Provider Role and Its Dysfunctional Consequences." *Sociological Focus* 5 (Winter 1971–72): 10–18.

Hacker, Helen M. "Women as a Minority Group." *Social Forces* 30 (1951): 60–69.

Hedblom, Jack. "Social, Sexual, and Occupational Lives of Homosexual Women." *Sexual Behavior* 2 (October 1972): 33–37.

Homans, George. *Social Behavior: Its Elementary Forms.* New York: Harcourt, Brace and World, 1961.

Hooker, Evelyn. "The Homosexual Community." In John Gagnon and William Simon (eds.), *Sexual Deviance,* pp. 167–184. New York: Harper and Row, 1967.

Jones, Beverly. "The Dynamics of Marriage and Motherhood." In Robin Morgan (ed.), *Sisterhood Is Powerful,* pp. 46–61. New York: Vintage Books, 1970.

Koedt, Anne. "Can Women Love Women?" *Ms.* (Spring 1972): 117–121.

Komarovski, Mirra. *Blue Collar Marriage.* New York: Vintage Books, 1967.

Laws, Judith Long. "A Feminist Review of Marital Adjustment Literature: The Rape of the Locke." *Journal of Marriage and the Family* 33 (August 1971): 483–516.

Lopata, Helena. *Occupation: Housewife.* New York: Oxford University Press, 1971.

Lowenthal, Marjorie Fiske, and Haven, Clayton. "Interaction and Adaptation: Intimacy as a Critical Variable." *American Sociological Review* 33 (February 1968): 20–30.

Marmor, Judd. " 'Normal' and 'Deviant' Sexual Behavior." *The Journal of the American Medical Association* 217 (July 12, 1971): 165–70.

Martin, Del, and Lyon, Phyllis. "Lesbian Love and Sexuality." *Ms.* (July 1972):74–77 and 123(a).

Martin, Del, and Lyon, Phyllis. *Lesbian/Woman.* New York: Bantam Books, 1972(b).

Millett, Kate. *Sexual Politics.* Garden City, N.Y.: Doubleday, 1970.

Nadle, Marlene. "Prostitutes." In Sookie Stambler (ed.), *Women's Liberation: Blueprint for the Future,* pp. 51–56. New York: Ace Books, 1970.

Newcomb, T. M. *The Acquaintance Process.* New York: Holt Rinehart & Winston, 1961.

O'Neill, Nena, and O'Neill, George. *Open Marriage: A New Life Style for Couples.* New York: M. Evans & Co., 1972.

Papanek, Hanna. "Men, Women, and Work: Reflections on the Two-Person Career." *American Journal of Sociology,* 78 (January 1973): 852–72.

Peck, Ellen. *The Baby Trap*. New York: Pinnacle Books, 1971.

Pogrebin, Letty Cottin. "Competing with Women." *Ms.* (July 1972): 78–81 and 131.

Reiss, Albert J., Jr. "The Social Integration of Queers and Peers." In John Gagnon and William Simon (eds.), *Sexual Deviance*, pp. 197–228. New York: Harper and Row, 1967.

Safilios-Rothschild, Constantina. "Companionate Marriages and Sexual Inequality: Are They Compatible?" In Safilios-Rothschild (ed.), *Toward a Sociology of Women,* pp. 63–70. Lexington, Mass.: Xerox College Publishing, 1972.

Scanzoni, John. *Sexual Bargaining: Power Politics in the American Marriage*. Englewood Cliffs, N.J.: Prentice-Hall, 1972.

Sexton, Patricia Cayo. *The Feminized Male*. New York: Vintage Books, 1969.

Shelley, Martha. "Lesbianism and the Women's Liberation Movement." In Sookie Stambler (ed.), *Women's Liberation: Blueprint for the Future*, pp. 123–29. New York: Ace Books, 1970.

Shelley, Martha. "Women of Lesbos." In *Up Against the Wall, Mother: On Women's Liberation*. Beverly Hills, Calif.: Glencoe Press, 1971.

Simon, William, and Gagnon, John. "The Lesbians: A Preliminary Overview." In Gagnon and Simon (eds.), *Sexual Deviance,* pp. 247–82. New York: Harper and Row, 1967.

Simon, William, and Gagnon, John. "Psychosexual Development." In Gagnon and Simon (eds.), *The Sexual Scene,* pp. 23–41. Chicago: Aldine Publishing Co., 1970.

Strong, Ellen. "The Hooker." In Robin Morgan (ed.), *Sisterhood Is Powerful,* pp. 289–97. New York: Vintage Books, 1970.

Thibault, J. W., and Kelly, H. H. *The Social Psychology of Groups*. New York: John Wiley & Sons, 1959.

Tiger, Lionel. *Men in Groups*. New York: Vintage Books, 1970.

Chapter 6

Conclusion: Masculine/Feminine or Human?

It was the best of times, it was the worst of times; it was the age of wisdom, it was the age of foolishness; it was the epoch of belief, it was the epoch of incredulity; it was the season of Light; it was the season of Darkness; it was the spring of hope; it was the winter of despair; we had everything before us; we had nothing before us; we were all going direct to Heaven; we were all going direct the other way.

Charles Dickens, *A Tale of Two Cities* (1859)

In the same manner that Charles Dickens introduced his classic novel about the French Revolution, we can begin our discussion of the social ferment of the past several years in our own society. Dickens's message is that periods of radical social change are never easy for a society. They cause despair and frustration in proportion to the hopes they raise, and they spawn wickedness and stupidity to match the moral upsurge and intelligence that also emerge in such times. Times of deep social ferment force members of a society to examine the presuppositions upon which they have based their lives and the collective activities of the whole, causing people to question their deepest values, their most habitual responses, and the very reasons for their existence. In such a time do we live today, in a full-scale crisis of legitimacy for all social institutions. Sex role stereotypes, the gender caste system, the entire constellation I have called the sex role status quo are very much part and parcel of this ferment.

Social change is a difficult concept with which to come to grips. How much change in institutional structures, norms, values, and individual behavior needs to occur before we can say that there has really been a radical alteration in the status quo? Incremental, evolutionary change is always occurring in every society, no matter how static that society may appear on the surface. The total effect of such changes, however, may only amount to "adjustments" by which the most fundamental aspects of the status quo are buttressed. Such, for instance, was the basic impact of the New Deal *vis-à-vis* capitalism; changes necessitated by economic disaster served in the long run to give new life and vigor to the institution of private enterprise. Moreover, there is a very real question as to whether it is possible for social institutions to alter themselves radically in response to social strains or new social currents, or whether such change can only result from conflict between these institutions and forces outside the system. Will those who profit from the status quo willingly alter the situation in any way that might seriously undermine their own position, or must such changes be wrested from them by the "have nots"?

Most of this book has been devoted to documenting the existence of sex role stereotypes, examining the many ways by which they are reinforced and passed on through the generations, suggesting who profits from them, and delineating the individual as well as social costs of the sex role status quo. The future of our species depends in large measure on our collective ability in the next several decades to control population growth, prevent further ecological deterioration, and avoid war, especially a nuclear holocaust. To accomplish these in the context of modern technology, our age-old notions of masculinity and femininity must be fundamentally altered. Moreover, given the fact that our major social institutions reflect and support the sex role stereotypes and profit from their continuation, to the extent that such stereotypes significantly change our institutions will be altered in profound ways. In short, such changes, if they occur, will constitute a veritable "revolution." The questions for this final chapter thus concern those trends already existing in American society that may encourage such sex role changes. What are they? Who is involved in them? What kinds of changes are likely to produce what kinds of results?

Before attempting the difficult task of surveying the contemporary scene for indications of such trends, a crucial point that is all too frequently ignored in sociological writing and even activistic planning must be made. This is the need for utopian thinking. Change does not mean the same as progress; our society has too long obscured the difference, to its own detriment. When social institutions, norms, or values are altered, things do not become *ipso facto* better. First of all, what is defined as better or progress is a matter of values, of who is doing the defining. From the vantage point of one person's or group's values and/or interests, a given change may represent progress; to someone else it spells disaster. When we actively engage in efforts to bring about some sort of change in the status quo we should have in mind some idea of what we would define as progress, or a better state of affairs. In other words, it is not enough to reject the present. To guide the future we need a positive image of how it might look if our goals and values should be embodied. That is utopian thinking.

In the context of this book, understanding the damage created by our current sex role stereotypes constitutes an impetus to change the situation. Next we need to develop some alternatives: a utopia. This cannot consist merely of concrete suggestions like "equal pay for equal work" and more day-care centers, important as such things are. We need a vision of what it would mean to be a society not of feminine and masculine creatures, but comprised of humans. The truth of the matter is that we have no real notion of what it means to be human, divorced from notions of masculinity and femininity. Traditionally, human has largely meant masculine; all too often today we make the same error, and, for many, women's liberation becomes merely a question of how females can acquire those prerogatives traditionally allocated to males. I for one do not wish to trade the disadvantages of the feminine sex role simply to be burdened with those of the masculine role. Therefore, in reviewing recent trends it is important to search for an emerging definition of humanness and to try to envision a world in which we might want to live in the magical year 2000.

A Brief History Lesson

Before we can assess where we might be going, we must examine where we have been and are. In the preceding chapters historical changes that have occurred in recent decades and even centuries have been suggested in passing. These will be brought together here to develop a somewhat more systematic picture.

The secular changes brought about by the Industrial Revolution of the 19th century and the postindustrial "revolution" of the 20th have profoundly altered the way in which members of Western societies function in virtually every aspect of their social existence. Some significant changes even date back to the sharp increase in trade and urbanization in Northwestern Europe in the 17th century. Those most relevant for our purpose include: (1) changing demographic rates, (2) change in family structure and functioning, (3) alterations in the nature of productive work, (4) sharply increased production in the quantity of goods and services available to most members of society, and (5) the development of new forms of institutional organization. These are all highly interrelated phenomena; incremental changes in one tend to produce alterations in the others which, in turn, feed back in an almost perpetually accelerating progression.

Before about 1650 Europeans and the few "Americans" lived in extended family networks in primarily rural settings. The birth and death rates were very high; it was not uncommon for a woman to bear 10 or 15 children, of whom only a couple would survive to reach reproductive age themselves. Thus, the rate of growth of the total human population was incredibly slow. The population of the entire world in 1650 totaled only about a half a billion, of which only about 100 million inhabited Europe and North America. In the next three centuries the world population increased sixfold, while that of Europe and North America increased to more than eight times what it had been (Wrong, 1968, p. 13). This demographic "revolution" began primarily because better sanitation facilities and methods of food distribution resulted in a slow decline of the death rate, while the birth rate remained stable. Death rates dropped off even more sharply in the West with the advent of modern medicine in the first part of the century and in the so-called "undeveloped" countries after World War II. In Europe and the United States birth rates also finally began to decline, and during the Great Depression of the 1930s total population actually decreased in some Western nations.

Many demographers attribute the declining birth rate in the West to the combined effects of urbanization and industrialization. On the farm, children were an economic asset and cost very little to rear. After the passage of child-labor laws, the situation for urban dwellers was reversed: children earned nothing and cost a lot. In addition, parents began to understand that they could provide the resources for their children to become upwardly mobile, but only if they kept their families small. Members of urban industrialized societies ceased, by and large, to produce large numbers of children because they were provided with increasingly effective birth control methods, assured that most children would survive to adulthood, and offered the prospect of economically prosperous offspring. Families became as we know them today: small, mobile units free to follow economic opportunities from city to city, leaving kin behind in the process.

While families were shrinking and becoming geographically mobile, they were also losing most of their functions. In the eons before modern times, families functioned as a productive *unit* in which all but the very youngest were involved in activities needed to supply the goods and services upon which their lives depended. Training and "education" were part of life; children learned from older people—parents, kin, and older siblings—in the course of their everyday lives. The Industrial Revolution took production out of the family, moved it spatially, and later restricted the entry of children into the factory. Thus one's life work could no longer be learned within the bosom of the family. Moreover, the age at which it was learned was increasingly postponed. Together, childhood and adolescence were created as a long period of dependence without serious responsibility.

The nature of productive labor also changed with industrialization. Most people were henceforth restricted to a single, repetitive task, usually requiring little skill and, increasingly over time, little physical strength. Nothing in most jobs intrinsically required one gender rather than the other. A minority controlled the daily functioning of the work force in the ever more complex, immense, and powerful bureaucratic structures of technocratic society. Organizations came to "own" their employees, especially those at the top, moving them at will and often impinging on many aspects of their private lives. Economic institutions and bureaucracies developed their own paradigm of rationality based on a cost accounting ethos in which corporate profits and the machinelike efficiency necessary to produce them became the most important considerations, even long after individual entrepreneurs had ceased to own companies (Harrington, 1969, chap. 1; Roszak, 1969, chap. 1). For society as a whole this became translated into an overwhelming emphasis on a rising gross national product and a balanced budget.

"Rational" administration, coupled with science, has brought us to a stage of technological development that is truly astounding. It has created the weaponry to destroy ourselves, a glut of goods designed to be replaced every three years (to "keep the economy going"), foul air and water, and the marvelous potential to someday shape our lives to gain maximum personal fulfillment. Technology has opened up the future possibility and, to a considerable extent, the present reality of large quantities of leisure and a decent standard of living for all. Everyone need not be productive today, and producers need not spend 70 or more hours a week at their labor, as they did in the past. But the system that has done this has allowed a sizable minority to continue to exist in poverty. It has led many of us to lose our capacity to enjoy leisure. It has provided most of us with goods that obviate the necessity of hard work and increase the potential pleasure we can derive from our hobbies and pastimes, but it has ruined the land, air, and water we would want to use in doing so. It has frustrated, bored, and alienated many of those who staff its assembly lines and offices. In short, our species has created a radically new world for itself but has not yet learned how to use it to develop its human potentials; it is strangling us rather than being controlled by us.

While the very foundations of human existence have been altering in such radical ways, our sex role stereotypes, as we have had ample opportunity to note, remain pretty much the same as those extant eons ago. Females are still enjoined to devote their lives to families, shrunken and stripped of functions though they may be. They are not taught to develop the attributes that would enable them to function well in the economy, although those attributes are irrelevant to gender. Males are still enjoined to be rugged, aggressively competitive, and productive in a nation gagging on its affluence, a world threatened by nuclear holocaust, and a society ruled by all-powerful institutions that are no longer under identifiable human control. We are enjoined to do things with the bulk of our lives that no longer make any sense. Indeed, in some ways at least, the feminine role is ironically more "traditional" than tradition itself! To understand this we need to look more closely at the recent past, particularly the post World War II history of our society.

Demographers are hard pressed to explain the postwar "baby boom" of the late 1940s and 1950s in this, the most industrialized nation of the world, but it really isn't difficult to understand if we go back a bit in time. Beginning with the Seneca Falls Convention of 1848, or even earlier with Mary Wollstonecraft's *A Vindication of the Rights of Women* published in 1792, women's rights has become a public issue. The history of the first Woman's Rights movement is as frustrating to read about as it is glorious to contemplate (Flexner, 1968; O'Neill, 1969; Sinclair, 1965). The important fact for our purposes is that gradually this social movement spawned many young women who, especially after World War I, were anxious to create a place for themselves outside the home. During the closing years of the 19th century and first two decades of the 20th, educational institutions and many occupations and professions were opened to women for the first time, and the vote was finally gained. The cultural heroine of young women in the era between the two World Wars became the ambitious career woman, as demonstrated by the popular movies of this era. Even if most females continued to marry, have children, and stay home, models of females doing other things were evident and increasingly acceptable.

Women entered the job market in tremendous numbers and attained positions new to their gender during World War II when *man*power was short. It looked like a new era had finally arrived for females. The very small families characteristic of the depression years, coupled with new employment opportunities, seemed to herald a time when females could truly enter the mainstream of society. Then V-J Day arrived and the soldiers came home. Ultimately millions of women were fired from their jobs to be replaced by these veterans, even though many of them had earlier expressed a desire to continue working after the war (Trey, 1972). In the two years following the termination of hostilities, the number of females in the labor force declined by about two million. The marriage rate soared and so did the birth rate, as if to make up for lost time. But it did more than that. The middle-class family that had two children in the 1930s gave way a decade or so later to an ever-expanding number of families averaging almost four children.

With the help of a more advanced, less labor-intensive technology developed during the war, the economy had little need for female employees over and above males. Moreover, it did not take industry long to discover that prosperous families with females at home producing lots of children spelled marvelous profits. If the housewife was bored and frustrated in her suburban "cell," she would buy goods in those shiny new suburban shopping centers to relieve her frustrations (bad moods could always be changed with the acquisition of a new hat). Insecure females, isolated in their homes, could be counted on to try that new hair product or deodorant that promised a "new, more lovable you." Create a product, create a new female insecurity, and increase your profits. Children? You can't deny them the many material benefits technology has to offer. And so we get the feminine mystique which encourages females to stay home and have children—created by industry and Madison Avenue, nurtured by all the media, supported by "science" and believed by almost everyone: housewifery, motherhood, but, most of all, *consuming* is FULFILLMENT. Never before had these tasks been expected to alone fill the lives of most females; never before had they been so romanticized and glamorized. But then, never had they been so profitable, either.

The so-called "sexual revolution" that was also occurring in these years, far from liberating females, bound them more tightly to the mystique. Sure, women, like men, were freed to enjoy sex, and thank heaven for that. But mostly this simply meant that the housewife had to spend the money and effort to appear the glamorous mistress to her husband after spending ninety-some hours a week on household drudgery. "Respectable" women were freed to enjoy sex, but the price they paid was to add "sex object" to the list of their obligations to males.

What was happening to males during this period? The masculine mystique was little changed during any of the period under consideration. Perhaps males' dedication to work increased slightly, if for no other reason than to supply the funds for their burgeoning families' burgeoning consumption habits. Male executives were encouraged by the new human relations school of corporate management to develop some expressive skills in order to function better in bureaucratic settings, and these undoubtedly carried over to their private lives. Males were under increased pressure to perform well sexually in order to satisfy the newly liberated sexuality of their partners. However, crew-cutted and attired in grey suits, white shirts, and nondescript ties, tied to their corporate offices or an assembly line, males continued to be suppressed by age-old notions of masculinity based essentially on an agrarian existence.

By the late fifties and early sixties some things started happening that were to burgeon, in a very few years, into a veritable social upheaval. One of the first of these things was that the postwar brides, now with children mostly grown and realizing that they still had 35 years or so to live, began returning to the job market to help the family acquire all the "goodies" shown on TV. In a decade the working wife went from a statistical rarity to practically a majority. Likewise, these women have been returning to school in dramatically increasing numbers. But it was the children of this generation, the enormous generation of the baby boom now grown, who really began to foster potentially far-reaching social changes.

Decade of Upheaval

Significant numbers of the baby-boom children have taken two directions upon reaching adolescence that may possibly spell the beginning of a radically new type of society: males have rediscovered sensuality and emotional caring and expression, and both sexes have rediscovered what it means to have a social conscience. Both developed in part as direct reactions against the stifling existence these young people knew as children in affluent, middle-class homes, and in larger part as the logical expression of the point to which our society has come. For social scientists, the most appalling thing is that in the late fifties and early sixties the discipline apparently had no inkling of what was brewing; it expressed little more than smug satisfaction with the state of affairs that existed.

Given the isolated nuclear family and contemporary sex roles, parent-child relationships suffer from a variety of pressures tending to produce strain, as noted in the preceding chapter. First Elvis Presley and later acid rock and the Rolling Stones, marijuana, long hair on males—all of the symbols of the youth subculture—were designed to infuriate middle-class parents trapped in their own roles. If father and mother seek their vicarious thrills from junior's academic and economic successes and constantly apply pressure toward these goals, what better rebellion than "turning on and dropping out"? If father is a chemical engineer, how better can you reject him than by turning anti-intellectual, rejecting science and reading your stars? If mother wants young Jane to snag a prosperous WASP lawyer, the latter can say no by sleeping around and ending up living with a dropout, or better yet, a black man.

But mere rejection of parents cannot entirely explain the "youth phenomenon" now occurring in most industrial societies. The nature of the technocratic society in which this generation grew up was radically unlike that which existed in their parents' youth, and their parents' own behavior at least dimly reflected the changes that had occurred. Nurtured on a work ethic crucial to earlier stages of industrial development, the fathers continued to half-heartedly espouse productivity and economic success as the highest virtues. Yet increasingly the work week was shortened and the quantities of consumer goods available vastly increased, along with the pressures to consume, and the parents' lives and behaviors reflected these phenomena. They pampered their children, gave into their whims, supplied them with huge allowances, and gave them little if any real responsibility. Moreover, the postwar babies grew up watching television and receiving the message that to *consume* is the highest good; leisure is the most meaningful part of life; constant adventure is fun and available to all. The realities of postindustrial (capitalistic) society are such that the role of humans in productivity is less important than previously and consumption more so (for the sake of the GNP), and youth has learned that "message." Moreover, life, as depicted on the TV screen, is constant excitement and new experience, a far cry from the daily routine of middle-class existence. The children themselves never knew financial adversity, the most formative experience of their parents, who reached maturity during the depression. In addition to substantial allowances, these young people enjoyed considerable leisure, arising in large measure from virtual enforced absence from the labor market until well into their twenties. It is little wonder, then, that this generation is characterized by a mentality that says work is acceptable only if it is personally satisfying and challenging and holds consumption, leisure, and action as the highest values.

This mentality which, for want of a better term will be called a "consumption mentality," is very different from the older production-oriented one. The latter is usually associated with a kind of Puritanism (very evident today in such production-oriented societies as the U.S.S.R. and Communist China) that calls for a denial of both sensuality and emotional expression. Work is done because it must be done, and those who will not work at whatever job is available are morally culpable. A consumer orientation encourages hedonism; enjoyment of life becomes the highest value, and such pleasure is bound to be linked to sensuality and freer emotional expression, as it has long been for our primary consumers, females. It is equally bound to be divorced from the straitjacket of a rigid work schedule, not to mention the alienation of the assembly line. Work per se is not rejected, only the dullness of fixed schedules, routine or "irrelevant" tasks, and so forth. To be worth doing, work must be "meaningful" to the worker, and substantial numbers of youth are willing to live in poverty rather than work under circumstances not to their liking. To their own generation they are not morally culpable in refusing routine work.

This general shift in orientation became patently evident when first the beatniks and later the hippies exploded onto our TV screens.

Young, white males were shown rejecting serious study as promulgated in our educational institutions, as well as the straitjacket of formal jobs, not to mention careers. They were depicted as sensual, emotional, and free-spirited, given to enjoying sun, nature, and bright colors, drifting around the country and world "grooving" on some wild musical form, and escaping from rationality through a mystifying variety of drugs. Their parents' tentative steps toward the consumer mentality with martinis, barbiturates, high levels of material consumption, and long weekend parties in the country found a logical extension in their children with pot, LSD and full-time leisure. The straight male world was carried along to a limited degree, as bright colors replaced the grey flannel and white shirts, hair began to reach to the collar and sprout on the face, and many turned to marijuana on Saturday night. The first little crack in the masculine mystique was becoming evident.

If jewelry-bedecked, emotionally expressive male hippies represented a new kind of male, their female counterparts did no such thing with reference to the feminine sex role. Garbed in long peasant dresses, making their own bread, the "flower girls" were steeped in "femininity." Indeed, the entire phenomenon is one of reinforcing "feminine" values and extending them to males. They may have been more sexually liberated than their mothers or straight sisters, but in practice for most that merely meant that the legalities were dispensed with, not monogamous (if serial and somewhat short-lived) relationships, and not their relative caste position.

While many male youths were becoming emotionally and physically free of a number of the arbitrary restrictions under which their fathers labored, young people of both sexes were also becoming more socially conscious. The adults of the fifties had centered their entire existence on the family and its status and security—on "togetherness." Smugly convinced that the United States was then the "best of all possible worlds," white adults during the Eisenhower years virtually ignored social issues, until Martin Luther King began forcing the nation to open its eyes. The Civil Rights movement of the early sixties gave to many white middle-class youth of both genders a sense of excitement and purpose for the first time in their routinized, organized, and overplanned lives. Unlike their parents, who had experienced the Great Depression, many postwar youths have known nothing but physical security and comfort since infancy. Thus they were psychologically equipped to temporarily or even permanently reject material comfort in the name of "social injustice." Indeed, it may be precisely because of boredom induced by a lack of challenge that they were so willing to take up a social cause. Their parents' most meaningful experiences were depression and war. They had to fight to acquire material goods, and to them "heaven" was withdrawing into the comforts of a financially secure family life. To the most energetic of their offspring there seemed to be no challenge in taking up where their parents had left off; in continuing to chase economic success, material comfort, and security. Opulence bred its own antithesis.

The Civil Rights movement was the impetus for this social conscience, but it took Vietnam to produce a relatively widespread involvement, at least among middle-class college youth. It was at this juncture that the developing social conscience of the generation linked up with its developing sensuality and emotional expressiveness. Males openly proclaimed in large numbers that war, far from being a test of one's masculinity, was (in this case) immoral; that the heretofore "feminine" values of peace, love, and sensual enjoyment were more important. Most were probably not pacifists opposed to all wars; they were opposed to what they perceived to be an aggressive war based on some antiquated notion of honor. Their view of war began to coincide with what has long been the characteristic female response, as discussed in Chapter 4. Here again their parents' generation tentatively followed suit, until the majority of the population began to disown the war. Another crack in the masculine mystique seemed to have appeared, although the history of the Nixon years may show this to have been a temporary phenomenon.

The generation was now "tuned in" to social issues, and it did not take long for their analysis of the corporate role in war, racism, and poverty to spread to the environmental rape that was rapidly destroying our national resources. Ecology became an issue as youths, followed somewhat by their parents, questioned the right of corporations to pursue profits at the expense of our national environmental heritage. The entire notion of continued productivity for its own

sake, the ever-expanding GNP, became suspect as another fundamental aspect of the masculine stereotype came under fire.

Closely related to ecological questions were those pertaining to
population growth. It became clear that 200 million Americans consuming resources at ten times the rate of peoples in underdeveloped
lands was, if not too many people, at least enough. Serious questions
were raised about the morality of having more children than the two
who would replace the parents, regardless of how well the parents
could "afford" children. The value of motherhood was questioned as
people began wondering if it is wise to advocate that all females
must engage in it—and often. A chip was chiseled out of the feminine stereotype.

Young females had been involved in these various social movements from the beginning. However, as pointed out in Chapter 4,
they were relegated to the boring tasks, perceived as sexual objects,
and refused entry into the decision-making ranks. The human rights
for which the multitude of different groups were ostensibly fighting
were obviously to be equal rights and freedom for all males only.
And so in the mid sixties a handful of activist women skilled in
organizational techniques withdrew to their own enclaves to discuss
their status and role as females. They began to realize that while they
were fighting male death in Southeast Asia, no one was fighting the
greater number of female deaths resulting from bungled illegal abortions; while they were clamoring for better jobs for blacks, females
were receiving less pay than white *or* black males. Simultaneously, a
group of older career women was reaching essentially similar conclusions about the relative position of women in the economy and in
society. By 1972 these two streams had coalesced into a full-fledged
social movement with hundreds of groups around the nation and
rapidly increasing numbers of adherents. In early 1972, when the initial edition of *MS.,* the first major national women's liberation magazine, appeared, all 300,000 copies were sold off the newsstands in
eight days. The social movement that had died after passage of
women's suffrage, leaving most of the crucial issues unsettled, was
given new life by the suffragists' granddaughters and was quickly
joined by females of all ages, marital statuses and, to a lesser degree,
social classes and racial and ethnic groups.

The New Feminism

It is impossible to make truly accurate generalizations about any social movement. With that in mind, I will nonetheless proceed to attempt to generalize about the new feminism. Women's liberation is today a full-blown social movement, many if not most of whose adherents are oriented to nothing less than changing the basic values, as well as the norms of this society. While involved in attempts to bring about a wide variety of specific legal and institutional changes, this movement goes further, to question some of the core values of our society and its definition of appropriate behavior for both genders. Rather extensive normative changes can occur without basic value alterations in a society; in fact, they can serve to bolster the most fundamental aspects of the status quo. However, the opposite is not possible; value changes will, sooner or later, necessarily entail normative ones. Another way of looking at the overall goals of the movement was expressed by Constantina Safilios-Rothschild in these terms:

> Liberation . . . means freedom from stereotypic sex-linked values and beliefs restricting the range of socially acceptable options for men and women because some options are considered to be inappropriate for one or the other sex. Liberated men and women living in a liberated society have equal access to the range of options and may make any choice according to their particular inclinations, talents, wishes, and idiosyncratic preferences. . . . A major goal . . . of emancipation was to give women as many privileges as men, while the major goal of liberation is the elimination of social, cultural and psychological barriers in the way of *both men and women's* realization and, therefore, benefit both men and women (1971–72, p. 71).

In his theory of collective behavior, Neil Smelser (1962, p. 124) delineates a number of stages, which, if followed sequentially, will give rise to a value-oriented belief system as the basis of a value-oriented social movement. The first of these pertains to the existence of a social strain, which, as we have seen, clearly emerges from both sex roles. In stage 2 this strain gives rise to anxiety. It is clear, again, that both genders manifest anxiety over their respective sex roles in contemporary society. Stage 3 consists of a "generalized belief that agents are responsible for [the] anxiety-producing state of affairs." It is here that the genders part ways. Today it is primarily females involved in some way with women's liberation who attribute their sex role problems to specific agents, namely, male-dominated institutions and/or males in general ("male chauvinism"). The next two stages consist of a "generalized sense of social disharmony [and] failure of institutional life," and a "generalized belief in [the] degeneration of values." Such beliefs characterize the thinking of most females involved in the movement, who view both the norms and the values of the society as wrongly reflecting masculine interests and supporting patriarchy to their own detriment and that of society at large. Stages 6 and 7 stress the belief in the possibility of regenerating values and norms, in short, some degree of optimism in the possibility of meaningful social change. The last two stages involve the conviction that value changes will in fact "destroy, remove, damage or restrict the responsible agents," and a new and better society will be forthcoming.

Smelser goes on to explain that value-oriented social movements, as opposed to social movements merely directed to altering norms, "arise when alternative means for reconstituting the social situation are perceived as unavailable." Smelser gives as examples of this the following:

> (a) The aggrieved group . . . does not possess facilities whereby they may reconstitute the social situation; such a group ranks low on wealth, power, prestige, or access to means of communication. (b) The aggrieved group is prevented from expressing hostility that will punish some person or group considered responsible for the disturbing state of affairs. (c) The aggrieved group cannot modify the normative structure, or cannot influence those who have the power to do so (1962, p. 325).

As we have seen, females rank as a lower caste, deprived of wealth, power, and prestige. They are trained psychologically so that direct expression of hostility toward males is virtually impossible. Excluded from the power structure of all major institutions, their opportunities to change the normative structure of the society are very limited. In short, they are prime candidates for a value-oriented movement.

The social movement known as women's liberation consists of a wide diversity of groups which, for the purpose of simplicity and clarity, can be roughly divided into two types. Some, like the National Organization for Women (NOW), Women's Equity Action League (WEAL), the national and local Women's Political Caucuses, Welfare Rights groups, and the women's caucuses of a variety of professional associations are oriented primarily to normative changes or "bread and butter" issues. They are the rough counterparts of the National Association for the Advancement of Colored People and the Southern Christian Leadership Conference. These task-oriented groups are generally patterned on the usual structure of voluntary organizations in our society, with elected officers, dues, newsletters, and often constitutions. They address themselves to legal changes, such as the Equal Rights Amendment and, earlier, abortion repeal legislation. Some engage in litigation, such as suits against corporations for failure to comply with the Civil Rights Act. Most propose new programs such as the creation of low-cost day-care centers or the revision of school texts and curricula. Generally, these organizations consist of a relatively large number of usually white, middle-class females. The bulk of the members are employed outside the home, many as "career women." Most allow male membership.

A much larger number of usually nameless women's liberation groups or "cells" are quite different in nature, however. They often number little more than a handful of females at any one time (usually 10 to 15), and they bar male membership or even presence. They lack formal structure or formalized national ties, although they are in communication with one another. Characteristically, they have a constantly shifting "membership." With some frequency they come into being and break up, only to form again with somewhat different people. Such groups are primarily composed of young females, often college students or dropouts who are generally politically radical and who come together first and foremost to "rap" and "raise consciousness." Their concern is less with normative changes (which they do, however, usually actively support) than with "head" changes, namely, alterations in the value premises upon which our sex role stereotypes and patriarchal institutions are based, as well as our day-to-day behavior. They range from the overly publicized, militant, man-hating groups to the far more prevalent type consisting of many who are trying to live with a male and yet break out of the old stereotypes they have internalized. Some groups have quotas establishing the proportion of "members" who can be living with a male at any given time; some are lesbian groups; some are communes.

Let us take a somewhat closer look at how many of these rap-type groups function, since they generally attempt to put into practice the kinds of radical changes they propose for society at large. Such groups function primarily for what Barbara Polk (1972, p. 322 ff.) has termed "personal liberation/consciousness raising" purposes. The "members" attempt, by rapping, to come to a more complete understanding of what the current sex role status quo (male chauvinism) has done to their own personal thinking and behavior, in which they ultimately hope to make fundamental changes. In short, these groups serve a resocializing function. However, Polk notes that "The purpose of these groups is not therapy; it is to develop both an analysis of the society and an appropriate politics based on the experience of being female—the personal becomes the political" (pp. 323–24). For this reason, at the local level many of the more formal organizations have also created rap sessions, for their new members especially. Because of the ingrained psychological aspects of "femininity," most participants feel that they cannot fully and adequately express themselves in the presence of males; they have internalized passivity and submissiveness toward the opposite sex too strongly to work through these problems in their presence. Thus for most groups the exclusion of males is not based on manhating but on practical necessity if they are to accomplish what they have set out to do.

To the extent that many females are more or less passive, afraid to express their opinions, and so forth, a variety of techniques have been developed to overcome these traits. These groups define traditional organizational structure as a masculine, middle-class phenomenon in which a small number of articulate members compete for dominance over a larger number of passive followers. Having rejected this model, they conspicuously avoid creating formal structures. There are no presidents or chairpersons. Tasks are frequently allocated by lottery, thus rotating among all members. Each must take her turn at the dull typing and stamp licking, as well as at public speaking. In addition, many have instituted some form of system to ensure broad participation (Polk, 1972, p. 327). In the disk system, each member receives a limited number of disks upon arrival at the meeting. Each time she speaks she spends a disk; when she runs out she may no longer speak. This system encourages all members to develop confidence and poise in speaking to a group, while discouraging dominance by a few. In these ways some feminists are attempting on a small scale to develop new modes of organization and interaction that they feel will put their beliefs into practice. However, it is questionable whether such organizational looseness can be effective in striving for concrete, normative changes. It is likely that feminist groups will increasingly combine elements from both wings of the movement, utilizing traditional forms to organize for concrete goals and maintaining the nonstructured form for ongoing consciousness raising.

The future of the new feminist movement, like that of all social movements, is unclear. There is the ever-present danger that, like the earlier Woman's Rights movement, it will succeed in extracting certain concessions (more and better jobs for equal pay, more and better child care centers, and abortion law repeal) at the expense of truly fundamental alterations in the sex role status quo. In short, there is the danger that feminists will be "bought off" with what amount to token changes, as they were when women's suffrage was passed. Avoiding this minimally entails emphasizing the value-oriented aspects of the movement as the ultimate goal and viewing the normative or utilitarian goals as mere beginning steps.

The real question, and the one for which there is no pat answer, pertains to how the movement might go about altering the value premises underlying the sex role stereotypes. Females are increasingly in a position to extract some normative changes by use of traditional conflict strategies and tactics. As more come to understand their caste position, they can utilize the ballot box to extract legal changes and the courtroom to follow them up. The fact that one third of the delegates to the 1972 Democratic National Convention, as well as a number of important chairpersons and the runner-up vice-presidential nominee, were female is a sign that women are becoming a political force to be reckoned with. As they continue to increase as a proportion of the labor market, especially if they continue to be concentrated in a relatively small number of occupations, they can use the labor strike as a tool. As they have more disposable income of their own, they can use the economic boycott. They can refuse to buy products whose advertisements degrade and insult their gender or to patronize stores that discriminate against females in hiring, promotions, salaries, or the granting of credit.

With the exception of a few male spin-off groups, comprised mostly of mates of active feminists, men have yet to become seriously involved in any *collective* way with the issues inherent in the sociology of sex roles. Many individual males are quite ready to advocate some or many of the goals of feminism (although not necessarily of "male liberation"), sensing that their future prospects will be far happier if a few changes are made. Increasingly, husbands can see that bored, frustrated wives trapped at home lead to poor marital relations and severe emotional burdens. They can see that their collective disposable income would be much increased if wives worked and received equal pay for their labors. Many support child-care centers so their wives can go to work. Some even perceive the fact that a wife with a decent-paying career can relieve them of the necessity of engaging in highly paid occupations which they don't like rather than pursuing their own "thing," regardless of income. A few years ago a couple comprised of two professionals, each of whom alone earned enough to support the family, found themselves in such a situation. The male had a number of job offers but really wanted to take a year off from work (after 30-odd years of either being a student, working, or both) to catch up on reading, communicate with his young son, and so forth. That, in fact, is how he spent the year, but it took him several months merely to overcome anxiety about the fact that he, a male, was not gainfully employed.

Thus, on the basis of personal interest (and maybe a twinge of conscience), increasing numbers of males at least pay lip service to many of the concrete demands made by feminists. However, these same men, when acting as corporate employees or union members instead of thinking as husbands, maintain the kind of mental set and priorities that result in *de facto* discrimination against women. They are frequently unwilling to accept truly *equal* responsibility for and involvement in housekeeping and child rearing; without this, the result is a double burden for women, who must carry the full-time household role on top of their full-time jobs. The habits of a lifetime continue to encourage these would-be supporters of feminism to attempt to dominate the females with whom they come in contact. Feminists may find males useful allies in some concrete endeavors, but until the latter begin to collectively reexamine their own masculine behavior patterns and value premises and perceive the *long-term* advantages to be gained by changing them, that alliance will be fragile at best. The *short-term* advantages to males in maintaining the most fundamental aspects of the sex role status quo are simply too great to expect most men to knowingly and willingly undermine them. Most will gladly trade the necessity of opening the car door for females for the knowledge that they need not compete with them for their jobs.

The question of how fundamental *value* changes can be wrought has still not been answered. This process, which will probably involve at least a generation or more, may result from the confluence of a wide variety of changes, many of which are ostensibly based on other issues. Earlier in the chapter we saw that the various social movements of the past decade contributed to chipping away some of the traditional stereotypes of masculinity and femininity and the values implicit in them. You simply cannot clamor for zero population growth and still define the highest mission of females primarily in terms of motherhood, or fail to provide viable alternatives for females. Nor can you demonstrate for peace and not eventually come to reject the more aggressive and even violent aspects of the masculine stereotype.

To the extent that the concrete, utilitarian demands of feminism are met, there is a fair probability that values will also alter to some extent. For instance, if females are the equal of males in the economy, the idea that masculinity is mainly expressed through the function of provider will probably decrease. If, given increased opportunities for rewarding careers, females take work outside the home seriously as a major life commitment, then there is a good chance that many will simply refuse to carry the lion's share of responsibility also for the full-time job of housekeeping and child raising, and thus they will come to question the overwhelming emphasis on being a good homemaker. If females function outside the home, in school, office, politics, and so forth, as the equal of males, they are less apt to defer to male opinion just because it is male and are more apt to question the feminine "virtue" of passivity *vis-à-vis* males. In short, because of normative changes people may come to behave in ways that belie the stereotypes, and there is a good chance that their attitudes will follow suit.

The social-psychological theory of cognitive dissonance (Festinger, 1957) maintains that in an attempt to avoid that uncomfortable psychological state known as dissonance, once we have made some sort of commitment to a course of action we will readjust our thinking to support it. However, the other implication of this theory is that those who have had long-standing commitments to established patterns will avoid considering changes that would create dissonance. Thus, for instance, the middle-aged housewife is hardly in a position to redefine the role of females when in so doing she risks seeing her life as in some manner a waste or failure.

The crucial changes, however, will come about (if, indeed, they do) because we rear a new generation with different values; because the cracks that appeared in the sixties become the crevices of the eighties. If mother has a commitment (not necessarily a "job") to the world beyond the home, children of both genders will no longer be taught that "woman's place is in the home" and that the greatest virtue a female can have is to stay there. If mother earns as much as father or more, children will learn that earning and providing are irrelevant to gender. If we have male kindergarten teachers, homemakers, and secretaries and female astronauts, plumbers, and corporate executives, children will learn that all manners of life are open to all who are suited by inclination and aptitude. If father cooks dinner regularly and transports the children to the dentist (because mother's outside commitments are less flexible than father's), the message will be clear: housework and child rearing are everyone's responsibility. If parents disavow an aggressive war fought for "honor" and corporations that pollute for the sake of an expanding

GNP, children will learn that, regardless of gender, production without social conscience or purpose and fighting for reasons other than defense are wrong. If boys as well as girls get dolls to play with, if both are given Erector sets and science kits and neither receive toy weapons, if everyone is encouraged to develop their bodies for pleasure and to keep healthy, children will learn radically new notions about "appropriate" behavior.

Children learn from the *actions* of their parents and other adults with whom they come into contact. What we do with great effort and psychological cost to overcome sex role stereotypes will become our children's habitual responses. Changes in our behavior today will create new values in our children which, in turn, can be expected to lead to further changes in norms and institutions. A male social worker, married to a physician, recounted a discussion he overheard between his preschool-aged son and seven-year-old daughter. They were discussing what they wanted to be when they grew up. The daughter proclaimed that she was going to be a "doctor, like mommy." The son thoughtfully stated that he supposed that he, like daddy, would go into social work. It never occurred to either child that both parents were engaged in occupations more or less extraordinary to their gender in contemporary America. As these children reach maturity, the chances are that this will not be so unusual.

It is not easy for parents to encourage attitudes and behaviors in their offspring that essentially make the latter "social deviants" among their peers and in their schools. In fact, the pressures on children outside the home may all but cancel many lessons being conveyed by parents. In most neighborhoods today the boy with his doll or the girl who demands of the boys the opportunity to play the doctor, not always the nurse, will either spend many lonely years as an outsider or change to conform to traditional patterns. There is undoubtedly some critical proportion that must be reached before such children can find enough others reared the same way to reinforce the messages being taught by parents who would radically change sex role stereotypes. Without that proportion of peers, such children are asked to pay a substantial personal price. There is no assurance that such a critical level will be reached in most places, and the existence of such antifeminist groups as the "Pussycats," cutely proclaiming that "the lambchop is mightier than the karate chop," bears that out. There are, after all, very large segments of our population to whom any social change appears threatening, and changing sex roles may appear more dangerous to them than most other phenomena. However, the number of young females in the childbearing years, and even some of their mates, who espouse an ideology based on change in both sex roles is rapidly increasing.

It should be clear that the costs of *conformity* to both sex role stereotypes are terribly high for individuals and for society at large. Nonconformity is never easy, and the costs entailed in it are only too obvious to all who have ever broken relatively important social mores. The problems arising from conformity are far less obvious; indeed, they are usually not perceived as such by most members of society. Moreover, particularly in the case of the feminine role, recent changes and suggestions for change are very threatening to substantial numbers of people of both sexes. The threat to males is obvious; change entails a loss of many concrete prerogatives and an automatic ego haven, namely, their designation as intrinsically "superior" to half the human species. The threat to females is less obvious. First, women who conform need not seriously question the manner in which they have spent their own lives or those of their loved ones. Although a woman may be unhappy due to the pressures of her sex role, she also basks in an illusive kind of security. She need never explore the limits of her abilities, and in so doing risk failure; she need never live under personal or social pressure to fully exert herself in any endeavor; she need never, in the final analysis, take the full and terrifying responsibility for her own personal destiny. That she receives none of the immense personal satisfactions of standing as a self-fulfilled, independent adult may be, for many, unnoticed, or at least of little importance. In short, to ask people who have been trained to be dependent and of whom little has been expected to make the real effort to be independent and competent is to ask a lot; to ask this when it also entails the obvious costs of nonconformity seems almost ridiculous. Yet the fact of the matter is that increasing numbers of females are demanding precisely this of themselves.

Social Institutions and Changing Sex Roles: A Glimpse at Utopia

What might some of our most fundamental social institutions look like in the year 2000 *if* significant changes occur in the sex role status quo? To the extent that males and females are truly released from their stereotyped roles, the family, economic, and political institutions, at the least, will very likely be radically altered in the process. In turn, such institutional changes would feed back and further reinforce the changes in our sex role definitions.

The Family

The most basic social institution is usually considered to be the family. Already a wider diversity of living arrangements is being tried than was true a decade ago. There are a larger number of one-parent families due to the rising divorce rate and an increasing willingness on the part of unwed mothers to keep their children, questioning the sexual double standard that labels them immoral and their offspring illegitimate. Communal living arrangements, ranging from the "back to nature" rural communes of the counterculture to small urban communes consisting of a few usually young, often professional families, are proliferating. Even within the nuclear family, many are attempting to radically alter the old presuppositions and create what Nena and George O'Neill (1972) have termed "open marriages." Increasing numbers of young people are choosing not to have children, and many are no longer bothering to legalize their sexual relationships, either. The minority now experimenting with a variety of new forms of living together can be expected to grow into a large number by the year 2000, when living arrangements may reflect the personal needs of those involved more than the social and legal prescriptions surrounding the contemporary nuclear family.

Young people today are increasingly aware of the necessity to restrict the number of children they have to two or fewer. Moreover, as females increasingly take life outside the home more seriously, they will be further encouraged to have few or no children. Already during the past couple of years our national birth rate has plummeted to a record low level, below even that of the depression of the thirties. In the last chapter the argument was made that the kind of "hothouse" attention that almost necessarily becomes focused on children in small families can result in disaster for both parents and children. Many solutions to the dilemma of how to raise children in small families are possible. The society could encourage a small number of couples to have large families, make that their "livelihood," and encourage everyone else to have none. That is an unlikely solution, however, and one that would deprive most people of the very real rewards entailed in child rearing.

More promising are various communal arrangements consisting of a number of adults, married and single, with and without children, living as an extended family based on choice rather than "blood." This is already occurring, but the practice cannot become widespread until architectural forms are developed to accommodate such arrangements. Residential architecture in the present and recent past has overwhelmingly reinforced the isolated nuclear family structure with relatively small, single-family dwellings and apartments designed for a series of separate families. Each unit is fully equipped for independent functioning, with great expenditure of resources and to the substantial profit of industry.

The advantages of communal living are potentially enormous if sufficient space and privacy can be provided. Those without children can benefit by partaking in the experiences of child rearing without contributing further to the population problem, and those with children can benefit by sharing the burdens of child rearing. The children benefit from daily contact with both other children and a variety of adults. The burdens and expenses of housekeeping can be lightened for everyone. As a society, we would benefit by decreasing the rapid expenditure of our resources; only one of each appliance would be needed, instead of one per family if each family were living separately. Presumably, all tasks pertaining to home and children would be assigned or rotated without regard to gender, thus releasing all to function more readily in the world outside the home. Finally, the kind of ingrown relationship that springs up between mates and serves to stifle both parties can more readily be avoided. Everyone can be more free to pursue his or her own interests without worrying about a mate's "sacrifices." Dick is less apt to demand that Jane be home for dinner every night if Alice and Ted and Bob and Mary also eat with him; Jane is less apt to get angry that Dick is too tired to listen to her or to go to a movie or a party if someone else is readily available.

Another mechanism by which families with a small number of children can overcome their shortcomings is through inexpensive, well-run child-care centers. To the extent that they are adequately funded and staffed with members of both sexes who are emotionally stable, competent people who enjoy their work, such centers have tremendous advantages over the home. The child has better recreational and educational facilities, more playmates, and probably as much real attention from adults. Since it is not a burden to a harried mother, the child will not find itself cast in the role of the most available recipient of her frustrations. Infant and child centers need not turn out assembly-line children who think and act alike, although they might if such centers continue to be funded at the abysmal level characteristic of most social services. There is nothing *inherent* in such centers, however, that must result in this. The children of Israeli kibbutzim are not drab, maladjusted, totally conformist, or emotionally disturbed, as visualized by many Americans contemplating collectivized child rearing for anyone other than the poor. Indeed, children raised in such settings are probably more socially adept and adjusted and less egocentric than those brought up in an isolated nuclear family (Bettleheim, 1962). In such centers, child rearing would no longer be learned by the young as a "feminine" function (not to mention the primary one), and there is the obvious freedom to engage in other activities that these centers provide for the parents. Perhaps the greatest benefit, however, arises from the fact that parents and children, being less of a burden to one another, would probably relate better during the time they did spend together.

Thus we can anticipate that in 2000 A.D. families will be small, and a greater number of them will live communally, so that adults of both sexes will be freed to pursue their own interests. In the utopia that may develop if sex role stereotypes disappear, most children will be raised in a collectivized setting of one variety or another. It is also likely that fewer people will actually marry in legal terms. As people forego the assumption that relationships will last " 'till death do us part"; as many opt not to have children; as females become economically independent of males; and as the sexual double standard crumbles, there will be less and less reason to become involved in the legal "hassles" that surround marriage and, ultimately, divorce for so many. Men and women will increasingly come together as independent human beings who truly love and respect one another's individuality, form close relationships, live together, share together. This relationship will last until one or the other changes or moves geographically and they find it to be no longer tenable.

Such relationships, which are already relatively widespread among the young, tend to be more "open" than marriage. Each feels more free to pursue independently her or his own interests, to spend time with others of both genders, to share equally in the housekeeping tasks. In short, each is free to grow and change and explore potentials. Legalizing the union, however, as the O'Neills point out (1972, pp. 139–40), often produces profound changes as both become psychologically bound by traditional notions of matrimony (the "closed" marriage). Such notions include a more strict division of labor by gender and the presentation of a "couple front," in which each is more or less bound to be with the other and share all activities and relationships. An open *marriage* is prescribed by these authors as the solution to the stagnation and ultimate deterioration of such relationships. Increasingly, people can be expected to question the need to legalize it at all.

If the outward *form* of the contemporary family is valued as intrinsically sacred, then the kinds of changes discussed above will, by and large, be repugnant. However, if the *substance* of family living is considered more important, such changes should be greeted with cautious optimism. In postindustrial societies, the fundamental function left to the family is the provision of warm, open, close, primary relationships. Secondarily, the family is supposed to provide a modicum of security. Taken together, these functions should enable the family to serve as a springboard from which individuals can develop their own personal potentials and interests to their fullest. The isolated nuclear family structure increasingly fails to fulfill these functions. It seems to me that any hope for their fulfillment must reside in the emergence of a variety of new forms, offering more choice to people to suit their changing personal needs at various points in their life cycles.

The Economy

The logical question that arises at this point is: If we free everyone from full-time housework, how is the economy going to absorb all of the adults in our society? The answer is that it will not. Moreover, our definitions of work, occupation, and leisure will have to change quite substantially. It is a commonplace today to predict that technological changes will, within the next several decades, restrict the number of jobs in the economy. Indeed, the facts that we forcibly retire most people at age 65 and keep young people out of the labor force and in educational institutions (where they learn little if anything directly pertaining to their future work) until well into their twenties indicate that this trend is well underway. So too do the shortened work week and the increasing amount of holiday and vacation time being provided.

In the year 2000 many people may spend their time "unemployed" in the sense that they will not be in the labor force because it will have no jobs for them. However, if sex role stereotypes have disappeared, there would be no reason why it should be females who absent themselves from the labor market more frequently than males. Both will be equally free not to work. There are also a variety of arrangements by which more people could be employed in a given number of jobs. For instance, a male could work mornings, his mate or friend afternoons; or she could work January through May, he the other six months; or two or a group of people could work six months together while another couple or group were off, and not be part of the labor force the remainder of the year when the second crew was. Such arrangements would clearly require the cooperation of industry to hire and train two or more people to do essentially one job. This would not be the most profitable course, but, as shall be argued shortly, if sex role stereotypes have really changed, other considerations may enter corporate policy decision making.

Whether or not the members of our society approve, we will eventually have to support people at a decent standard of living who are either not part or are only intermittently part of the labor force. Society will also have to "create" jobs, which, given pressing social needs, should not be too difficult. Well-staffed child-care centers will require relatively large numbers of people to run them; school classes could be cut to an educatable 10 to 15 students; jobs could be created involving reading to the blind, transporting the disabled, and providing similar services. In short, the affluence created by cybernetics could be used in the service sector of the economy to help people, thus employing in meaningful ways large numbers of both females and males. To cope with the economy of the future, however, involves a willingness on the part of members of our society and its leaders to relinquish some of our most cherished notions about rewarding productivity and punishing those who are not employed. Similarly, it will involve a willingness to radically increase government spending to finance new types of jobs which will yield no one individual or group a profit in strictly economic terms. Such changes almost presuppose the demise of some aspects of the masculine mystique.

There exists, however, a more profound question: Just what do work and productivity mean? Today we tend to define these in terms of having a paid job: you do some work, have an occupation, and in return receive income and some degree of social recognition and prestige. The person who is doing volunteer work at a hospital today is not "working"; he or she does not have this activity as an occupation. The same is true of the individual who sews at home for family members or makes a cabinet for the house.

It can be assumed that, given our level of intellect as a species, humans are somehow impelled to try to express themselves creatively by making an impact, however small it may be, on their world. Our mental health probably requires some sort of challenge which demands a physical and/or mental expression of our abilities. If society fails to provide such challenges, it risks creating a vast number of alcoholics, drug addicts, mentally ill, and so on, due largely to boredom. Technological society poses relatively few challenges for many people, and it is not difficult to discern the effects of this shortage.

As more people spend less time on jobs, there is an increasing likelihood that this problem will increase. This is because, the multi-billion-dollar entertainment and leisure industries notwithstanding, Americans have not learned how to use large amounts of leisure in noncompulsive, personally satisfying ways. Our culture encourages us to do only those few things we do well. We have all dropped pastimes which gave us great joy but which we nonetheless did poorly.

In adjusting to the future, the concepts of occupation, work, and leisure must essentially disappear. Most humans will have to learn to spend most of their time doing that which they enjoy (and, of course, first they must discover what that might be), regardless of whether or not it is rewarded monetarily; income will no longer be an indicator of the value of an activity. When we are all occupied less, we will need to redefine the bases upon which we distribute scarce and valued resources such as prestige and income. Humans of both genders will engage in activities that are meaningful and challenging to them, but they may or may not be engaged in occupations. They will spend some or much of their time actively exploring and expressing their potentials and, in the process, growing, changing, and developing as humans. But will this be "work" or "leisure"?

There is another way in which the economic complexion of our society may change if sex role stereotypes disappear. Assuming that as females enter the decision-making ranks of corporations they do not become engulfed in the essentially masculine emphasis on productivity for its own sake (and that males retreat from this orientation), there is the possibility that the kinds of policies characteristic of our contemporary economic institutions may change. Goods may be built to last rather than to wear out and require replacement; ecological issues may become more central to policy decisions, not just advertisements. In short, industry may become more humane and socially oriented, as it already proclaims it is, and considerations other than spiraling profits based on spiraling production may come to play a major role. If that comes to pass, efficiency may not be the only concept determining work schedules and the deployment of our human resources.

Political Institutions

As sex roles change, females should take their place as leaders in the various political units of society. Again the assumption is made that in doing so they will not become completely "masculine" and that males will have lost some of their stereotyped attributes, while taking on some aspects of the "feminine" personality. If this is the case, wars for honor and aggressive purposes will decrease, and decision making in the context of saving face will no longer be salient to our national heritage.

In the process of these changes, a greater proportion of our national resources will be available for government to steer into human development rather than arms development. Schools, social services, hospitals, day-care centers for the very young and very old, housing, and public transportation are likely candidates for the lion's share of expenditures. In all likelihood the firearms which many American males cling to as an expression of their virility will be stringently controlled, if not altogether outlawed. And, perhaps most generally, politicans will begin to seek power not as a goal in itself but as a means to accomplish social goals.

To Be Human

The last sections of this chapter have focused on females taking on previously male functions and vice versa, as females enter the mainstream of life outside the home and males learn to partake more fully of both the dull tasks of housekeeping and the potentially rewarding and enriching duties of child rearing. Changing sex roles mean males becoming more sensual and emotional as females become more rational and psychologically and intellectually confident and competent. Evolving into a society of humans undoubtedly entails the breakdown of the traditional division of labor and personality by gender, as the choices open to all are expanded. The term "unisex" is often used to convey this phenomenon; depending on the author, this possibility is greeted with glee or dismay. I feel that progress in achieving a better society will only be made when and if *all* ascribed characteristics, including gender, are irrelevant to the way in which people spend their lives, the manner in which they are taught to view themselves and others, and the kinds of emotional and intellectual responses that are deemed appropriate.

A mere swapping of sex role traits, however, is not enough in our world today. Are we any better off in the long run, individually or collectively, if females begin to fight for glory; if they learn to dedicate their lives to productivity for its own sake and to compete for power, dominance, and status at the cost of all else? For that matter, is monetary payment for housekeeping chores more to be desired than questioning the values that place so much emphasis on money in the first place? Would it be any improvement if males, in the process of rediscovering their expressive faculties, surrendered their willingness and ability to be analytical on occasion? Does it help if they learn to be so vain about their appearance that they spend billions on it; if they ignore completely the joys that can come from creative production, embrace passivity, and forsake all competition, even that which spurs humans to their finest endeavors?

In short, we lack a full-blown definition of "humanness" divorced from masculinity and femininity. At best we have a definition that allows any and all to choose to manifest the traits heretofore reserved for only half. But merely allowing males to get into the costly "bag" females have long been in, and vice versa, is no solution. We must also unlearn some traits almost completely, while tempering others. It is the task of the future to come to grips with this problem; to develop a viable definition of humanness that will enable us to live in personally and collectively rewarding ways in postindustrial society. It is the task of all of us to decide whether our society is to be comprised of people who are masculine/feminine or human.

References

Bettleheim, Bruno. "Does Communal Education Work? The Case of the Kibbutz." *Commentary* 33 (February 1962): 117–25.

Festinger, Leon. *A Theory of Cognitive Dissonance*. New York: Row Peterson, 1957.

Flexner, Eleanor. *Century of Struggle: The Woman's Rights Movement in the United States.* New York: Atheneum Publishers, 1968.

Harrington, Michael. *Toward a Democratic Left.* Baltimore, Md.: Penguin Books, 1969.

O'Neill, Nena, and O'Neill, George. *Open Marriage: A New Life Style for Couples.* New York: M. Evans & Co., 1972.

O'Neill, William. *The Woman Movement: Feminism in the United States and England.* Chicago: Quadrangle Books, 1969.

Polk, Barbara Bovee. "Woman's Liberation: Movement for Equality." In Constantina Safilios-Rothschild (ed.), *Toward a Sociology of Women,* pp. 321–30. Lexington, Mass.: Xerox College Publishing Co., 1972.

Roszak, Theodore. *The Making of a Counter Culture: Reflections on the Technocratic Society and Its Youthful Opposition.* Garden City, N.Y.: Anchor Books, 1969.

Safilios-Rothschild, Constantina. "The Options of Greek Men and Women." *Sociological Focus* 5 (Winter 1971–72): 71–83.

Sinclair, Andrew. *The Emancipation of American Women.* New York: Harper and Row, 1965.

Smelser, Neil J. *Theory of Collective Behavior.* New York: Free Press, 1962.

Trey, J. E. "Women in the War Economy—World War II." *The Review of Radical Economics* 4 (July 1972).

Wrong, Dennis. *Population and Society.* New York: Random House, 1968.

Index

THE BOOK MANUFACTURE

Masculine/Feminine or Human? was typeset, printed and bound at Napco Graphic Arts, Inc., New Berlin, Wisconsin. Internal design was by the F. E. Peacock Publishers art department. Cover design was by Graphic Arts International. The type is Times Roman, with Spartan Medium Italic display.